SO-BBC-235

Contents

Continued

Part II Canadian Cross Country Skiing Directory 93

Preface

Over four million people currently practice the sport of cross-country skiing in Canada. If you are one of the many Canadians or visitors to this country who want to get the most out of skiing, this book is for you.

Basic information on cross-country skiing in the first section of this book is oriented toward novice and intermediate skiers. This introductory section covers all the essentials for a safe and enjoyable outing. The second part of the book is a directory containing data on over 500 cross-country ski areas across Canada.

Information is provided on location, facilities and activities for most ski centres. Every attempt has been made to ensure that these listings are current but, obviously, such data is subject to change. To avoid any inconvenience, call ahead to ensure that the ski centre you wish to visit is open and the services you require are available. Listings will be updated in future editions of this book, any contributions from readers are welcome, whether about listed or unlisted ski areas.

Happy Trails!

Leon Ferrari

Disclaimer

Mention of any company, good or service in this book does not constitute an endorsement and is provided as general information only. Verify the qualifications and financial background of any business before making any substantial expenditure.

Ski with care!

Cross-country skiing is a sport that comprises some degree of inherent danger. Take all the necessary safety precautions before setting out on any ski trip. Skiing at any area listed in this handbook can be hazardous due to bad weather, snow conditions, isolation or poorly marked trails. Ski with a group and always be prepared to deal with mishaps, such as getting lost or injured.

Acknowledgements

Many people have contributed directly or indirectly to the preparation of this book. My thanks to Jacinta Ferrari, Louis Piché, Tom Silletta, Toni Scheier, Anthony Singelis and Gail Tedstone. A special thanks to the Randonnée Aventure outdoor club for all the wonderful trips that I have taken with them over the years. It was those excursions that provided the inspiration for this book.

Various divisions of Cross Country Canada provided some valuable advice about skiing in their regions. I would also like to express my gratitude to all the ski centre operators who provided information on their facilities particularly the Alberta Parks Service and Manitoba Natural Resources.

Finally, I am deeply indebted to my sister, Pepita Ferrari, for her support, encouragement and advice.

Photo credits

I
Cross Country Skiing
Basics

1 Skiing Past to Present

Skiing is thought to have originated over 4,500 years ago in Scandinavia as a means of winter transportation. In fact, the word "ski" originates from the Norwegian *skith,* meaning "snowshoe." Skis found in bogs in Norway and Sweden have been dated to 2,000 B.C. and 2,500 B.C., respectively. A petroglyph found on a rock wall in Norway, depicting a figure with two long skis (Figure 1.1), dates from about the same period. Ski-like artifacts have also been discovered in Asia, and there are references to skiing in Chinese writings as early as the seventh century.

Some stone-age skis, such as the Swedish relics, are short and wide, resembling wooden snowshoes, while the Norwegian artifacts are each over two metres in length. It is thought that in some regions, a short ski was combined with a long ski. The short ski would have been used for propulsion and the long ski for gliding.

Skis played an important role in two historic Scandinavian events, both of which inspired modern day touring races. In 1205, the infant heir to the throne of Norway was rescued by members of the Birkebeiner royal guard and carried from Oslo, north to Trondheim. Today, skiers in the Birkebeiner races carry a 5.5-kg (12-lb.) backpack over a 55-km (89-mile) course to commemorate the event.

In 1521, King Gustav Vasa, the founder of the Swedish monarchy, evaded his political assailants on skis. His 90-km (56-mile) escape route from Oslo is retraced in the annual Vasaloppet, the world's longest single-day ski event.

Figure 1.1 *Rock carving at Rødøy, Norway, circa 2000 B.C.*

Skiing in North America

The Vikings who established settlements on the Newfoundland coast in the 10th century may have been the first skiers in North America. However, no artifact has yet been uncovered to verify this theory.

Scandinavian immigrants introduced skiing to North America in the mid-1800s. One such immigrant, John "Snowshoe" Thomson, achieved legendary stature by providing the only overland link to the west coast. For 20 years, he made weekly 300-km (200-mile) return trips carrying mail over the Sierra Nevada mountains.

A Mr. A. Birch, a Montrealer of Norwegian origin, made the first recorded ski trip in Canada in 1879, travelling from Montreal to Quebec on a three-metre-long pair of "Norwegian snowshoes."

Herman Smith "Jackrabbit" Johannsen was one of the most inspirational figures in North American skiing history—not only for what he accomplished, but also for the life that he led. Johannsen emigrated as a young engineer from Norway, first to America in 1901, then to Canada in 1928. His agility on his skis earned him the name "Chief Jackrabbit" from the Cree Indians whom he encountered while selling heavy equipment to the railways.

After the Great Depression forced him into retirement in the Laurentians, Jackrabbit undertook the development of the 128-km (80-mile) Maple Leaf Trail almost single-handedly and without financial compensation. Eking out a living as a guide and a designer of ski jumps and trails, Jackrabbit exemplified the self-reliant outdoor lifestyle that he constantly espoused. Even after he hung up his skis for the last time at 111 years of age in 1986, his spirit of generosity and of adventure lived on.

Canadians were active at both poles during 1995. Richard Weber of Gatineau, Quebec and Russian Misha Malakhov accomplished the first unassisted return journey to the North Pole. Setting off in February 1995 from Ward Hunt Island, the most northerly point of Canadian land, they completed the gruelling thousand-mile ski trek in 107 days. In November of the same year, Quebecers Bernard Voyer and Thierry Pétry began a 1500-km (960-mile) expedition to the South Pole and were the first Canadians to accomplish the feat carrying all their supplies.

Recreational Skiing

Early ski equipment consisted of bent wooden planks up to 3.5-m (12-ft.) long, with crude toe loops and a single pole. Equipment remained primitive and skis were mainly considered a means of transportation until the mid 1800s, when Sondre Nordheim gave birth to the sport of skiing. Nordheim invented the heel strap and skis with sidecut that provided more turning control on downhill descents. Nordheim also discovered that landing from a jump was easier on a slope than it was on flat terrain, an important factor in the development of the sport of ski jumping.

In the late 1800s, Nordheim's innovative equipment was introduced to central Europe, where it was perfectly suited to the mountainous regions. In the 1930s, the new sport of "alpine" skiing flourished with the introduction of mechanical ski lifts and the Kandahar binding which kept the heel fastened onto the ski.

Skiing was initially a spectator sport, with large crowds turning out for ski races and jumping contests. Snowshoeing was a popular sport in Canada at the turn of the century and numerous snowshoe clubs were established across the country. These clubs

Figure 1.2 *Skiers at Rockcliffe Park, Ottawa in 1895.*

gradually adopted skiing and new clubs devoted to the sport sprang up across Canada, beginning with Revelstoke in 1890 and Montreal in 1904. During the twenties and thirties, Finnish-Canadians were very active in organizing ski clubs and races in northern Ontario.

Emphasis shifted to alpine skiing during the 1920s, with skiers taking to the hills in the Laurentians, in the Gatineau hills, north of Ottawa and at Collingwood, north of Toronto. Resorts and ski schools, with predominately Swiss and Austrian staffs, were widespread. Each weekend up to 25,000 people took the ski trains north from Montreal into the Laurentians.

Cross-country skiing went through a sudden growth spurt in the late 60s and the early 70s, spurred on by the fitness boom of that period. People thronged to the sport in large numbers as a means of getting into shape. Dozens of races and tours such as the Canadian Ski Marathon began during that decade.

Telemark skiing is another nordic sport that has enjoyed a recent upswing in popularity. Sometimes described as "cross-country downhill", it requires nordic-style equipment that allows the heel to rise off the ski as the skier performs the telemark turn.

Competitive Skiing

Military ski competitions in the late 1700s were the first to offer monetary prizes. One of the earliest civilian cross-country ski races took place at Tromsö, Norway, in 1843. The first big ski jumping competition was held at Oslo, in 1879.

In North America, Scandinavian miners and loggers staged downhill races and ski jumping contests in the late 1800s. Rossland, British Columbia was the site of the first Canadian professional ski competition, a nordic combined event, held in 1898. Ski jumping retained its popularity in western Canada until the thirties, with world records being set at Revelstoke from 1925 to 1933. A ski jumping contest, held in 1909 on Westmount Boulevard in Montreal, was the first Canadian ski championship.

The Federation Internationale de Ski (FIS) was established in 1924 as the worldwide governing body for both nordic and alpine sports. Today, most ski competitions follow FIS rules and regulations. An FIS-sponsored Nordic World Ski Championship is held biennially. Thunder Bay, Ontario was the site of the 1995 Nordic World Championships. The nordic events currently sanctioned by the FIS are cross-country skiing, ski jumping and nordic combined—a traditional Scandinavian competition that involves both a cross-country race and a ski jumping contest.

Telemark skiing and the biathlon are the only competitive nordic sports not regulated by the FIS. Each sport has its own governing body: the International Telemark Federation and the International Biathlon Union, respectively. World Championships are held annually for each skiing discipline. Al Pilcher was the first Canadian to break into the top ten ranks of a world championship cross-country ski race, finishing seventh in the 50-km race in 1989.

The World Cup is a privately-sponsored annual series of ski competitions, held mainly in European and North American countries. First held in 1967 for alpine skiing only, a World Cup series is now held annually in each skiing discipline. A title is awarded each year to the man and woman winning the most points in their discipline throughout the season. Canada's Pierre Harvey won three World Cup cross-country skiing events during 1988 and 1989, finishing sixth in the point standings for the

Winter Olympics

Summer Olympic Games have been held quadrennially since 1896. Winter Olympic Games began in 1924 and were held the same year as the Summer Games until 1992. Starting with Lillehammer, Norway in 1994, the Winter Games were rescheduled to take place two years after the Summer Games, at four-year intervals.

Men's cross-country skiing and ski jumping were among the events of the first Winter Games (see appendix). Women's cross-country racing was initiated in the 1950s. Skating technique was first permitted in certain events designated as "free technique" at the 1988 Olympics.

The year 1992 saw the introduction of the "pursuit"—a two-part event starting with a classic technique race, followed a day or two later by a free technique event. Medals are awarded for both the first and second legs of the event. With the exceptions of the relay event and the second leg of the pursuit, all other races are skied individually against the clock, with starts at 30-second intervals.

The biathlon first appeared as an Olympic medal event for men in 1928, but was dropped after World War II because of anti-military sentiment. It was reinstated at Squaw Valley, California in 1960, but it was not until 1992 in Albertville, France that women could compete.

Each nation is restricted to a maximum of four entrants (not including the previous year's winner) in any Olympic, World Championship or World Cup event. Canada's current criteria for Olympic team selection is such that few skiers qualify for the team.

Canada and the USA have remained almost medal-less in Olympic cross-country skiing events. Bill Koch of Vermont is the sole exception, having won a silver medal in the 30-km event at the 1976 Games. Myriam Bédard of Neufchtel, Quebec was the first North American to win an Olympic medal in the biathlon, taking home a bronze for the 15-km event in 1992. She crowned it by winning gold medals in both the 7.5 and 15-km events at Lillehammer in 1994.

Further Reading

The Legendary Jackrabbit Johannsen by Alice E. Johannsen, 1993, 312 pp, McGill University Press.

2 Equipment Selection

Until the turn of the century, it was easy to select ski equipment—the same wooden skis were used for jumping, cross-country and downhill. Skiing has since fragmented into an array of specialized sports, with equipment designed for each of several alpine and nordic disciplines. More recently, the sport of cross-country skiing has been revolutionized by the skating technique and has seen a return to its roots with the current growth in backcountry touring.

When choosing the ski equipment that suits you best, there are several factors to take into consideration: the type of skiing you intend to do, your level of skiing ability and your credit card limit.

Categories of Nordic Equipment

There is no universal classification standard for nordic equipment. Different publications and manufacturers use different designations. SALWI is an international system of classifying all nordic equipment (with the exception of ski jumping equipment) according to target groups (the designation used in this guide appears in brackets):

- **Specialist**—for competition by serious racers on challenging, groomed trails (racing)
- **Advanced**—for skilled recreational skiers on groomed trails (sport)
- **Learner**—for inexperienced skiers on groomed trails (light touring)
- **Wanderer**—for backcountry skiing on challenging untracked snow (backcountry)
- **Individualist**—for telemark skiing and ski mountaineering (telemark).

Racing and sport equipment are designed either for skating or for classic technique. "Classic" is the term used to differentiate equipment intended for the diagonal stride from that designed for the newer skating technique. Equipment for light touring and backcountry skiing are both designed for the diagonal technique.

Skiers who wish to alternate between skating and classic techniques have the option of buying combination equipment. A person who only skates occasionally may decide to purchase short or mid-length classic skis.

Light touring equipment is intended for entry-level skiers or for use on groomed or lightly packed trails over easy-to-moderate terrain. Of heavier construction than sport equipment, light touring gear delivers less performance, but is less expensive.

Backcountry equipment is of more substantial construction than the preceding categories, but is lighter than equipment intended exclusively for telemark skiing. Backcountry and telemark skis have metal edges for better control on hills. Telemark gear is primarily designed for downhill performance rather than cross-country technique.

Classic Vs. Skating Technique

Classic and skating techniques use two completely different methods of propulsion. Wax applied to the centre portion of the classic ski base grips the snow to prevent the ski from slipping back as the skier kicks off into the glide phase. Skating technique, on the other hand, is similar to the stride used in ice skating. Just as in ice skating, the edge of the ski is set into the snow to provide traction as the skier pushes off from it.

Skating technique is faster than classic but may require a greater physical capacity to maintain momentum and glide, depending on the snow conditions. On the other hand, skiers using the classic technique, can shuffle along at whatever pace suits them. Skating derives about half of its propulsion from poling, as compared with 10 to 20 percent in the diagonal stride.

In skating technique, unlike classic, skis are never parallel but are always at an angle to the direction of travel. Skating technique, therefore, requires trails that are groomed flat for at least two metres in width. Many ski centres provide a skating lane alongside some of their classic trails.

Since the skating technique is a fairly recent development, skating trails are not as plentiful as classic trails. Before buying skating equipment, check that enough trails in your area are groomed for the technique.

A major advantage of skating over classic is that grip wax is not needed—a real plus on granular snow where grip wax quickly wears off. On the other hand, when snow is fresh, it can make skating awkward because glide is reduced—especially when temperatures are cold.

Physical Characteristics of Skis

The key features of ski design are width, sidecut, length, weight, flex, construction and base material. Ski weight is dependent on the width, length and type of construction. Weights can range from 800 g (1.75 lb.) for a pair of high-performance racing skis to over 2,500 g (5.5 lb.) for metal-edged backcountry touring skis.

Width and Sidecut

Wide skis float better than narrow ones on unpacked snow and prevent you from sinking. Skis designed for off-track skiing are therefore relatively wide. Wider skis are also more stable and make it easier for novice skiers to keep their balance.

An undesirable feature of wide skis is that they decrease glide because of the friction caused by the larger surface in contact with the snow. Wide skis also weigh more than narrow skis. That's the main reason that racing skis are narrow—to reduce weight.

 Tip *Novice skiers should choose a ski of about 50 mm in width for skiing on groomed trails. A ski that is wider than 55 mm will be difficult to manoeuvre in machine-set tracks.*

Sidecut is the difference in the width of a ski from the tip to the waist, with the waist generally being narrower, as illustrated in Figure 2.1. A ski with sidecut edges will turn to one side when the skier's weight is shifted to that side. Skis with a large sidecut, such as those designed for off-trail skiing, will turn more easily

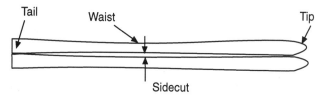

Figure 2.1 *Ski nomenclature.*

than a ski with little sidecut, but they may tend to wander. High-performance racing and recreation skis are usually of uniform width or have a slightly narrower tip so that they will track in a straight line.

General Characteristics of Nordic Skis

Ski Type	Weight/pair (200 cm) g	Waist width mm	Sidecut mm
Racing	800-1200	43-45	0
Sport	1000-1300	44-45	0
Touring	1300-1900	45-50	0-6
Backcountry	1700-2500	50-55	4-5
Telemark	2000-3500	55-70	5-10

Length

Skis have traditionally been produced in a variety of lengths ranging between 185 and 215 cm, in 5-cm increments. The once popular belief that "longer is better" has been challenged in recent years. Sport, light touring and backcountry skis are now available in short and mid-length sizes between 145 and 190 cm. Racing skis are normally only produced in longer lengths, to meet the FIS specifications.

Very short backcountry skis may not be suitable for deep powder snow, as they may bog down more than regular-length skis. Short skis are easier to turn than long ones, so are particularly suitable for the novice skier. They are, however, harder to control at high speeds. Longer skis are thought to be faster gliders, depending on snow condition. On hard-packed snow, there is little difference.

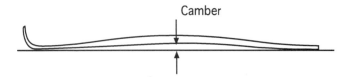

Camber

Figure 2.2 *Side view of unweighted ski, showing camber.*

Skating skis are generally 10 to 15 cm shorter than classic skis, ranging in length from 175 to 205 cm for regular models. Short skating skis, 146 to 180 cm in length, are particularly popular because their lightness and manoeuvrability make skating a breeze.

Camber and Flexibility

All skis have profiles that curve up in the middle when they are not supporting any weight, as in Figure 2.2. The gap under the middle of the ski is called camber. Its purpose is to compensate for the deflection caused by the weight of the skier, thereby allowing the ski to lie relatively flat. Skis used for classic technique have a residual camber (sometimes called "double camber") when supporting half the skier's weight, as shown in Figure 2.3(a). Skating, telemark and alpine skis are single-cambered, i.e. they have no residual camber.

Double camber prevents the grip wax that is applied to the middle of the ski from making contact with the snow when the skier's weight is evenly distributed over both skis, as happens when gliding. If the ski flattens under half the skier's weight (Figure 2.3(b)), the flex is too soft. A flex that is too soft will slow the skier's glide and quickly wear off the grip wax.

When the ski supports the full weight of the skier it should lie flat, as shown in Figure 2.3(c). Classic skis that are too stiff will prevent the wax pocket from making contact with the snow when supporting the entire weight of the skier, keeping the wax from gripping the snow, as shown in Figure 2.3(d).

Stiffer skis are preferable for hard-packed snow and skating. Soft skis, on the other hand, make turning easy in soft snow. Stiffness of tip and tail are also important considerations. A tip that has a

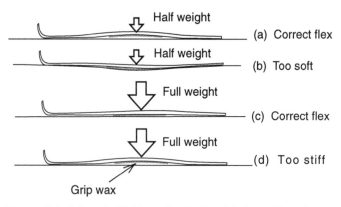

Figure 2.3 *Soft and stiff skis vs. the ideal model when fully and partially weighted.*

soft flex is easy to turn and rides over bumps more easily. A hard flex is usually desirable in the tail of skating and telemark skis to maintain edge control.

Another type of flexibility is the twist that a ski allows. A ski that is torsionally rigid resists twisting and transmits more energy to the edge of the ski—an attractive feature for both skating and telemark skis.

Construction

Modern skis have, until recently, been made up of a sandwich-type composition with an inner core, usually consisting of a wood and foam laminate covered by a protective top and sidewalls (Figure 2.4). A recent innovation, borrowed from alpine ski design, is cap construction—a torsionally rigid box covered by a one-piece shell over the top and sides of the ski.

The torsional rigidity of cap construction provides better edge control, without increasing the stiffness of the ski. Note that some skis are cosmetic caps that have a one-piece shell, but lack the inner torsion box.

Backcountry touring skis usually have steel edges to provide better control when stopping and turning while descending hills. Steel edges, however, need regular maintenance to stay sharp. They add extra weight and require major repairs if they happen to be dislodged by rocks. Some models have steel edges only along the middle of the ski to save weight.

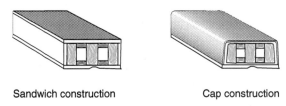

Sandwich construction Cap construction

Figure 2.4 *Types of ski constructions.*

Ski Bases

Bases are composed of either polyethylene (P-tex) or a graphite composite. Polyethylene bases are produced in a rainbow of colour combinations. Graphite bases are made of a carbon and polyethylene compound that glides better than standard polyethylene at warmer temperatures.

Many skis have bases that are sintered, meaning they are cut from a block of polyethylene. Sintered bases have a better finish than extruded bases and a flatter surface that glides better. They absorb wax more readily, and therefore retain wax longer. Some high-end skis are manufactured with bases that have been structured with tiny grooves to increase glide.

Some skis have "waxless" bases—fishscale-type patterns that are molded into the middle section of the base material to provide grip. While these so-called waxless skis do not require grip wax, they do require glide wax on the tips and tails of the base. Waxless skis are noisier and less efficient gliders than skis with plain bases because of the friction of the grip pattern. They are, however, handy for problematic snow conditions, particularly soft wet snow that sticks to the grip wax of classic skis.

Ski Selection

In the early days, when all skis were made of solid wood, ski length was determined by simply holding your arm in the air and measuring from the floor to your wrist. Wood has predictable flexural properties so it was easy to predetermine the handling characteristics of a ski.

Nowadays, with dozens of different design and construction combinations, skis are manufactured to suit different purposes. With such a variety of skis to choose from, the first consideration is that the ski suits the type of skiing you are going to do.

Once you have decided what type of skiing the skis are to be used for, you may choose short, mid-length or regular-length skis. Most manufacturers produce models in each of the three length ranges. Most ski shops, however, don't carry every make and model, so you may have to shop around. Once you have found the model you want, you must check that the flex suits your weight and ability.

Checking Ski Flex

When shopping for a pair of skis, it is best to go to stores that specialize in cross-country ski equipment rather than large general sports equipment retailers. A salesperson at a ski shop will likely be more knowledgeable about ski equipment. Ski shops have a better selection and should have camber-testing equipment. A salesperson will be able to guide you in finding the appropriate ski for your ability and the type of skiing you intend to do.

Some shops are equipped with pressure gauges to measure the force required to flatten the camber out of a ski. A graph is then consulted to see if the flex is suitable for the buyer's weight and ability.

The Paper Test

The most commonly used method for checking ski flex is the paper test. It determines two things: the length of the wax pocket and the flatness of the ski when supporting the full weight of the skier. Since skating skis do not have wax pockets, it is only necessary to ensure that the ski is stiff enough to support the full weight of the skier.

The Paper Test

Remove all grip wax from the bases of the skis and lay them down on a clean, flat surface. Stand with your weight slightly forward and evenly distributed on both skis, positioning your toes behind the balance points of the skis.

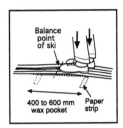

Have someone slide a strip of paper under the midpoint of the ski. A classic ski should have enough residual camber in the ski so that the paper can be slid beneath the heel and 400 to 600 mm (16 to 24 in.) in front of the heel before meeting resistance. This area is called the wax pocket or grip zone.

The next step is to ensure that there is residual camber in the ski when it is fully weighted.

Slide the strip of paper under the midpoint of one ski.

Stand with all your weight on that ski. If it is difficult to remove the paper from under the ski, the flex might be suitable for a beginner skier, especially on soft snow.

For more advanced skiers, there should be some resistance when you try to remove the paper.

If the paper is pinned to the floor, the flex is probably too soft.

Now raise the heel so that your entire weight is bearing on the ball of your foot. If the paper cannot be removed or comes out with difficulty, the flex is right for an intermediate to advanced skier.

If the paper can still be slid out with little or no resistance, the flex may be too stiff, unless the ski is for an expert skier with a powerful kick.

Flex and camber can vary widely for skis of the same length and model, so it is important to test both skis. Skis of equal flex are paired together by the manufacturer and are kept in matched pairs in better ski shops.

The wax pocket should be approximately the same length for both skis and it should take about the same effort to remove the strip of paper from under each ski. Mark the limits of the wax pocket on the sides of classic skis to delineate between grip and glide zones.

Bindings

Until the 1980s, most bindings were the three-pin model, sometimes referred to as 75 mm bindings. Three pins on the base of the binding clamp into holes in the extended sole of the boot (see Figure 2.5(c)). A heel support plate attached to the ski is intended to constrain lateral movement, but is not generally very effective when used with lightweight boots. In addition, the binding is wider than most skis so it drags against the snow. A more substantial version of this binding is, however, quite effective when used with heavy telemark or backcountry boots.

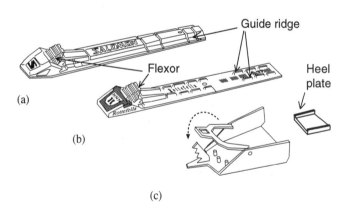

Figure 2.5 *Binding systems (a) SNS Profil, (b) NNN II and (c) three-pin.*

Today's most popular cross-country bindings are NNN (New Nordic Norm) II, made by Rottefella and Salomon's SNS (Salomon Nordic System) Profil. They are narrow enough to fit on the skinniest skis and provide better control than three-pin bindings when used with lightweight boots.

NNN and SNS bindings are both part of similar, but incompatible, boot-binding systems. A mechanism in the binding locks onto a horizontal metal bar under the boot toe, while a ridged base plate meshes with the sole of the boot. The combination of locking bar and ridged base plate help to keep the skier's heel on the ski when used with torsionally-rigid boots.

The SNS Profil model has a single wide ridge, while the NNN II binding incorporates a pair of narrow ridges. Ridges on both systems run from the toe to the heel and were developed from models with very short guide ridges (SNS and NNN). The original bindings may still be available as entry-level touring models but are not compatible with the newer systems. Both Salomon and Rottefella produce backcountry bindings featuring wider guide ridges to provide better control.

NNN II and SNS Profil touring bindings attach automatically and can be released with the tip of a pole. They are, however, occasionally prone to freezing up. Skate, classic, combi and backcountry bindings must be set and released by manipulating a lever.

Bindings for skate and classic techniques differ in the firmness of the rubber flexors located against the toe of the ski boot. As the boot is lifted during each stride, the flexor rebounds, rotating the ski into position under the skier's foot. Skating technique requires a firmer flexor for faster ski rebound. Backcountry bindings have even harder flexors, to provide better ski control.

Bindings are usually mounted so that the point of rotation of the binding is directly over the balance point of the ski. Chances are good that you will damage your skis if you try to mount your bindings yourself, so have them mounted by a reputable ski.

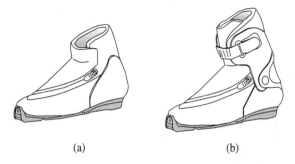

(a)   (b)

Figure 2.6 *Cross-country ski boots: (a) classic and (b) skating.*

Boots

Cross-country ski boots are designed to be used with a specific binding system that is incompatible with other systems. SNS Profil and NNN II boots both have a horizontal bar in the toe of the boot which, together with the thick grooved sole, help to restrict the lateral movement of the skier's heel. Boots for three-pin bindings have extended soles, with three holes underneath that mesh with pins on the binding when clamped in place.

Classic boots are low-cut to allow some forward rotation of the ankles during the classic stride (see Figure 2.6). Soles of classic boots have a supple flex for a more efficient kick.

Skating boots are usually high-cut, with stiff ankle supports to provide lateral stability when skating and going down hills. Since skating requires consistent use of the ski's edges, boots have rigid soles to support the foot laterally.

Combination boots can be used for both skating and classic, but usually make compromises. Some of the sole stiffness and ankle support that is desirable during skating may be sacrificed to allow freedom of movement during the diagonal stride. Some combi boots have plastic ankle stabilizers that can be removed for classic technique.

Backcountry boots are high-cut and heavy to provide control on ungroomed trails. Telemark boots are of even heavier construction for easy downhill turning.

Comfort is the most important factor to consider when shopping for boots. When trying on boots, wear socks of the same thickness as you would normally wear when skiing. Make sure that your heel cannot lift away from the insole. Check for pressure points that may cause discomfort. Any minor discomfort should not be overlooked—after several hours skiing, it will probably become quite painful. As with hiking boots, it takes some time for boots to adapt to the shape of your foot (or vice versa, as the case may be).

Your comfort also depends on warmth, so make sure the boots that you buy have adequate insulation. Many of the of the mid- to higher-priced boots have zippered closures over the laces for protection against cold and snow.

 Tip *First-time skiers should consider buying a mid-priced boot as they are generally better insulated. A boot made for the NNN II or SNS Profil binding system will provide good control and allow the skier to upgrade to better equipment without changing bindings.*

Poles

Originally, poles had bamboo shafts and round baskets. Today's pole shafts are made of fibreglass or aluminum (for recreational use) or of lightweight carbon composite material (for racing). Pole shafts should be as stiff as possible to prevent loss of energy when the pole flexes. Stiffness is especially important in skating poles, since they are longer and provide more propulsion than those designed for classic technique.

Poles intended for use on machine-groomed trails have small asymmetrical baskets so that when the pole is leaned forward the basket does not pry the pole tip out of the snow or catch the snow as the pole is pulled out. Poles for skiing in loose snow have large round baskets that prevent the pole from sinking too deep. Pole tips should be made of carbide rather than steel to retain sharpness.

Hand grips are made of either cork or molded plastic. Straps should be as wide as possible to support your hand comfortably and prevent the constriction of circulation.

Classic poles should be long enough so that the attachment point of the wrist strap is between your armpit and your shoulder when the points are resting on the floor. Skating poles should reach your chin or mouth, to provide extra upper-body leverage. Telescopic backcountry poles can be adjusted according to the depth of the snow, and for climbing and descending hills.

Recommended Pole Lengths

Body Height		Pole Length (cm)	
ft.- in.	cm	Classic	Skating
6-1	185	155	165
6-0	182	152	162
5-11	180	150	160
5-10	177	147	157
5-9	175	145	155
5-8	172	142	152
5-7	170	140	150
5-6	167	137	147
5-5	165	135	145
5-3	160	130	140
5-1	155	125	135
4-11	150	120	130

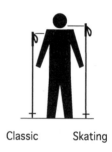

Classic   Skating

Points to Remember

- Determine the type of snow conditions for which your equipment is to be used.
- Decide on the length of ski you want, then check that the flex is suitable for your weight and ability by means of the paper test.
- Select boots and bindings that are compatible.
- Classic poles should reach to between your armpit and shoulder. Skating poles should reach to between your chin and mouth.

Further Reading

Cross-Country Ski Gear, second edition by Michael Brady, The Mountaineers Press.

Cross Country Skier, Ski Trax and *Explore* magazines all publish annual equipment guides.

3 Clothing

Canadian skiers face a wide range of weather conditions—anything from mild spring-like temperatures to arctic blizzards—sometimes on the same day. But, as Marty Hall, a former Canadian National Ski Team coach, is reputed to have said, there is no such thing as bad weather, only bad clothing.

Body Heat

Warmth should be the primary goal of dressing for skiing, over and above your desire to make a fashion statement. Dressing appropriately will reduce the loss of body heat by regulating the main avenues of escape:
• conduction through moisture in contact with the skin
• radiation of heat from the body
• convection cooling by air circulation.

To control heat loss, clothing should prevent moisture from accumulating next to the skin, provide insulation to keep heat in and reduce air circulation around the body.

It is important to strike a balance between your level of activity and the amount of clothing you wear. The more intensive the activity, the lighter your clothing should be. Heat loss can be regulated by selecting appropriate clothing to match the body's heat output.

Some skiers are active enough that they are comfortable wearing just a thin ski suit over long underwear in temperatures as low as -15°C (5°F). Overdressing can cause excessive sweating and actually lead to a cooling of the body.

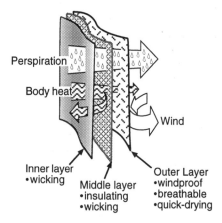

Figure 3.1 *Layering system for active winter sports.*

Layering System

Cross-country skiers usually wear several separate layers of clothing, the thickness of which may be chosen according to air temperature and their normal level of activity. Each layer should perform a different primary function in controlling body warmth (see Figure 3.1). The advantages of the layering system are:
• Air is trapped between layers providing extra insulation.
• A layer can be removed or added to adjust comfort level.
• Separate layers can be dried faster than a single thick layer.
• Unused layers can be stowed compactly in a knapsack.

Inner Layer

Perspiration is a very efficient method of cooling that the human body has evolved to rid itself of excess heat. When internal temperatures rise, moisture forms on the skin as means of expelling excess heat. Heat is transferred much faster through a liquid than it is through air. Cold spots are therefore felt wherever sweat remains in contact with the body, particularly when your activity level decreases.

Comfort level is, to a large extent, determined by the millimetre-thick zone between skin and fabric. When excessive amounts of moisture remain in contact with the skin, hypothermia may result, even on a mild day. The primary function of the inner layer should be to keep the skin as dry as possible.

Clothing made of materials such as cotton tend to retain moisture and should be avoided, particularly next to the skin. Polypropylene and polyester are materials that "wick" or draw moisture away from the skin. Both materials are durable and fairly comfortable to wear. Wool retains its insulative properties when wet, but may irritate the skin.

A wide selection of poly-knit underpants, long johns and long-sleeved undershirts are available in several thicknesses and in a variety of colours. Most cross-country skiers will find lightweight material best suited to their level of activity. Underwear made of thicker material is suitable for less consistently active sports such as downhill skiing or ice climbing. Look for a brand that provides antibacterial protection to help prevent odour build-up.

Middle Layer

The middle layer of clothing should provide insulation while allowing perspiration to escape. Fabrics with wicking properties are desirable here also, but are not as vital as in the inner layer.

A top made of fleece or wool may be best for colder days and for less active skiers. More active skiers may find that a thin jersey suits their needs or may decide to forego a middle layer entirely.

Cotton/polyester blends are satisfactory as a cheap alternative to polypropylene. A turtleneck or high collar is recommended to keep the neck warm. For colder temperatures, an extra middle layer, such as a vest, can be worn.

Legs don't require as much insulation as the upper body, so a pair of long johns is usually sufficient as a middle layer. In colder weather, fleece pants or a second pair of long johns may be added.

Outer Layer

Wind draws heat from the body, increasing the severity of the cold (see Figure 3.2). Your outer layer of clothing should, therefore, provide protection against the wind. Shells of nylon and Lycra™ are good windbreakers, yet breathable enough to let moisture escape. They are also fast drying and water-resistant enough to prevent moisture accumulation caused by falling snow—or from falling *in* the snow.

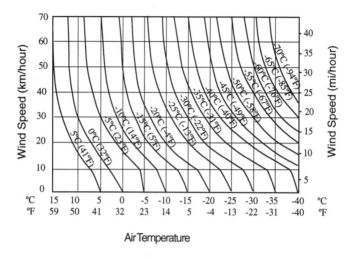

Figure 3.2 *Wind chill factors.*

Waterproof breathable materials, such as Gore-Tex™, are often not porous enough to vent the perspiration given off during high-exertion activities. If you do decide to buy a microporous jacket, make sure that it has air vents in the back, front and under the arms.

Jackets and pants can be stretchy and form-fitting or on the baggy side (for more modest individuals). Stretchy material may be too tight to maintain an adequate insulating layer of air or may restrict movement. If your clothes are excessively baggy, they may allow air to circulate too freely. Overalls and one-piece suits prevent entry of wind and snow around the waist, but can be inconvenient when nature calls.

 Tip *If you are properly dressed for medium or high levels of activity, you will probably feel a bit of a chill when you first start out on a cold day. To avoid discomfort, wear a vest or extra jacket until you warm up. A knapsack, containing extra clothing, should always be carried to be put on when stopping for a break or in case of an emergency or a sudden drop in temperature.*

Hands and Feet

Your hands and feet can also be covered in layers. Polypropylene or wool liners are usually worn under unlined gloves or mittens. Gloves allow fingers more freedom of movement but mittens provide more warmth. A good compromise is to wear gloves and carry a pair of large mittens to slip over them when needed.

Mitts and gloves can be made of leather or synthetic materials, such as nylon or Lycra™. Synthetic gloves and mitts should have leather palms for durability.

A thin liner sock of polypropylene is usually worn under a wool outer sock to prevent moisture build-up around the foot. Keeping the feet dry is especially important to avoid blistering and frostbite.

Insulative boot covers are ideal for extra warmth. Gaiters (nylon covers worn around the calf and over the top of the boot) are another useful item to have. They will keep snow out when skiing ungroomed trails and also help keep your ankles warm.

Head Covering and Eye Protection

Due to the high volume of blood circulating in your head, about half of your body's heat may be lost when your head is uncovered. Wear a headband or toque to keep your head and ears warm. Head coverings made of a wicking material will help keep your head drier than will hats made of wool. You can wear a head band along with a hat if it gets very cold. In extremely cold conditions, it may be necessary to wear a face mask or balaclava to prevent your face from freezing.

Sunglasses are not just a fashion accessory, they are a necessity to prevent sun blindness when skiing in open terrain. Yellow or rose tints provide the best contrast and depth perception in open areas. Green or gray lenses distort colours less and would be suitable if you mainly ski on forest trails.

Good quality shatterproof plastic lenses can meet high optical standards while weighing less than glass lenses. Glass, however, is more resistant to scratches. Side shields or wrapped-back lenses help block wind and ambient light. Frames should be made of sturdy plastic or composite materials rather than metal, which can easily be deformed. Use an elastic retaining strap to keep glasses in place.

Points to Remember

- Dress in layers:
  - inner layer of wicking material
  - middle insulating layer(s)
  - outer wind-stopping layer
  - inner and outer gloves and socks.
- Wear a hat or head band and sunglasses.
- Carry extra clothing in a knapsack.

4 Maintenance and Waxing

Elite ski racers choose from among a dozen or so pairs of skis and use hundreds of dollars worth of wax to prepare for a single race. Technicians grind the bases of each pair of skis to suit a particular type of snow. On the day of the race, the racer tries dozens of different ski and wax combinations to get optimal performance.

If you are like most skiers, you won't have such extravagant resources and will likely have to make do with one pair of well-worn skis and three or four waxes. Even so, you can still get decent performance from your skis by taking time to properly prepare them. A good knowledge of waxing fundamentals can make the difference between a good day and a lousy day on the trails.

Maintenance

A good time to examine and repair the bases of your skis is just before applying glide wax. Look for gouges in the base material. Gouges can be filled with epoxy or by melting a P-tex stick, both of which can be obtained from any ski store.

If you have metal-edged skis, check to see whether the edges are dull or rusty. Edge sharpness can be tested by rubbing with the back of your fingernail—if shavings are produced, the edge is sharp. Sharpness should be tested near the middle of the ski since it is standard practice to dull the edges at the tip and tail to make turning easier. Edges can be sharpened with a standard bastard file or a special edge-sharpening tool. If you don't like to get your hands dirty, an alpine or cross-country ski shop can do the job for you.

Skis with wooden bases require an occasional application of pine tar to prevent the wood from absorbing water or drying out. Pine tar should be applied hot for best results.

Structuring the Bases

Contrary to what you may think, skis with smooth bases are not the most efficient gliders. Research has shown that skis with structures or patterns embedded in their bases glide faster.

When temperatures are warm, a film of water is created by the pressure of the ski on the snow. It is thought that suction forces between the water film and the base of the ski reduces glide. Tiny grooves, or rills, reduce these adhesive forces and provide channels where water can collect. In colder weather, when snow is drier, structuring reduces the surface area of the ski that makes contact with the snow, thereby reducing friction.

Expert skiers who want optimum performance can structure the bases of their skis to match the texture of the snow: coarse grooves for wet or coarse snow, fine grooves for cold powdery snow. Some ski manufacturers produce skis with bases structured for warm or cold conditions.

Structuring can be done by a variety of means. Sandpaper, metal scrapers, rillers and brushes can all be used to produce short irregular rills. After structuring, deburr the bases by rubbing them with a fibertex pad to remove polyethylene hairs. Rilling tools embed structures in the base, without creating burrs or hairs.

More demanding skiers can have their ski bases prepared by one of the handful of ski shops equipped with a special stone grinder. Depending on the depth of the structure, changing it to meet a different temperature range may be difficult and can wear away the thin layer of base material.

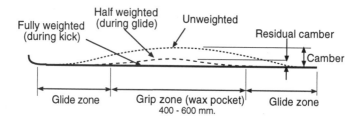

Figure 4.1 *Relationship between wax zones and the camber of a classic ski.*

Wax Zones

Classic skis have two wax zones: a grip zone in the middle of the ski and a glide zone on the tip and tail, as shown in Figure 4.1. During the kick phase of the diagonal stride, the entire weight of the skier is shifted onto one ski, flattening the whole length of the ski against the snow, as shown by the solid line in the diagram. Grip wax applied to the middle portion of the ski base should grip the snow, preventing backslip as the skier pushes off from it. Grip wax also helps to avoid backsliding when striding up gentle inclines. The fishscale pattern of "waxless" skis performs the same function as grip wax.

When gliding down hills or double-poling, the skier's weight is distributed over both skis so that there is some residual camber in each ski (middle line in Figure 4.1). Residual camber creates what is sometimes referred to as a "wax pocket," where the grip wax is prevented from making complete contact with the snow and slowing glide.

The length of a wax pocket is not written in stone and can be varied according to snow conditions. For example, some backcountry tourers find that a longer wax pocket provides better grip when climbing, and more control going down hills. On unpacked snow, glide is reduced anyway, so an extra-long grip zone will not affect glide as much as it would on groomed trails. On the other end of the scale, a shorter-than-normal wax pocket is recommended when applying klister, since it goes on thicker than hard wax.

Skating skis have no wax pocket; the glide zone covers the entire length of the ski. Combination skis (used for both classic and skating) should only have grip wax applied if they are to be used for classic technique. When skating, the grip wax will make contact with the snow and reduce glide. A cold-temperature grip wax can be applied to the grip zones of combi skis to protect the bases when the skis are used for skating.

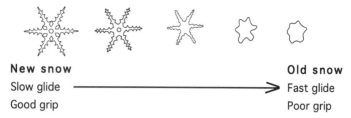

New snow   **Old snow**

Slow glide ⟶ Fast glide

Good grip   Poor grip

Figure 4.2 *The transformation of snow crystals and the effect on grip and glide.*

Glide Wax

Glide wax, as the name implies, helps the ski slide over the snow. In actual fact, the ski floats upon a thin film of water created as the pressure of the skier's weight melts the snow. The thickness of the water film varies according to the temperature of the snow.

As snow crystals age over several days, they transform, becoming rounder (see Figure 4.2). Under colder conditions, the crystals remain pointed for a longer period of time and the thinner water film under the ski allows the crystals to cling to the ski base. Glide is therefore reduced on new snow, especially at colder temperatures, when the snow creates greater friction.

Glide wax acts as a water repellent to prevent adhesion of the water film to the base and also helps prevent penetration of the snow crystals. Most of the more expensive waxes have fluorine additives that enhance glide by increasing water repellency and preventing dirt build-up.

A universal glide wax that covers the widest range of temperatures is ideal for beginner and intermediate skiers. If you do a lot of skiing, you may decide to buy warm-temperature wax for the start and end of the season and a cold wax for midwinter.

Glide wax helps protect the bases against abrasion and prevents them from drying out, or "oxidizing." Since glide wax is quite durable, it may only have to be applied a few times a year, depending on how much you ski, the desired performance and the abrasiveness of the snow. To check whether skis need waxing, place a drop of water on the base. If a bead doesn't form, the ski needs wax. Ski bases that have discoloured patches at the tip and tail are long overdue for a wax job.

Glide wax should be applied hot to penetrate the pores of the base. Many people find hot waxing such a tiresome chore that they prefer to have it done by a ski shop. Glide waxes are available in liquids and sprays that are easy to apply, but are not as durable as ironed-on wax.

Glide Waxing Equipment

If you are doing the hot waxing yourself, you will need:
• wax remover and wiping cloths
• a work bench with vise, wooden blocks and a drop cloth
• glider wax
• an iron to heat the wax
• a Plexiglass scraper.

Wax remover, lint-free Fibrelene cloths, glider wax and scrapers are all available from ski shops. Biodegradable citrus-based wax remover is preferable as it does not leave petroleum residues in the pores of the ski base which can prevent wax absorption.

Waxing is best done on a special ski form which will support the ski along its entire length. If no such support is available, a work bench with a standard vise can be used instead. Support the tip and tail of the ski with blocks of wood. If you don't have a vise to hold your skis in place, scraping them will be difficult. Place a drop cloth under the ski to catch wax drips and shavings.

Glide wax should not be applied to the grip wax pocket when waxing for classic technique, as it prevents grip wax from adhering to the base.

 Tip   *Mark the ends of the grip zone on the sides of the ski during the paper test.*

Preparation for Glide Waxing

Skis should be allowed to warm up to room temperature before waxing or the wax will not penetrate the base. Before waxing, scrape off as much old wax and embedded dirt as possible. Clean the base with a liquid wax remover and brush. Wipe off the remaining liquid and set the skis aside for about half an hour or so to let the wax remover evaporate before waxing. Another method of cleaning is to apply a layer of soft wax with the iron, then scrape it off before it cools.

33

Application of Glide Wax

IMPORTANT: Do not use an open flame to apply fluorinated waxes as toxic gases are created by burning fluorocarbons. Wax your skis in a well-ventilated area to avoid inhaling fumes.

Clamp the ski with the base facing upwards and above the top of the vise. Take care not to clamp the vise too tight and damage the edge of the ski.

Set the iron to a low temperature to start.

Hold the stick of wax against the iron a few inches above the ski. If the wax doesn't melt at the rate of several drops per second, increase the temperature.

Carefully monitor the iron temperature—too hot an iron can damage the ski base. If the wax starts to smoke, reduce the temperature setting.

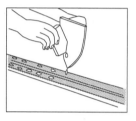

Starting at one end of the ski, direct the melting wax onto the base on each side of the centre groove.

Keeping the iron a few inches above the ski, move the iron and wax stick together along the ski so that a drop of wax falls every few centimetres along the glide zone on each side of the groove.

When the glide zones are evenly covered with drops of wax, use the iron to smooth the wax out over the base, within the glide zones. Keep the iron moving so that the base doesn't burn.

Make another pass with the iron to ensure that as much wax as possible has permeated the base.

Put the ski aside to cool at room temperature for about half an hour.

When the skis have cooled, scrape the base with the Plexiglass scraper until no more wax shavings are produced. Classic skis should be scraped from the wax pocket out towards the ends of the skis.

Gouge the wax out of the centre groove with a round implement, such as a klister applicator.

Wax can be applied with either an electric or a blowtorch-heated iron. Electric irons are best since they have a stabler heat output. Unless you can afford over a hundred dollars for a special wax iron, a second-hand iron will do the job. Check out garage sales for a travel iron or an old-fashioned iron without steam vents.

A Plexiglass scraper works best to remove as much wax as possible and can be kept sharp by occasionally running it over a sanding block. A scraper with a rounded corner is handy for gouging wax out of the centre groove of the ski.

Brand-new skis should be waxed and scraped three or more times to saturate the bases with wax. To provide optimal glide, the bases should be brushed to remove wax from the structures of the base. Use a brush with nylon bristles or a nylon scrubbing pad before polishing with a Fiberlene cloth to accentuate the structure.

Before storing skis for the summer, coat the bases with a layer of soft wax and leave them unscraped to prevent the base material from oxidizing over the summer.

Grip Wax

Grip wax and kick wax are both terms for the same stuff that you put on the grip zone of skis to provide traction during the diagonal stride. Grip wax must have both grip and glide properties: it must be soft enough to allow snow crystals to penetrate deep enough into the wax to provide grip (see Figure 4.3(a) and (b) below), but not so soft that the crystals remain embedded when the ski is gliding (Figure 4.3(c)).

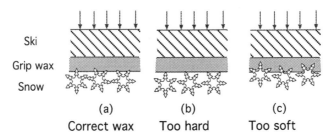

Figure 4.3 *Action of different grip waxes during the kick phase of the diagonal stride.*

Temperature Ranges of Grip Waxes

°C	-30	... -20	-18	-16	-14	-12	-10	-8	-6	-4	-2	0	2	4	... 10

Hard Waxes

Rode
- Blue
- Yellow
- Alaska
- Green
- Violet Multi
- Special Green
- Multi Blue
- Violet
- Super Blue
- Red Extra
- Red

SWIX
- Polar
- Violet Special
- Green Special
- Violet
- Green
- Violet Extra
- Blue Special
- Red Special
- Blue
- Red
- Blue Extra
- Red Extra

SWIX Cera (Low Fluoro)
- VF20 Green/Blue
- VF30 Blue
- VF40 Blue/Violet
- VF50 Violet/Red
- VF60 Red/Silver
- VF80 Titan Basebinder

TOKO Dibloc (Snow Temp.)
- Green
- Dark Blue (Old Snow)
- Yellow
- Bright Blue (New Snow)
- Dark Red (Old Snow)
- Bright Red (New Snow)

Klisters

SWIX
- Green
- Blue
- Violet
- Pink
- Red

SWIX Cera (Low Fluoro)
- Red Special
- Red
- Silver
- Universal

TOKO Dibloc (Snow temp.)
- Viola
- Orange
- Multirange

°F	-22	...	-4	0	3	7	10	14	18	21	25	28	32	36	39	... 50

36

At cold temperatures, the crystals are sharply pointed and require a harder wax to prevent them from penetrating too deeply into the wax. Warm temperatures require a softer wax that will stick to the rounded snow crystals.

There are two types of grip wax: hard wax and klister. Hard wax, the most commonly used of the two, comes in a cylindrical stick and is used for powdery snow. Klister, a very sticky paste wax, is used for old snow that has become granular or icy.

Due to its stickiness, klister will last longer than hard wax under the abrasive action of hard snow. A base layer of binder wax or cold-temperature wax, followed by several layers of the wax of the day, is sometimes used as an alternative to klister under such conditions.

Both hard waxes and klisters are coloured according to the temperature range that they cover (see chart on previous page). Each wax manufacturer uses different colours for different temperature ranges.

Hard Wax

Waxes formulated for cold temperatures are generally harder than warmer-temperature waxes. Novice skiers often opt for a two-wax system—one wax for moist snow and one for dry. More advanced skiers use three or more waxes, each of which covers a temperature range of several degrees.

Manufacturers specify their waxes according to air temperature, except for Toko which classifies its waxes according to snow temperature. You will have to carry a thermometer if you are using a snow-temperature wax, since ski centres usually post air temperature only.

Most ski centres have a waxing room, where it is easier to apply grip wax while your skis and wax are warm. If your skis are cold from being outside, wait 20 or 30 minutes for them to warm up to room temperature. A layer of condensation will probably form on the bases of the skis as they warm up. Wipe off the moisture with a cloth before waxing. Apply grip wax to your skis before driving to a ski centre so you don't have to wax cold skis or wait for them to warm up.

To apply grip wax you will need a metal or plastic scraper, a cork to smooth the wax and some grip wax. Metal scrapers are more effective than plastic for removing old wax. Contrary to what the name implies, most waxing corks are no longer made of cork, but of synthetic foam. Try to select a wax with a temperature range that includes the current temperature and the forecast high of the day. For example, if the current temperature is -10°C (14°F) and the forecast high for the afternoon is -6°C (21°F), you might select Rode Green or SWIX Green.

Application of Grip Wax

Scrape off as much old wax as possible before applying new wax. You may decide to start with a layer of binder wax or colder-temperature wax to bind the wax to the ski base.

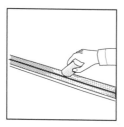

The first layer may be ironed on.

Crayon the stick of wax over the wax pocket until there is enough wax to smooth out over the pocket. When using harder waxes, you may have to crayon several times to get enough wax on the base.

Use a cork to smooth the wax over the base. Friction from rubbing will soften the wax, making it easier to spread.

Apply several layers of wax, rubbing each of them in with the cork. As many as six or eight layers may be needed, depending on the hardness of the wax and the amount of skiing you intend to do.

Place the skis outside to cool for at least five minutes before using them, or snow will become embedded in the warm wax.

If the skis do not have enough grip, try the TLC formula.

Add a Thicker layer. If that doesn't work, try extending the grip zone Longer towards the tip of the ski. And finally, if that doesn't work, Change to a warmer-temperature wax.

If snow embeds and builds up in the grip zone, preventing glide, you will have to remove the wax and apply a colder-temperature wax. It is difficult to apply wax for cold temperatures over that for warmer temperatures because the warm-temperature wax is softer—it's like trying to spread peanut butter over jam.

A few inches of warmer-temperature wax applied to the middle of the wax pocket over the wax of the day may improve grip.

If you are continually having a problem getting grip, you should check that the flex of your skis is not too stiff for your weight. Use the paper test to ensure that the middle of the ski is making contact with the snow when all your weight is bearing down on it. If there is no contact, the grip wax cannot do its job.

Always take a scraper, an assortment of grip waxes and a waxing cork on the trail with you, in case you have to change wax or add more wax.

 Keep short stubs of wax for use on the trail to reduce your load. Carry the wax near your body to keep it soft. Before applying the wax, wipe off any snow, then rub the wax pocket of the ski with the cork to warm up the base.

Klister

Klister has earned itself a bad reputation because it sticks to everything, especially clothes, and once it has been applied it is difficult to remove. With careful application, however, klister can be used without too much trouble.

 Since klister applies in a thicker layer than hard wax, the wax pocket should be shortened by 5 to 15 cm (2 to 6 inches). You may find it easier to remove klister outdoors, when your skis are cold.

At room temperature, klister can be squeezed from the tube, but will solidify when cold. If you are trying to apply klister under cold conditions, place the tube in your armpit for a few minutes to warm it up. Remember to first put it in a plastic bag to avoid getting any klister on your clothes.

Application of Klister

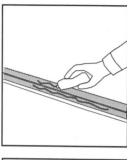

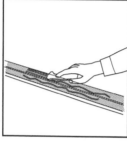

Scrape off the old wax or klister.

Squeeze a line of klister down each side of the base in the wax pocket. To begin with, apply only about half of what you think you will need.

Spread the klister out as thinly as possible with the plastic applicator provided by the manufacturer. An iron can be used to smooth out the klister and make a better bond with the base.

Use long strokes in one direction, from tip to tail, to smooth it evenly.

Normally, one layer is enough.

Put the skis outside to cool a few minutes before using them.

If backslip occurs, add a layer of warmer-temperature klister.

If snow crystals embed in the klister and prevent glide, the klister will have to be removed and replaced with a colder-temperature klister.

Points to Remember

- Glide wax is ironed onto the glide zones of classic skis and along the entire length of skating skis.
- Grip wax is applied to the wax pocket of classic skis—klister for hard or wet snow, hard wax for soft snow.
- If the wax doesn't grip, try TLC: apply a Thicker layer, make the grip zone Longer or Change to a warmer-temperature wax.
- If snow builds up on the grip wax, scrape off the wax and apply a colder-temperature wax.

Further Reading

Nordic Ski Preparation by SWIX.

Wax Book by Toko.

Waxing and Care of Cross Country Skis by Michael Brady.

5 Skiing Safety

Before setting off on a skiing trip, whether on groomed trails or into the backcountry, it is important to take the proper precautions to avoid injury or mishap.

At least one person in a group should carry a first-aid kit. The size of the kit depends upon the number of people in the group. For small groups, a basic kit should consist of adhesive bandages, gauze, disinfectant, cloth bandages and aspirin.

Ultra-Violet Radiation

In recent years the ozone layer in the upper atmosphere has rapidly become depleted, letting more of the sun's ultraviolet rays pass through to the earth's surface. Long-term exposure to high UV levels has been linked to an increase in skin cancer and eye cataracts.

Although the sun is lower in the sky in winter than in summer, the effects of the sun's rays are intensified by reflection from the snow. In winter, just as in summer, it is important to protect your eyes and skin from the sun's rays.

A sunscreen with a Sun Protection Factor of at least 15 should be applied before starting out, even on an overcast day. Choose one that protects against both UVA and UVB.

Snow blindness can occur when eyes are unprotected for a few hours in an open snow-covered area. This condition be described as a sunburn of the cornea—somewhat painful, but likely to clear up within a few days. Wearing sunglasses will help to prevent snow blindness.

Most sunglasses have a tag or sticker attached indicating 100% UV protection. There is, however, no standard UV-rating test, so be aware that the rating may be questionable. High-quality glasses are most likely to provide the best protection.

Hypothermia

Hypothermia is caused by the lowering of the body's energy levels to a point where it can no longer maintain body temperature levels. Hypothermia can not only happen at extremely cold temperatures, but may also occur at temperatures above freezing. Once hypothermia starts, it progresses at a rapid rate. Symptoms of hypothermia usually occur in the following order:

- Uncontrollable shivering—the body's way of producing heat, but it also uses up valuable energy.
- Fumbling, stumbling, mumbling—blood circulation to hands and feet is reduced in order to keep the core warm thereby causing a loss in fine motor skills.
- Incoherence and loss of judgement—both signs are difficult to recognize in yourself, so watch for these and other symptoms in others in your group.
- Drowsiness—the victim starts to enter a metabolic state with a drop in pulse and respiration. At this point, the victim requires immediate medical attention in order to survive.

Prevention of Hypothermia

- Dress appropriately for the weather and level of activity to avoid getting too hot or cold. Use the layering system of dressing to regulate heat loss.
- Avoid over-exertion. Profuse sweating will cause rapid heat loss. Too much exertion also drains the body's energy stores, reducing its ability to produce heat. Take your time on long climbs so that you don't overheat.
- Eat and drink at regular intervals to maintain energy levels.
- Stay dry. If your clothes get wet from rain, snow, perspiration or falling through thin ice, stop and change into dry clothes or dry out wet clothes at the nearest shelter.
- Watch for the symptoms of hypothermia in others in your group. The nature of the condition makes it difficult to recognize the symptoms in yourself.

Treatment of Hypothermia

- Get the victim sheltered from wind and cold. Assist the victim to the nearest windbreak, such as a stand of trees or snowdrift.
- While one person looks after the victim, another should build a shelter with branches or by digging a snow cave.
- Light a fire or stove and heat up some water.
- If the victim is conscious, feed him or her warm sweet liquid to heat up the body core. **Do not provide alcoholic drinks as they reduce the body's ability to generate heat.**
- Remove wet clothes from the victim and wrap him or her in a sleeping bag or emergency blanket with bottles of warm water.
- If there is no sleeping bag or emergency blanket available, replace the victim's wet clothes with dry ones. Add as many layers as possible.

Frostbite

Frostbite generally attacks either exposed face and ears or the hands and feet where the body's heat mass is lower. The stages of frostbite are:

- White patches on face or ears. Hands or feet feel numb.
- Ice crystals form inside skin cells making affected area feel stiff. When the area is warmed a clear blister forms.
- Freezing progresses deeper. A blood-filled blister may form when the area is warmed. There may be extensive loss of tissue.
- Tissue becomes frozen and hard to the touch. Chance of recovery of the frozen tissue is minimal.

Prevention of Frostbite

- Avoid skiing on extremely windy or cold days. Over-exertion at temperatures below -20 °C (-4 °F) can freeze lung tissue.
- Dress appropriately for the weather and your level of activity.
- Monitor your hands and feet for numbness and check others in your group for white spots on exposed skin. Take immediate action to halt the progression of freezing by seeking shelter or adding clothing. Windmilling your arms will usually get the blood circulating faster to warm your hands.
- Carry extra hat, gloves, socks and a face covering such as a balaclava in case of a sudden drop in temperature. Some people use petroleum jelly to protect their faces when it is very cold.
- If you get wet, change into dry clothing.

Treatment of Frostbite

Do not rub or massage a frostbitten area. Manipulation may cause the ice crystals that have formed inside the cells to damage the surrounding tissue.

Slowly warm up the injured part by bringing it in contact with something warm, such as an armpit, either your own or that of an obliging friend. Face and ears can be warmed by gently placing a hand against them. Warming the frostbitten area with anything that is more than a few degrees warmer than normal body temperature, or about 35°C (100°F), may harm the tissue.

Avalanches

Each year in Canada up to a dozen or more lives are claimed by avalanches, mainly in the western provinces. Many other close calls occur; just how many is not known, since not all are reported.

Avalanches can occur both in loose snow and in snow that has consolidated. Avalanche prediction is a complex science that depends upon a variety of factors, such as terrain, weather and snowfall. An estimate of avalanche probability in regions of Alberta and BC can be obtained from the Canadian Avalanche Association and from park wardens (see BC and Alberta listings).

Avalanches can be triggered by the weight of a single person, so your choice of route is an important consideration. Avalanche awareness courses incorporating route finding, stability analysis and rescue techniques are taught by several organizations. The best insurance for a safe trip is to hire a guide who has avalanche safety training and who is familiar with the area.

Avalanche Safety

When travelling in mountainous regions where there is danger of avalanches, take the following precautions:
- Check the avalanche report to see if snowpack conditions are stable before leaving home.
- Travel in groups of three or more.
- Know how to identify danger zones. Choose a route to avoid avalanche-prone areas, if possible.

Figure 5.1
Avalanche beacon.

- If a hazardous area must be crossed, only one member of the party should cross at a time. Remove your pole straps and undo your backpack belt. Bindings with safety releases and without safety straps are recommended so that you are not dragged under by the skis in the event of an avalanche.
- Carry avalanche rescue equipment. Each member of the party should have a beacon, a collapsible probe and a shovel and should be proficient in avalanche rescue procedures.

Beacons are transceivers that can be set to either broadcast or detect a signal to help locate buried avalanche victims. Make certain that everyone in the group has a compatible beacon. Older beacons may use the outdated 2.275 kHz signal, while the newer ones are on a 457 kHz frequency and may not be able to detect the older model.

Beacons are always turned on and set to broadcast mode while skiing in avalanche country. If someone is unfortunate enough to be swept away by an avalanche, the other members switch their beacons to receive mode. After verifying that the slope is safe, a zig-zag search pattern is traced out below where the victim was last seen. As the buried skier is approached, the signal broadcast by his beacon indicates his general position. Probes are then used to determine the exact location of the victim.

If caught in an avalanche, try to stay at the surface by making swimming or rolling motions. Most deaths occur by asphyxiation, so when you feel your movement slowing, try to keep your nose and mouth covered with your hands to block snow from entering. Once you have come to rest, it may be possible to dig your way to the surface, but the snow usually packs solidly making it impossible to move. To determine which way is up, let a drop of saliva dangle from your mouth.

Beaver Fever

Water from a stream or lake may contain giardia or cryptosporidium—protozoa from animal or human sources. Giardiasia is sometimes called "beaver fever" because the animal is a common carrier of the bug. Symptoms include fever and diarrhea. Cryptosporidium causes diarrhea, vomiting and nausea. Both illnesses may last a week or more.

To avoid getting the runs, water from streams or lakes must be purified by filtering, boiling or adding iodine tablets. Iodine takes about 15 to 30 minutes to destroy any harmful parasites but leaves a bad taste and may not be completely effective, especially at cold temperatures. Boiling water for about 10 minutes will kill any nasty bugs, but requires extra fuel.

Filtering is a good way to purify water, although it can be tedious to process large quantities. Filter systems weigh from 0.5 to 0.75 kg (1 to 1.5 lb.) and range in price from about $50 to about $300. Filters must have a pore size of 2 microns or less to remove protozoa. Water is pumped through the filter manually, at the rate of about 0.5 to 1 litres per minute.

Emergency Repair Equipment

At the beginning of the winter, on one of those cold rainy afternoons, take some time to put together an emergency repair kit. It should include the following basic items:

- a cigarette lighter or waterproof matches
- two or three candles to provide heat and light
- a lightweight emergency blanket
- a whistle (in case you happen to get lost or injured, three short blasts will alert searchers of your location.)
- a pocket knife with a screwdriver blade
- a replacement ski tip, pole basket and replacement screws
- a roll of duct tape (to repair just about anything).

Safety Precautions

To avoid problems and to be prepared to deal with any difficulties that may arise, follow these safety guidelines:

- Let someone know where you will be skiing and what time you are returning, particularly when going into backcountry areas.

- Check your equipment before leaving home, to ensure that it functions properly.

- When venturing into avalanche country, follow safety procedures and carry avalanche equipment.

- Carry a map of the area where you are skiing. A compass will also be needed, especially if trails are not marked.

- Wear a backpack containing extra clothing, food and liquid, a waxing kit, emergency equipment and a first-aid kit.

- Know your limitations—both in terms of trail difficulty and distance—and ski on trails that are within your ability.

- Ski in groups of three or more, especially when venturing into backcountry areas. If someone is injured, one person can stay with the victim while the other goes for help.

- Know the symptoms and remedies for frostbite and hypothermia.

- Eat and drink at regular intervals to maintain energy and hydration levels. Physical activity suppresses the appetite, so eat a few mouthfuls of food and take a few swallows of liquid every half hour or so—even if you're not hungry or thirsty.

- Before crossing the ice over lakes or streams, make certain that the ice is thick enough to support your weight. Ski centres will usually warn their clientele about thin ice. Several weeks of continual sub-freezing temperatures are needed to build up a safe thickness of ice.

Skier Etiquette

Following these guidelines will help make skiing a safer and more pleasant experience for everyone:

- Step off the trail when stopping to let other skiers pass.
- Ski single-file on double-tracked trails unless overtaking.
- Move to the right when a skier behind calls out "track" to allow them room to pass.
- Avoid cutting off other skiers when entering trails or overtaking another skier.
- Ski in the specified direction on one-way trails.
- Descending skiers have right-of-way on hills. Climbing skiers should move to the right as descending skiers approach.
- Fill in sitzmarks after falling on trails.
- Pack out any garbage that you have brought with you. Leave nothing but tracks, take nothing but pictures.
- Don't walk or snowshoe on ski trails—footprints decrease grip and glide.
- Leave your dog at home—it not only leaves pawprints (and other more unpleasant things) but may also cause an accident.

Winter Driving

Driving a car in winter can be hazardous, especially for those who are unprepared. Don't wait until snow flies to get your car winterized. Have a mechanic check your car's battery, brakes, exhaust system, antifreeze and oil and have winter tires mounted before it snows. If you do a lot of driving, a membership in the Canadian Automobile Association might come in handy.

Before heading out on a long winter trip, listen to the weather forecast to find out if a snow storm is expected. A blizzard is classified as a combination of falling or blowing snow, winds of 40 km/hr (25 mph) or more, visibility of less than 1 km (0.62 mi.) and temperatures below -10°C (14°F), lasting six hours or more. It doesn't have to be snowing for weather to be disruptive. Winds in open areas can create havoc by blowing snow over the road. When in doubt, call for a road report.

Preparation for Winter Travel

The well-prepared winter driver should carry in his car the following items, in case of emergency:

- a shovel
- sand
- tire chains
- booster cables
- fire extinguisher
- tow chain
- warning flares
- tools and a flashlight
- fuel line antifreeze
- windshield washing fluid
- windshield scraper and brush
- candles, a candle holder and matches
- emergency food and drink
- a sleeping bag or blankets
- warm clothing and snowboots.

On the Road

Winter driving can be treacherous, especially during and after snow storms. Black ice is one hazard that may be lying in wait of unsuspecting drivers. When temperatures are below -10°C (14°F), the thawing effect of salt on snow and ice is greatly reduced.

Regulate your speed according to weather conditions. Speed limits are set for ideal conditions. If it is snowing, reduce your speed to a level that allows you to maintain adequate traction and visibility. If conditions are so bad that visibility is less than 30 metres (100 feet), pull off the road and wait out the storm or turn back, if you haven't gone too far.

Proper braking procedure depends on the type of braking system your car is equipped with. Anti-lock Braking Systems require that you maintain constant pressure on the brake pedal in order to keep the car from skidding when slowing or stopping. For cars not equipped with ABS, it is suggested that the brake pedal be pumped to avoid skidding.

Should you become stranded during a snow storm in an unpopulated area, stay with your car unless you know for certain that you can reach help nearby. **Do not run the motor to keep warm**—deadly carbon monoxide may build up inside the car. Instead, bundle up and light a candle for heat.

If, as a last resort, you must run the motor to keep warm, do so sparingly. Make certain that the exhaust pipe is clear of snow and keep a window partially open on the downwind side of the car.

If you feel cold, keep moving your hands and feet and watch for signs of frostbite. Don't fall asleep. Watch for snow plows or searchers and turn on your four-way flashers and dome light if you hear someone approaching.

Points to Remember

- Wear sunblock and sunglasses, especially in open areas.
- Watch for signs of frostbite and hypothermia in yourself and others in your group.
- Travel through avalanche-prone regions only during low-risk periods and with the proper equipment and know-how.
- Follow safety procedures and carry a backpack containing clothing, food, drink, a first-aid kit and emergency equipment.
- Carry emergency equipment in your car for winter travel.

Further Reading

Avalanche Safety for Skiers and Climbers 2nd Edition by Tony Daffern, Rocky Mountain Books.

How to Stay Alive in the Woods by Bradford Angie, Collier Books.

Winter Survival in the Backcountry, a booklet available from Kananaskis Country.

6 Basic Technique

Skiing, like many other things in life, is much more enjoyable when the proper technique is used. You can improve your technique much faster by taking lessons with a qualified instructor. A local ski club or a large cross-country ski centre are your best bets for finding qualified ski instruction. Video taping and analysis of your technique can prove very helpful once you have learned the basics.

Starting Out

If you are on skis for the first time—or even if you are an experienced skier—walking and gliding without poles helps to establish a sense of rhythm, weight transfer and balance as well as a feel for the gripping action of the wax.

On flat terrain, start by walking on your skis, much as you would normally without skis, letting your arms swing naturally. As you move each ski forward, do not lift it up, just slide it along the snow. As one ski slides past the other, you push off with the rear leg. You should feel the grip wax on the rear ski grip the snow. Let your arms swing as they would when walking.

Once you have mastered this first manoeuvre, add a little glide to your step. As you bring your rear leg forward past your other leg, push off from the stationary leg. Transfer your weight to the ski that is being moved forward as you glide. Keep your weight balanced over the forward ski as you glide.

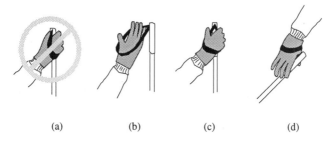

(a)	(b)	(c)	(d)

Figure 6.1 *How to attach wrist straps and grip the pole.*

Gripping the Pole

Most novice skiers tend to slip their hand through the top of the wrist strap and grip the pole tightly (Figure 6.1(a)). Not only can this position cause the hand to cramp, but it also restricts follow-through while poling. A light grip on your pole is required only when carrying it forward to be planted; the rest of the time your hand is supported by the wrist strap.

To properly attach the straps, pass your hand through the loop from the bottom, as illustrated in Figure 6.1(b). Bring your thumb down over the strap on one side of the pole and your fingers over the strap and around the other side of the pole. Adjust the length of the strap so that your hand is supported on the grip of the pole (Figure 6.1(c)). Your grip should be fully relaxed when you push-off with your poles (Figure 6.1(d)).

Technique for Flat Terrain

Diagonal Stride

Diagonal striding uses the same natural rhythm as walking with each arm swinging in the same direction as the leg on the opposite side. Your trunk should be leaning forward from the hips, with your lower spine straight and your upper spine curved slightly forward. Your knees should be kept slightly bent.

Forward momentum is provided by two propulsive forces: the initial kick-off from the weighted ski (position 1 in Figure 6.2), followed by your push-off with the pole on the opposite side (position 4). As one ski glides forward, your other leg kicks to the rear (position 2). Grip wax under the kicking ski resists the kick, causing you to be propelled forward.

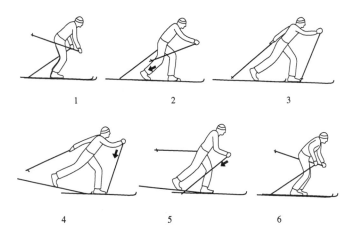

Figure 6.2 *Diagonal stride, showing kick with right leg.*

Follow through so that your kicking leg becomes almost fully extended, but without locking your knee. Your head, torso and extended leg should almost form a straight line (position 4). As your glide begins to slow, plant your forward pole even with your leading foot and push on it to add extra impulse to the glide (position 4).

Many novice skiers make a slapping noise with the rear ski as they bring it forward. The noise is caused either by a stance that is too upright, or by poor balance. In both cases, weight is transferred onto the ski when it is too far back to be positioned flat on the snow. The tail of the ski is still in the air when it is slapped down on the snow by the skier's weight.

Keeping your hips forward will position the ski further forward when weight is shifted onto the ski.

If the problem is loss of balance, learning to glide with your weight balanced on one ski will prevent the premature weight transfer occurring as you struggle to maintain your balance.

Figure 6.3 *Incorrect stance at position 5 of Figure 6.2.*

Figure 6.4 *Double pole.*

Double Pole

The double pole is a technique for flat or gentle slopes. Your weight should be evenly distributed on both skis. Plant both poles next to your feet at a slight forward lean, as in position 1 of Figure 6.4. Keep your elbows bent at approximately 90 degrees. While keeping your back straight, bend forward from your hips to gain extra leverage on the poles (positions 2 to 3). Follow through by pushing down and back on the poles. Exhale as you bend down and breathe in as you straighten up.

Step Double Pole

When momentum slows while double poling, a kick can be added to increase speed. After double poling, kick off as you would for a diagonal stride. As you kick, swing both poles forward to plant them, then double pole as before.

Uphill Techniques

Uphill Diagonal

When executing the diagonal stride to ascend a gradual incline, you will find that your kick is not getting enough grip and backslipping occurs. By adjusting your stride, you can climb slightly steeper slopes than with the regular diagonal stride.

Keep your upper body more upright than in the regular diagonal stride and plant your poles further back, near the heel of your gliding foot. Since glide is reduced, the tempo of this stride is quicker, with less time for follow-through with the poles.

Herringbone

Hills that are too steep to climb with the diagonal stride are ascended using the herringbone.

Facing up the slope, angle your skis outward in a "V" formation without crossing the tails. The angle between the skis is increased according to the steepness of the hill. As you lift one ski and move it forward, backsliding is resisted by setting the edge of your other ski into the snow and simultaneously pushing on the poles.

Figure 6.5
Herringbone.

Repeat for the other ski and continue until the top of the hill is reached.

Side Stepping

If the hill is too steep for the herringbone, the slower side stepping method can be used.

Point your skis perpendicular to the slope and set the edges into the snow.

Move your uphill ski further up the hill and set its edge into the snow, while using your poles to maintain balance.

Move your downhill ski and pole closer to the uphill ski and repeat the procedure until the hill is crested.

Figure 6.6
Sidestep.

Downhill Techniques

If you are intimidated by the pitch of a slope, don't be ashamed to remove your skis and walk down the hill, off to the side of the trail. Just think how much more embarrassing it would be to be carted off on a sled by the safety patrol.

Falling and Getting Up

If you find yourself travelling down a hill at an uncontrollable rate of speed and you are unable to slow down, it's time to bail out. Falling is the most effective way of stopping—it's as easy as sitting down. Select a soft landing spot, away from any trees or rocks, then sit down to the back and one side of the tails of the skis, keeping your poles pointed in the air.

To get up after a fall, swing around so that your skis are on the downhill side perpendicular to the slope. Remove the wrist straps of your poles. Bend your knees to get your centre of gravity as low as possible.

Push against the snow, or against your poles if the snow is soft, so that you roll upright, into a squatting position. Fill in the sitzmark left by your fall so that it doesn't cause someone else to fall.

Figure 6.8
Getting up.

Downhill Stances

When schussing down hills, maintaining a stable position will help to keep you on your feet. Your skis should be shoulder-width apart to provide good balance. Your weight should be evenly distributed between your skis and balanced over the balls of your feet.

Keep your knees slightly bent so that they can absorb the shocks caused by bumps. Rigid legs will throw you off balance when you hit a bump. Keep your back straight and inclined slightly forward from the hips. Your hands should be in front of you and the tips of your poles pointing behind.

Figure 6.9
Downhill stance.

Figure 6.10
Downhill tuck.

Maximum speed can be attained by getting into a tuck position to minimize wind resistance. Bend your back nearly horizontal, leaving space between your chest and knees for your legs to absorb shocks. Your hands should be held in front of you and your poles tucked under your armpits. Your body weight can be shifted slightly to the rear to relieve the pressure on the tips of the skis thereby allowing them to float more easily over the snow.

Snowplow and Stem Turn

When schussing down hills, it is also important to know how to stop so that you don't become intimately acquainted with a tree. There are several methods of turning and stopping when descending hills. The suitability of each method is determined by the snow conditions and steepness of the slope.

Figure 6.11
Snowplow.

On packed trails of moderate pitch, the snowplow (also known as the "wedge") is most often used to turn, slow or stop. To execute the snowplow, bring the tips of your skis together, while maintaining an angle of 45 to 60 degrees between your skis. Your knees should be slightly bent. To slow down in a straight line, keep your weight balanced evenly on your skis.

To turn, place more weight on the ski that is pointing in the direction of the turn and twist your upper body in the direction of the turn. The effectiveness of the snowplow is improved by turning your ankles inward so that the inside edges of your skis dig into the snow.

Stem turns are similar to the snowplow turn, the only difference being that the more lightly weighted ski is kept parallel to the direction of travel. When you want to slow or stop on a track-set trail, take one ski out of the track and do a half-wedge.

Other Methods of Slowing

On an open, packed slope you can use the snowplow or stem turns to make a series of linked S-turns down the hill. Travelling at an angle to the fall-line, or "traversing" as it is sometimes called, reduces the steepness of the line of travel thereby slowing the speed of descent.

On hills where there is no room to turn or snowplow, you will have to find another method of slowing down. It may be possible to ski in the unpacked snow on the sides of the trail to decrease speed. The sudden change in speed sometimes, however, results in a nose-dive. In deep snow, your ski tips may dig in, or "submarine", also causing you to make a face-plant.

Various methods of pole dragging are sometimes effective in controlling speed but may damage ski poles or cause injury. When using your poles to slow down, it is important to remove your wrist straps in order to avoid dislocating a shoulder if a pole gets caught on something. Use only sturdy, inexpensive poles for braking, as high-performance poles are too lightweight for this kind of abuse.

Step Turn

Gentle curves on flat or slightly sloping terrain can be negotiated using the step turn. As you approach the curve, shift your weight onto the ski that is on the outside of the curve (position 1 in Figure 6.13). Move your inner ski so that it follows the curve. Shift your weight onto your inner ski (position 2) and move your outer ski parallel to the inner ski (3). Repeat as often as necessary as you progress along the curve.

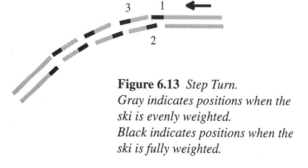

Figure 6.13 *Step Turn.*
Gray indicates positions when the ski is evenly weighted.
Black indicates positions when the ski is fully weighted.

Telemark Turn

A whole sport has evolved around the telemark turn. This alpine/nordic hybrid is used for descending hills at lift-serviced resorts and in the backcountry. Skiers who specialize in telemarking use metal-edged skis that carve easily and heavy boots that allow the heel to lift off the ski. It is possible, however, to execute the telemark turn on packed snow using regular cross-country gear.

Learning to telemark is easiest on a gently sloping hill where the snow has been packed. Begin the turn with a half-wedge turn (position 1), with the angled ski on the outside of the turn. Advance the outer ski until you are in the telemark position with your rear heel lifted and both knees bent about 90 degrees (position 3).

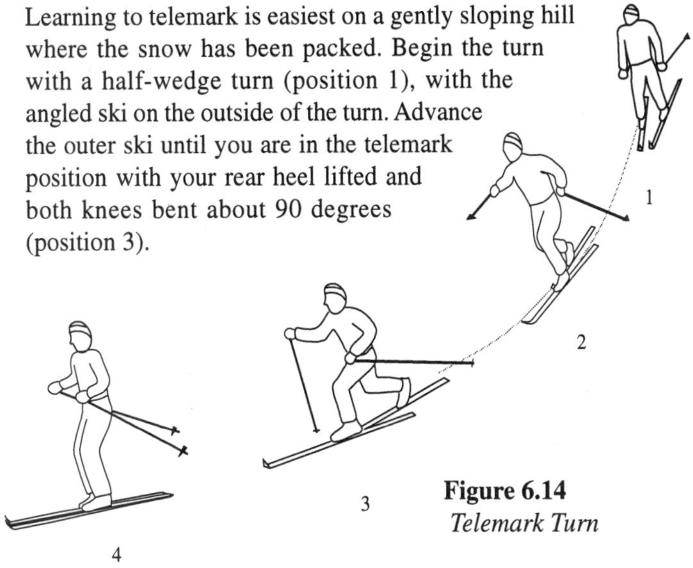

Figure 6.14
Telemark Turn

In the telemark position, your weight should be evenly distributed over both of your skis so that control of the trailing ski can be maintained. Both skis work in unison to act as a single ski with an exaggerated sidecut. Steering is initiated by pressing the toes and rolling your knees into the turn. At the end of the turn, rise to an upright position by bringing your trailing leg forward (position 4).

Skating Techniques

American terminology for most of the skating techniques differs from that used in Canada. The alternate name, if any, for the technique appears in parentheses in the heading. All skating techniques except the marathon are more easily performed on snow that has been packed flat at least two metres wide.

Marathon Skate

Also known as the half-skate, because it combines elements of skating and classic technique, the marathon skate is a good introduction to the art of skating. The marathon skate is intended for flat terrain and is the only skating technique that can be used where trails are groomed for classic only.

One ski glides in the track and the other ski is kept at an angle to the track. The edge of the angled ski is set into the snow to provide traction during the skating action (position 2). As you finish the skating action, transfer your weight onto the gliding ski and lift the skating ski up and forward (position 3).

Poles are used together in synchronization with the skating action. As in the regular double-pole, your upper body should bend forward at the waist to increase leverage on the poles.

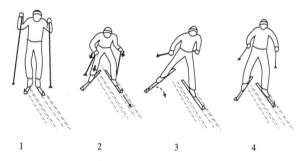

1   2   3   4

Figure 6.15 *Marathon skate.*

Free Skate

The free skate is used on gentle inclines where the speed of travel is too fast for poling. The free skate is a good introductory technique because it first concentrates on balance, rhythm and leg movements, without the added complication of poles.

Start off on a very gentle slope. Keep your skis pointed outward, on each side of, and at a slight angle to the direction you want to go. Push off using the inner edge of one ski, and glide on the other ski, just as you would on ice skates. As glide begins to slow, bring your rear leg forward to place it beside the gliding leg. Then push off from the gliding ski, before it stops completely, and glide on the other ski. To maximize glide, the gliding ski should be kept as flat as possible during all skating techniques.

One Skate (V-2)

The one skate is normally used on flat or slightly ascending terrain. There is one skating action for every double-pole, with poling occurring at the same time as the skate (see Figure 6.16). Since the rhythm of this technique is fast, there is little time for follow-through with your poles.

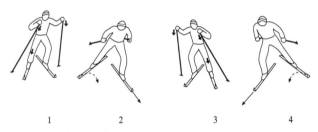

Figure 6.16 *One skate.*

Two Skate (V-2 Alternate)

The two skate is a slower-tempo skating stride for flat or slightly descending terrain, where glide can be maintained longer than in the one skate. It differs from the one skate in that there are two skating actions for each double pole and the first skate occurs midway through the double pole (position 2 below).

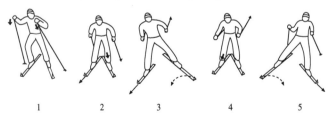

Figure 6.17 *Two skate.*

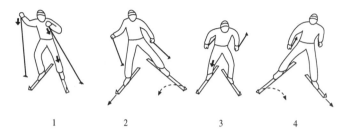

1   2   3   4

Figure 6.18 *Offset skate.*

Offset Skate (V-1)

With a similar rhythm to the two skate, the offset skate is primarily used to ascend moderately steep hills. It differs from the two skate in that the poles are not planted in line, but at an offset distance to each other. Placing one pole further up the hill than the other extends the double poling phase, thereby generating more propulsion.

The first skating action occurs with the leg that is on the same side as the downhill pole and coincides with the double pole (position 1 in Figure 6.18). A second skate occurs as the arms are brought forward (position 3).

Diagonal Skate (Diagonal V)

Best used on steep ascents, the diagonal skate is just the herringbone with a little glide added. As in the diagonal stride, your arms move in opposite directions.

Points to Remember

Each classic and skating technique is suited to a particular range of terrain steepness. Figure 6.19 indicates the relative order of usage of the techniques according to the slope of the trail. Actual application of all these techniques will vary according to the snow conditions and the kind of shape you are in.

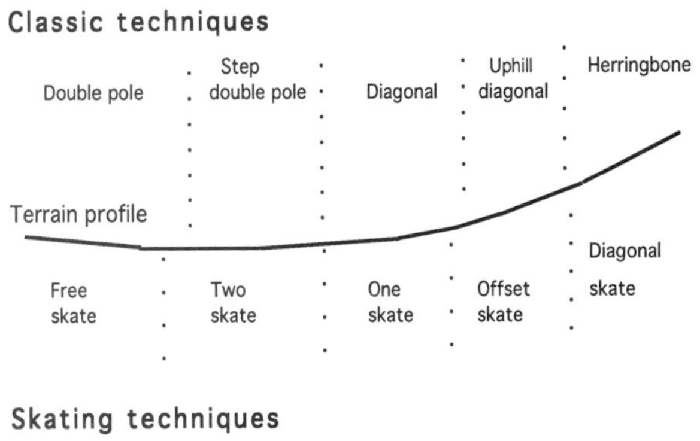

Classic techniques

Skating techniques

Figure 6.19 *Application of techniques according to the slope of the terrain.*

Further Reading

Cross Country Skiing Level 2 Technical Coaching Manual, Tom Silletta and Anton Scheier, 1995, Cross Country Canada

Free-Heel Skiing by Paul Parker, Chelsea Green Publishing.

Nordic Skiing Steps to Success, Laurie Gullion, 1993, Human Kinetic Publishers

The New Cross-Country Ski Book 8th Edition, John Caldwell, 1987, Stephen Green Press

Videos

How to Cross Country Ski, 1987, Karhu Canada, 30 min. (available from CANSI) presents a quick introduction to all the cross-country techniques.

Myriam Bédard presents Secrets of Cross Country Skiing (The Skating Technique), 1995, Vidéotron Ltd., 50 min., provides an excellent coverage of all the skating techniques.

7 Getting Ready

One of the great things about cross-country skiing is that it can be done anywhere there is snow—from your back yard to the backcountry. You will find places to ski just about anywhere in Canada, whether on groomed trails at ski centres or in wilderness areas.

Cross Country Ski Centres

Across Canada there are over 500 locations where cross-country skiers have access to groomed trails. Trail system operators fall into one of three categories: government organizations, private businesses or clubs.

Many municipal, provincial and national parks groom walking and hiking trails for cross-country skiing. Municipally-operated trails are usually free. Provincial parks often charge a flat rate per car, if they charge anything at all. At some provincial parks, a private concessionaire or club may operate the trails and charge fees. Some national parks charge an entrance fee for cars stopping in the park. An annual pass to the national parks in western Canada may be purchased for about $60.

Commercially-run centres are often full-service resorts with on-site restaurant and accommodation facilities. Some are operated in conjunction with an alpine ski centre where there is often a wide variety of hotels and condominiums. A few resorts restrict the use of their trails to guests only.

Many cross-country ski clubs operate their own centres on a non-profit basis with the help of volunteers. Some of these centres charge a daily trail fee, while others accept donations and request that you purchase a membership if you ski there frequently.

Trail Grooming

Trails can be groomed either by snowmobiles or with larger snow grooming machinery, most of which are manufactured by Pisten-Bulley or Bombardier. Snowmobiles are used to tow a track-setting sled and their smaller size allows them to fit on narrow, winding trails. Some people enjoy the intimacy of these types of meandering trails, while others prefer to speed along on faster trails.

Large snow groomers can only travel on trails that are fairly straight and wide—the super highways of the cross-country skiing world. The large groomers are wide and heavy enough to firmly compact the snow with just one pass, so are excellent for skating trails. Most have plows that can smooth out dips and bumps in the surface of the snow. Many are equipped with snow conditioners that can break up icy snow caused by midwinter rain.

Trail Systems

Trails that have been constructed solely for the purpose of cross-country skiing are generally laid out in some combination of loops. Often there are one or more main loops that start out from and lead back to the main lodge, as illustrated in Figure 7.1. Other loops may branch off the main loop, allowing you the choice of returning to the lodge or continuing your trip. Many trails are one-way, thus prevent you from retracing your path.

Multipurpose trails are used for biking or hiking in the summer and cross-country skiing in the winter. These types of trails are generally linear, leading either to a point of interest or to another access. In most national and provincial parks trails are linear, with trailheads scattered throughout the park. There is generally no central chalet or lodge where services can be obtained.

Just about every ski centre provides maps of their trails at no charge. The map should indicate the name, level of difficulty, length of each trail along with any hazards, trailside shelters or points of interest (see Figure 7.1). Some centres have a different name for each trail section between junctions, others name each loop that starts and ends at the day lodge. A ski centre that uses the latter naming system will appear to have fewer trails than those that use the former method. In reality, they may have the same total length of trails.

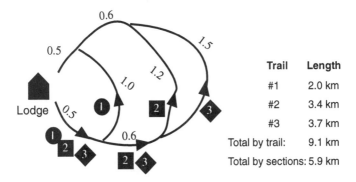

Trail	Length
#1	2.0 km
#2	3.4 km
#3	3.7 km
Total by trail:	9.1 km
Total by sections:	5.9 km

Figure 7.1 *Trail map of overlapping loops (stacked loops).*

Trail Lengths

Lengths of ski trails are almost always measured in kilometres and are usually indicated on the trail map and on signs. Some trail maps show distances between junctions of trails—a helpful feature for those who like to keep track of the total distance they ski each day.

Most centres indicate the total length of the trail system on the map and use that figure for promotional purposes. The total length of trails can be misleading because it can be calculated by one of two methods: either by adding up the lengths of each trail or by totalling up the lengths of individual sections.

Some commercially-operated ski centres use the more liberal method of simply totalling the lengths of all their trails. Since trails often partially overlap, these sections of trails are included more than once. In some extreme cases, the total length of the trail system calculated in this manner is more than double that calculated by adding the overlapping sections only once.

As an example, refer to Figure 7.2. Adding trail lengths yields a total that is over 50% greater than that calculated with no overlap. In short, when visiting a ski area for the first time, don't be surprised if the trail system is smaller than you were led to believe.

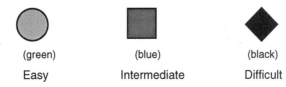

(green) (blue) (black)

Easy Intermediate Difficult

Figure 7.2 *Standard trail rating symbols.*

Trail Ratings

There are three levels of difficulty, each represented by a symbol, as shown in Figure 7.2: a green circle indicates easy; a blue square, intermediate; a black diamond, difficult. Rating levels may have different designations at different centres but the most common are "Easy," "Difficult" and "Most Difficult."

Trails are not always rated according to a standard specification. Often trails are rated relative to the other trails at the ski centre or according to distance. Determining if a trail is within your capabilities when you are skiing at an area for the first time may be difficult.

 If you are unsure about the rating levels at a new centre, start on a trail with a lower rating than you would normally ski.

Ski Clubs

Whether you are a novice skier or a veteran looking for new horizons, your local ski club has lots to offer. Most large cities have at least one ski club that arranges trips to different destinations by chartered bus or car pool. Clubs in more rural areas tend to operate out of a ski centre, often one that is run by the club itself.

Some clubs are geared towards adults only, while others are family oriented, with lessons and development programs for all ages. Joining a club is an excellent way to meet ski buddies of your own ability. When you hang out with a group of like-minded people you will learn by osmosis—everyone has their own bag of tricks that they are glad to share. Clubs also provide a great incentive to get out skiing, offering many activities throughout the season.

Over 300 clubs in Canada are associated with Cross Country
Canada and are run on a non-profit basis. Other clubs may be
run for profit and may charge more, but you are not expected
to volunteer your time to the operations of the club. Non-profit
clubs, on the other hand, have more of a community spirit
because everyone contributes. To find the club nearest you,
contact the division of CCC in your region or check your local
outdoor store for posters or brochures of outdoor clubs.

Packing List for Day Trips

When preparing for a day trip, check that you have the
following items to take on the trail with you:

- skis, boots and poles.
- ski clothes (including jacket, pants, hat and gloves).
- an extra layer of clothing in case of an incapacitating
  injury. (Even in an area with a ski patrol, it may take
  over an hour for help to arrive.)
- enough food for lunch and snacks plus extra food
  in case of emergencies. Trail mix, granola bars or
  dried fruit can be left in your backpack all season.
  Carbohydrates are the quickest source of energy.
- one to two litres of liquid, depending on the length
  of the trip. Juice or sports drinks such as Gatorade
  provide extra energy. Avoid caffeinated and alcoholic beverages.
- a waxing kit, consisting of two or three waxes, cork
  and a scraper.
- handkerchiefs or tissues.
- sunscreen, lip balm and sunglasses.
- your medicare card, money, identification and credit
  card in case of injury.
- a map and compass.
- a camera and film.
- an emergency repair kit and a first-aid kit.

Leave a change of clothing in your car to put on after
you have finished skiing—the journey home will be
more comfortable in dry clothes.

Backcountry Skiing

In recent years, there has a been a tremendous boom in the popularity of backcountry skiing. Sales of backcountry gear have been steadily increasing. It seems that more and more people are looking to get away from it all by venturing off the beaten path.

Backcountry touring can be done either on untracked trails through forests or across the wide-open areas above the treeline. Tourers in mountainous regions sometimes use alpine ski equipment with adaptable bindings that can be set to either allow free movement of the heel for ascending hills or to lock the heel for descents. Many mountain tourers attach climbing skins to their skis for long, steep ascents.

Getting lost has much more severe consequences in remote areas, where the chances of encountering another person are very slim. Skiing in an unfamiliar area where there are no trail maps or markers to follow requires a topographical map of the region, a compass and good navigational skills to keep on the right path.

Hiring an experienced guide is the best insurance for a trouble-free trip. Guided backcountry ski touring packages are offered by some commercial tour guides, lodge operators and outdoor organizations such as Yamnuska.

When planning a backcountry trip, allow extra time to reach your destination, as ungroomed trails are much slower to ski, particularly if you are breaking trail. As a rule of thumb, allow more than double the time it would take to cover the same distance on groomed trails, and more, if there is deep untracked snow or if the terrain is rugged.

Compasses and Topographic Maps

A topographic map describes the relief of the terrain within its boundaries by means of contour lines that join points of equal elevation (Figure 7.3). A map and a compass will help you determine your location and show the distance and the amount of climb or descent to get to your destination.

Topo maps covering most of Canada are produced by the Department of Energy, Mines and Resources. Of the two scales available, 1:50,000 and 1:250,000, the smaller scale is more suitable for backcountry travel. Each 1:50,000 map encompasses about 1,200 km^2 (500 mi.^{2}) with 50-m (164-ft.) contour lines.

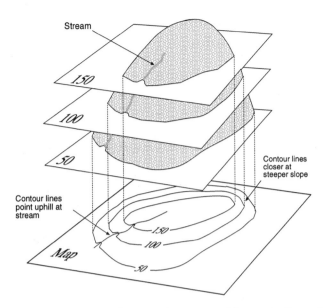

Figure 7.3 *Contour lines on the topographic map indicate the elevation of the terrain.*

Be careful about putting too much faith in maps, some contain inaccurate or incorrect information, such as errors in elevation. Maps can be ordered from EMR or your local map retailer.

Getting Your Bearings

One important detail to keep in mind about compasses is that they don't point to the true north pole, but to the magnetic north (see Figure 7.4). Maps, on the other hand, are drawn oriented to true north. Compass readings should therefore be adjusted by the angle of declination, particularly in the more easterly and westerly regions of Canada, where declination is greatest.

Magnetic north is about 1,500 km (1,000 mi.) south of true north, in the middle of the Canadian arctic. Declinations therefore vary from negligible amounts in central Canada to as much as 15 or 20 degrees in coastal regions. Most topographic maps show the declination for the region covered by the map.

To keep yourself on track, you must first determine your present location on the map. Turn the rotating ring of your compass so that the north arrow is set to the angle of declination. The north

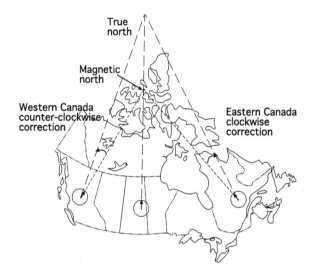

Figure 7.4 *Variation of magnetic declination across Canada.*

arrow will then point to true north and all compass readings will be adjusted to true north.

Hold your map so that it is aligned with the true north. Look at the countryside around you for topographical features, such as the lakes or peaks that appear on the map. Compass readings on several distant landmarks can be used to triangulate your position on the map. An altimeter is also useful for pinpointing your location.

Once your position on the map has been established, you can then measure the distance and the angle, or bearing, to your destination on the map. Set the directional arrow on the compass to your bearing. Pick out a distant landmark along that bearing and travel towards it.

A handy new navigational aid, the GPS (global positioning system), is an electronic device that reads satellite signals to determine your location and the bearing and distance to your destination. Waypoints can be stored so that you can retrace your path. Before spending several hundred dollars on one of these gadgets, make sure that it operates at cold temperatures. Carry a compass as a backup in case the device malfunctions.

Backcountry Lodges and Huts

Overnight trips in the backcountry are much more pleasantly spent in the comfort of a heated shelter than in a tent. Backcountry facilities, be they commercially operated or self-sufficient, can be rented for overnight accommodation in some areas. They are generally accessed by ski on ungroomed trails, but some are so isolated they can only be reached by helicopter.

Commercially-operated lodges offer many of the amenities of home—sometimes even hot showers and indoor toilets. Meals are usually catered and guides are sometimes provided. Most of the lodges in mountainous areas are only intended for alpine touring and telemark skiing, although some also offer treed terrain.

Huts are less expensive and more spartan shelters usually operated on a not-for-profit basis. Most huts offer dormitory-style accommodations and are equipped with wood-burning stoves that maintain temperature levels in the comfort zone. Some parks have several huts that can be used for hut-to-hut touring. Huts should be reserved well in advance as many are quickly booked up for the most popular periods as soon as reservations are accepted.

Overnight Backcountry Trips

Since most backcountry lodges supply catered meals and bedding, tourers making use of these facilities need only carry clothing and toiletry items and the usual equipment for a day trip. Much more gear is required for stays in backcountry huts. Each person will need to carry about 10 to 15 kg (20 to 35 lb.) of equipment, depending on the number of nights and the available amenities.

Some operations provide a baggage transport service to lighten your load. If you intend to carry your gear yourself, a frame backpack with a belt and chest strap and a capacity of a least 50 litres (3,100 in.^{3}) is an absolute necessity. Wide skis and heavy boots will help support the extra weight on ungroomed trails.

Hardy skiers wishing to camp in tents will need a very warm sleeping bag as the temperature in the tent will be about the same as outside. By morning, frost will have formed on every surface and will leave everything a little damp—even after being brushed off.

On backcountry sojourns it is easier to find water sources than to carry more than a day's supply. You can either make your own water by melting snow or purify water from a stream. If the weather is warm, you may be able to melt snow by continually adding it to a container that is partially full of water. When it's cold, you will have to heat snow which means that you must carry extra fuel. Water from a stream must be purified to remove parasites such as giardia (see Chapter 5).

For day trips in the backcountry, you may need (in addition to items for a day trip on groomed trails):
* gaiters
* climbing skins for mountainous regions
* avalanche rescue equipment when in avalanche country.

For overnight stays in backcountry lodges, you may also need:
* ear plugs for dormitory-style sleeping arrangements
* a flashlight, candles and a candle lantern
* toilet paper and toiletry items
* moleskins or adhesive bandages to protect blisters
* slippers and a change of clothes
* extra waxes, a thermometer, wax solvent and a wiping cloth.

If you are going on a self-sufficient trip, you may also need:
* a tent (a three-season or winter model)
* a sleeping bag and mattress
* a backpacker stove and fuel (allow extra for melting snow)
* waterproof matches
* a water purifier (if an unfrozen water source will be available)
* a large water container
* pots, pans and cooking utensils
* cups, plates, knives, forks and spoons
* a scrubbing pad and biodegradable dish soap
* food (preferably freeze-dried).

Points to Remember

* Lengths of trail systems sometimes include overlap.
* Trails are rated according to three levels of difficulty.
* Check that you have packed everything you will need.
* Carry a map and compass and know how to use them.
* Huts and lodges are available for backcountry stays.

Further Reading

Backcountry Skiing by Lito Tejada-Flores, Sierra Club Books.

8 Canadian Environment

Winter Climate

Of all the countries in the world, Canada has the most dramatic fluctuations in weather conditions. With the exception of coastal British Columbia, all regions are subject to markedly different seasons—from sweltering July heatwaves to frigid January blizzards.

West coast climate is dominated by Pacific air currents, keeping the weather relatively mild all year. Winters near the coast are typically quite rainy, due to the warm moist Pacific air currents that often penetrate to interior BC, bringing heavy snowfalls to the mountainous regions (see Figure 8.1).

Several times each winter, Pacific air masses infiltrate as far as the eastern foothills of the Rockies. These warm winds, or Chinooks, send temperatures soaring as much as 15°C (30°F) within hours. Chinook conditions are typified by a stationary arch of clouds over the foothills and may last for several hours or several days.

Winter on the prairies is dominated by Arctic air masses. Frontal disturbances, caused by the interaction of Arctic and Pacific systems, form over Alberta and travel eastwards producing, light snowfalls and leaving frigid temperatures in their wake.

Western winter disturbances moving into southern regions of Ontario and Quebec may be reinforced by warm, humid air from the south, resulting in heavy snowfalls. From time to time, storms formed in the mid-western United States also travel into the region and result in gale-force winds and heavy snowfall or freezing rain. Winters in southern Ontario and Quebec are subject to fluctuations in temperature and short cold spells, due

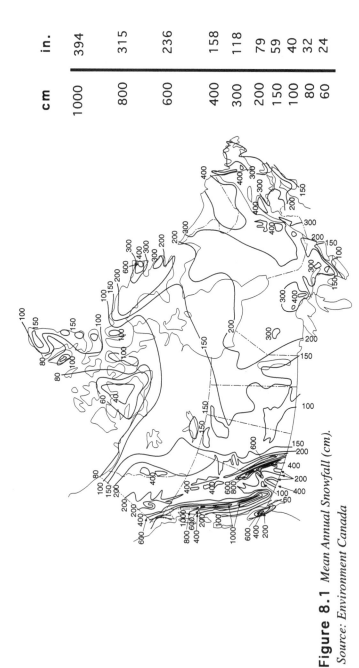

Figure 8.1 *Mean Annual Snowfall (cm).*
Source: Environment Canada

to the influence of the two weather-makers. The climate in the area immediately north of Lake Ontario and Lake Erie is moderated by the "lake effect."

Climate in the Atlantic provinces is influenced by three weather systems. In addition to disturbances from western Canada and central USA, storms may travel up the Atlantic coast. Despite its maritime location, the region has a continental climate owing to predominately eastward air currents. Only the southern coasts of Nova Scotia and Newfoundland are subject to the moderating influence of the ocean.

Topography and Vegetation

Topography and climate combine to influence the types of flora and fauna that grow in a particular region. Coastal rainforests are created by heavy rains wrung from humid Pacific air. As the warm, humid air rises over the coastal mountains, it cools, releasing huge snowfalls in winter (see Figure 8.2).

Buttressed between the coastal ranges and the Rocky Mountains are several smaller mountain ranges and the interior plateau. This region contains a wide variety of vegetation zones, such as the montane and sub-alpine regions. Vegetation in alpine zones above the tree-line is very similar to arctic tundra.

Canada's prairies stretch from the Alberta foothills to the southeast corner of Manitoba and as far north as Edmonton on the western edge. What was once rolling grassland is now mainly pasture and cultivated farmland. The only break in the region's relief are the Cypress Hills on the Alberta-Saskatchewan border, poking up several hundred meters above the surrounding plains.

Most of Canada is covered by boreal forest, sometimes called *taiga*, extending diagonally across the country from Alaska to Newfoundland. Bounded to the south by the prairies and Great Lakes and to the north by the Arctic tundra and Hudson Bay, it is composed of the northern, middle and southern sub-zones. The middle boreal region is mainly a mix of spruce, pine, fir and hemlock trees.

Figure 8.2 *Vegetation regions of Canada.*

In the southern boreal sub-zone there is a large proportion of deciduous trees such as birch, aspen and ash. In western Canada there is a southern transition zone of aspen and grassland along the border with the prairies. The northern boreal sub-zone is a mixture of forest and patches of tundra.

All of northern Canada above the boreal zone consists of arctic tundra, a treeless plain of permanently frozen subsoil covered with moss, shrubs and lichen. In the southern regions, close to the boreal forest, clumps of stunted spruce are interspersed with tundra.

Most of eastern Canada consists of the Canadian Shield—a complex of lakes, muskeg bogs, meadows and forest on glaciated rock with thin soil cover. In the southern regions, the milder climate sustains a greater proportion of deciduous trees. What little forest remains in the Niagara Peninsula region is almost entirely deciduous.

South of the St. Lawrence River, the Appalachian region stretches from North Carolina through New Brunswick to the west coast of Newfoundland. The steep hills, vales and low-lying plateaus of Appalachia sustain a mixture of hardwood and softwood forest.

Canadian Fauna

While skiing in the more isolated regions, you may have the good fortune (or, in some cases, bad luck) of encountering wildlife. More than likely, you will come across prints left by an animal. Some of the more common large mammals are described below.

Deer Family (Cervidae)

Caribou are found in regions of every province and territory in Canada, with the exception of Atlantic Canada. Two subspecies exist: barren ground and woodland caribou. Each spring, massive herds of barren ground caribou migrate several hundred kilometres from their winter feeding grounds to spend the summer in their calving grounds on the tundra.

Woodland caribou have short migrations, moving in small herds from higher elevations to the shelter of forests in winter. Unlike other members of the deer family, both males and females have antlers, those of the males being much broader and flatter.

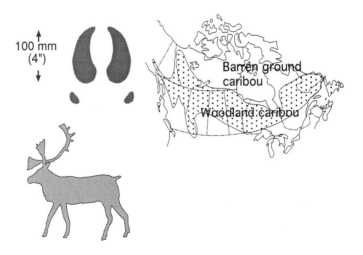

Figure 8.3 *Barren ground and woodland caribou.*

White-tailed deer inhabit the southern regions of every province except Newfoundland. During the winter, they usually seek the protection of the forest, although some roam in herds on the prairies. Their preferred winter diet consists of the twigs and the buds of hardwood trees. Lacking that, they will eat coniferous needles, sprouts, lichens and dead leaves. Their winter colouring is grayish with white around the eyes, chin and throat. When the deer is alarmed, it flips up the white underside of its tail to warn its herdmates.

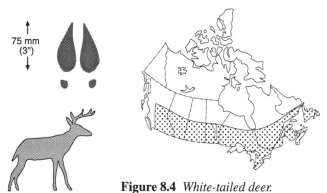

Figure 8.4 *White-tailed deer.*

Mule deer are denizens of the western provinces where their preferred habitat is the fringes of mountain forests. Mule deer differ in appearance from white-tailed deer in several respects: the mule deer is heavier, with larger ears, a black-tipped tail and Y-shaped antlers.

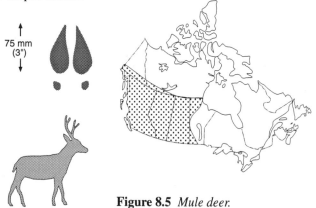

Figure 8.5 *Mule deer.*

Moose can be found in every province and territory. Males have large antlers that are a combination of round tines and shovel-like appendices. Antlers are shed around mid-December to mid-January and begin to regrow in April. Moose are generally solitary animals, although mothers will accompany their calves for almost a year. Females are very protective of their calves and should be avoided. Due to their massive size (300 to 550 kg, or 650 to 1,200 lb.), moose cause many fatalities and extensive vehicle damage when they encounter cars while crossing highways.

150 mm
(6")

Figure 8.6 *Moose*

Elk once ranged over much of North America. Now they are relegated to the Rocky Mountains and interior British Columbia. Summers are generally spent in alpine meadows. In winter, herds of elk are often spotted at lower elevations, along the highways. The elk's back and sides are light brown while their head, neck, legs and undersides are dark brown. Bulls carry antlers up to 1.8 m (6 ft.) long that are shed in February.

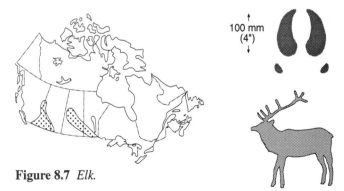

100 mm
(4")

Figure 8.7 *Elk.*

Canine Family (Canidae)

Coyotes range over much of Canada, from the Yukon to southwestern Quebec. They resemble medium-sized dogs with bushy tails. Mature coyotes weigh from 10 to 18 kg (22 to 40 lb.). Coloration varies greatly, from gray to light brown or yellow. Generally, the throat, chest and undersides are white.

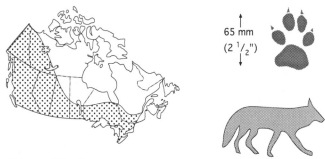

Figure 8.8 *Coyote.*

Red foxes make their home in a wide variety of habits—from tundra to mountains, prairies and forests. Red foxes, as you may have guessed, are reddish brown, except for their white neck, chest and undersides. They are small, weighing 5 to 6 kg (11 to 13 lb.), and sport bushy tails.

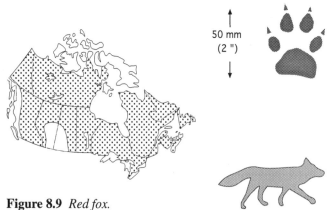

Figure 8.9 *Red fox.*

Wolves are similar in appearance to German shepherd dogs except for their larger heads and bushier tails. They hunt small animals and weaker members of the deer family. In spite of their reputation as killers, wolves are thought to be harmless to adult humans.

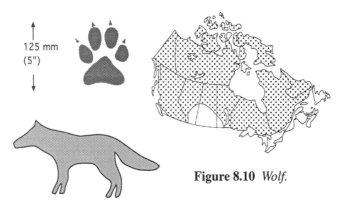

125 mm
(5")

Figure 8.10 *Wolf.*

Bear Family (Ursidae)

Black bears inhabit wooded areas of North America. They spend most of the winter hibernating in their dens. Males weigh an average of 140 kg (300 lb.) at maturity; females grow to about half that. As their name suggests, most black bears have black fur, but some are actually brown-coloured. They eat a balanced diet of insects, honey, berries and small mammals. They have a keen appetite for human's food and garbage.

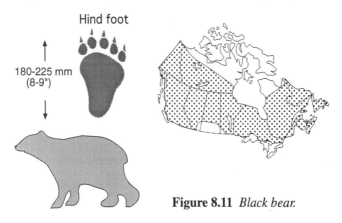

Hind foot

180-225 mm
(8-9")

Figure 8.11 *Black bear.*

Grizzly bears make their dens at elevations of about 2,000 to 2,400 m (6,500 to 8,000 ft.). Mature grizzlies weigh from 140 kg (300 lb.) for females to 350 kg (800 lb.) for males. Fur colours vary from gray to brown. Grizzlies can be distinguished from brown-coloured black bears by the hump on their shoulders. They also have a curved facial profile, unlike the flat snout of the black bear. Grizzly bears are short-sighted and are thought to be unable to discern anything beyond 100 m (300 ft.). They compensate for their myopia with their exceptional hearing and acute sense of smell.

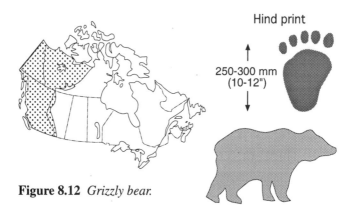

Hind print

250-300 mm
(10-12")

Figure 8.12 *Grizzly bear.*

It is unlikely that you will chance upon a bear in winter, as they are usually hibernating. If you do happen to encounter one, retreat slowly; bears are inclined to chase anything that runs from them, thinking that it is prey. Bears are very fleet-footed, able to run at speeds of over 60 km/hr (40 m.p.h.), so it is unlikely that you could outdistance it.

Further Reading

Climate Canada Second Edition, F. Kenneth Hare and Morley K. Thomas, John Wiley and Sons Canada Ltd, 1979.

Wild Mammals of Canada, Frederick H. Wooding McGraw-Hill Ryerson Ltd, 1982.

A Field Guide to the Mammals, William H. Burt and Richard Grossenheider, 1976.

9 Organizations and Events

Canadian cross-country skiing has been aided in its development by the support of several national organizations that promote different aspects of the sport. Annual events, such as the Canadian Ski Odyssey, also help to popularize cross-country skiing across the country.

Organizations

There are many associations in Canada devoted to the sport of skiing and to outdoor activities in general.

Ski Organizations

Biathlon Canada has as its mandate the promotion, development and administration of biathlon in Canada. It sanctions regional and national competitions held at various locations across the country. Each province and territory is represented by a member division. The national office of Biathlon Canada is located in the Canadian Sport and Fitness Centre at 1600 James Naismith Drive, Suite 407, Gloucester, ON K1B 5N4; (613) 748-5608; fax: (613) 748-5762.

Canadian Association of Nordic Ski Instructors (CANSI) is a non-profit group, founded in 1976 to certify nordic ski instructors. Courses and liability insurance are also offered to members.

There are four levels of certification in cross-country and three levels in telemark. Level 1 instructors are certified to teach beginners; Level 2, intermediate to advanced. Level 3 certifies the instructor to teach lower-level instructors. CANSI has regional offices in every province (see regional listings).

CANSI's national office is located at Suite 406A, 1600 James Naismith Drive, Gloucester, ON K1B 5N4; (613) 748-5893; fax: (613) 748-5730.

Canadian Association for Disabled Skiing helps people with physical disabilities learn to ski. Some have gone on to represent Canada in the World Championships and Paralympics.
PO Box 307, Kimberley, BC V1A 2Y9; (250) 427-7712; fax: (250) 427-7715.

The **Canadian Masters Cross Country Ski Association** encourages competition among skiers aged thirty and over. It is affiliated with the World Masters Cross Country Ski Association, founded by a Canadian, Bill Gairdner, in 1982. World Championship and regional competitions are held annually. Skiers compete within a specific five-year age bracket, according to their age. Competitions are open to all Masters members, regardless of level of ability. 5770 Seaview Rd., West Vancouver, BC V7W 1P8; (604) 921-0742; fax: (604) 921-0752.

The **Canadian Ski Association** is responsible for the development of all aspects of skiing, including cross-country, alpine, freestyle, ski jumping and nordic combined. Suite 406, 1600 James Naismith Drive, Gloucester, ON K1B 5N4; (613) 748-5660.

The **Canadian Ski Council** encourages participation in recreational skiing. It is the umbrella group for the various Canadian ski associations such as the Canadian Association for Disabled Skiing, CSA, CANSI and CSPS.
#412, 1220 Sheppard Ave. East, North York, ON M2K 2X1; (416) 495-4210; fax: (416) 495-4323.

The **Canadian Ski Patrol System** is mainly known for its patrols at downhill ski centres, but also organizes ski patrols at some cross-country ski centres. Volunteer patrollers are trained in first aid and the transportation of injured skiers.
4531 Southclark Pl., PO Box 921, Ottawa, ON K1G 3N3; (613) 822-2245; fax: (613) 822-1088.

Cross Country Canada is the governing body for the sport in Canada. It is responsible for the operations of the National Ski Team in the cross-country discipline. CCC also supports the development of clubs, coaching and officiating. Programs and resources are provided to clubs to attract members, thereby encouraging growth in the number of clubs and members.

CCC has also developed the following youth programs to encourage kids aged 4 to 16 to participate in skiing:
- The Jackrabbit Ski League for teaching the fundamentals of skiing while encouraging enjoyment of the sport.
- The Challenge program of activities that develop leadership skills, teamwork, fitness and competitive and recreational skills through pursuits such as ski orienteering and wilderness touring.
- The SchoolSki Program, a program offered through schools to introduce children to the sport.

For more information on any CCC programs, contact the CCC office in your area. Addresses of district offices can be found in the regional listings. The national office of CCC is located at Suite 407, 1600 James Naismith Dr., Gloucester, ON K1B 5N4; (613) 748-5662; fax: (613) 748-5703; Internet: canada.x-c.com; Email: xcski@CdnSport.ca.

Telemark Canada is dedicated to the development of telemark skiing in Canada. Suite 409, 1185 Eglinton Avenue East, North York, ON M3C 3C6; (416) 426-7260; fax: (416) 426-7346.

Outdoor Organizations

The **Alpine Club of Canada** provides backcountry huts and courses for hikers, climbers and skiers in the Rockies and in a few locations in eastern Canada. PO Box 2040, Canmore, AB T0L 0M0; (403) 678-3200; fax: (403) 678-3224

The **Association of Canadian Mountain Guides** certifies guides for hiking, climbing and skiing. PO Box 1537, Banff, AB T0L 0C0; (403) 678-4662.

The **Canadian Avalanche Association** provides bulletins on avalanche risk in the Canadian Rockies and conducts intensive courses for professionals. PO Box 2759, Revelstoke, BC V0E 2S0; (250) 837-2435; Internet: www.csac.org.

The **Company of Canadian Mountain Guides** is a cooperative of guides offering courses, trips and a referral service.
PO Box 1149, Canmore, AB T0L 0M0; (403) 678-4662.

The **Trans Canada Trail** is a 15,000-km (9,300 mi.) shared-use trail system that is currently being developed coast-to-coast and to northern Canada (see Figure 9.1). The TCT should not to be confused with the National Trail, a coast-to-coast hiking trail that is also currently under development.

Figure 9.1 *Proposed route of the Trans Canada Trail.*

The TCT is to be designed for five core activities: cross-country skiing, cycling, horseback riding, snowmobiling and walking. The trail will have a fairly flat grade, a gravel surface and will make using of existing abandoned railways, wherever possible. Trail construction is being overseen by regional associations that rely heavily on volunteer labour. For more information or to make a donation call 1-800-465-3636.

Yamnuska offers expeditions and courses for hikers, climbers and skiers. 1316 Railway Avenue, Canmore, AB T1W 1P6; (403) 678-4164; fax: (403) 678-4164.

Ski Museums

The **Canadian Ski Museum** offers an overview of the history of skiing for a small admission charge. Open from 12 to 4 P.M. Tuesday to Sunday at 457A Sussex Drive, Ottawa, ON K1N 6Z4; (613) 241-5832.

The **Jackrabbit Museum** houses artifacts of the legendary skier in the rustic cottage that was his home for the final 28 years of his life. Open by appointment only at 220 Beaulne, Piedmont, QC J0R 1K0; (514) 227-2886; fax: (514) 227-5500.

The **U.S. National Ski Hall of Fame and Museum** contains exhibits on the history of skiing from an American perspective. Admission is $3.00 for adults. Open from 10 A.M. to 5 P.M. daily. 610 Palms Avenue, PO Box 191, Ishpeming, Michigan 49849; (906) 485-6323; fax: (906) 486-4570.

Publications

Periodicals

Articles on cross-country skiing can be found in many magazines, but the following provide the broadest coverage:

Cross Country Skier is published five times annually with articles on the North American cross-country ski scene. PO Box 576, Mount Morris, Illinois 61054; 1-800-827-0607.

Explore publishes six issues a year covering a variety of outdoor sports. During the winter, most articles are about cross-country skiing. Suite 420, 301-14th Street N.W., Calgary, AB T2N 2A1; 1-800-567-1372 or (403) 270-8890; fax: (403) 270-7922.

Ski Trax publishes four issues annually for the competitive and recreational cross-country skier. 2 Pardee Ave., Suite 204, Toronto, ON M6K 3H5; (416)-530-1350; fax: (416) 530-1350

Back Country publishes four issues each winter on backcountry skiing only. 7065 Dover Way, Arvada CO 80004; (303) 424-5858.

Some divisions of Cross Country Canada publish annual magazines with information about clubs and events in their region.

Guidebooks

The following books offer an in-depth guide to cross-country skiing in some regions of Canada:

Exploring the Coast Mountains second edition by John Baldwin.

Summits & Icefields, Alpine Ski Tours in the Rockies and Columbia Mountains of Canada by Chic Scott, Rocky Mountain Books. #4 Spruce Centre, Calgary, AB T3C 3B3; 1-800-566-3336.

Ski Trails in the Canadian Rockies by Chic Scott, Rocky Mountain Books (see preceding reference).

Kananskis Country Ski Trails by Gillean Daffern, Rocky Mountain Books (see preceding reference).

Southern Ontario Cross Country Skiing Guide by Terry Burt-Gerrans, The Boston Mills Press.

Ski de Fond au Québec by Yves Séguin, Editions Ulysse.

Maps

The Department of Energy, Mines and Resources publishes topographic maps for all regions of Canada. Canada Map Office, 615 Booth Street, Ottawa, ON K1A 0E9; (613) 952-7000.

Events

National Ski Week

Look for special events at your local ski centre during the third week of January.

Ski Shows

When the autumn leaves start to fall, it's ski show season in all major cities across the country. Geared mainly toward the more lucrative downhill ski market, most shows still manage to squeeze something in for nordic skiers.

Canadian Ski Marathon

The CSM is not a competition, but a test of individual achievement. Medals are awarded for the number of sections skied, rather than the fastest times.

Divided into 10 sections, the 170-km (100-mi.) long classically-groomed course runs from Lachute, northwest of Montreal, to Gatineau near Hull, Quebec. In years ending with an even digit, the tour is run in the reverse direction. Montebello, located at the halfway mark of the course, is the focal point of the two-day event.

Participants register in either the touring class or the Coureur de Bois. Tourers start at 8:00 A.M. at any one of five sections each day, depending upon how many sections they plan to ski. At the end of each section, they can load up on carbos at feeding stations then continue on, or hop aboard a bus to return to town. Medals are awarded to tourers completing six or more sections over the two days.

Coureurs de Bois start at 6:00 A.M. and must complete five sections each day. As an added bonus, Coureurs de Bois in the gold category get to carry all their supplies and camp out overnight. Skiers in any category are restricted from entering a new section after a specified cutoff time.

Entry fees vary from about $60 to over $100, depending on the category and time of registration. Accommodation packages are available. Canadian Ski Marathon, PO Box 400, Gatineau, QC J8P 6T9; (819) 669-7383, fax: (819) 669-0826.

Canadian Ski Odyssey

The CSO is a series of loppets held at various centres across Canada, for both serious racers and avid skiers. Medals are awarded for top finishers in their age groups. Skiers not wanting to complete the entire distance have a choice of lesser distances. Entry fees vary from $20 to $40 for early registration. For more information about the competitions, contact the hosting ski centre.

Date	Event, Distance, Technique	Location
Mid Jan	Reino Keski-Salmi 40k C	Salmon Arm, BC
Early Feb	Canadian Birkebeiner 55k C	Edmonton, AB
Mid Feb	Keskinada Loppet 50k F	Hull, QC
Mid Feb	Red River Ski Fest 30k F	Winnipeg, MB
Early Mar	Yukon Gold Loppet 35k C	Whitehorse, YT
Early Mar	Tour of Hardwood 30k F	Hardwood Hills, ON
Early Mar	Vasaloppet Aventurier 42k F	Charlo, NB
Early Mar	Saskaloppet 55k F	La Ronge, SK
Early Mar	La Loppet Camp Mercier 65k C	Mont-Ste-Anne, QC
Early Apr	Great Labrador Loppet 54k F	Labrador City, Lab

C = classic technique, F = free technique.

Canadian Birkebeiner

Accredited by the Birkebeiner Society of Norway, the Canadian Birkie is skied over a traditional 55-km distance with a 5.5 kg pack. Over 2,000 participants ski various distances at the Blackfoot Recreation Area east of Edmonton, Alberta. Canadian Birkebeiner, c/o River Valley Outdoor Centre, 10125-97 Ave, Edmonton, AB T5K 0B3; (403) 496-7275

Worldloppets

The Keskinada Worldloppet (previously called the Gatineau 55) is one of a series of 13 loppets held in various countries around the world. As in all Worldloppets, skiers are seeded for a starting wave according to results obtained in previous loppets. Medals are awarded to top male and female finishers in their age brackets. At the end of the year, those who accumulate the most points earn the Worldloppet title.

Less ambitious skiers can compete in shorter distances. Apart from the 50-km freestyle, Keskinada offers 25-km skate, 25-km classic and 10-km freestyle courses in Gatineau Park. Fees for early registration are $10, $25 and $40.

Keskinada Loppet PO Box 554, Station A, Quebec J8Y 6P3; (819) 827-4641, fax: (819) 827-3337. American Birkebeiner, PO Box 911, Hayward, WI 54843; (715) 6344-5025, 1-800-872-2753 (USA only). For information about other Worldloppets contact the Keskinada office.

Date	Event, Distance, Technique	Location
Late Aug	Kangaroo Hoppet 42k F	Victoria, Australia
Late Jan	Dolomitenlauf 60k F	Lienz, Austria
Late Jan	Marcialonga 70k F	Moena-Cavalese, Italy
Early Feb	Konig Ludwig Lauf 55k F	Oberammergau, Germany
Mid Feb	Sapporo Skimarathon 50k F	Sapporo, Japan
Mid Feb	Tartu Skimarathon 60k C	Tartu, Estonia
Mid Feb	Keskinada Loppet 50k F	Hull, Quebec
Mid Feb	Transjurassienne 76k F	Lamoura-Mouthe, France
Late Feb	American Birkebeiner 52k F	Cable, Wisconsin
Late Feb	Finlandia Hiihto 75k C	Hameenlinna, Finland
Early Mar	Vasaloppet 90k C	Salena-Mora, Sweden
Early Mar	Engadin Skimarathon 42k F	Majola-Zuoz Schanf, Switzerland
Mid Mar	Birkebeiner Rennet 55k C	Lillehammer-Rena, Norway

C = classic technique, F = free technique.

Cup Races and Championships

Most divisions of Cross Country Canada and Biathlon Canada sanction a series of cup races in their region that are open to all skiers. Both organizations also host Canada Cups, a national series held at various ski centres across Canada. A regional championship event is held each year in both biathlon and cross-country.

Cross-country skiers who do well in races in their region may be invited to join that region's ski team and to train at one of three National Training Centres: Canmore, Thunder Bay or Mont-Sainte-Anne.

Canadian Junior Championships are held for three age levels: Juvenile, Junior Boys/Girls or Junior Men/Women. Top men and women may be selected for the National Junior Ski Team. North American and World Junior Championships are also held each year.

II
Canadian
Cross Country Skiing
Directory

10 Guide to the Directory

Information in the following sections is ordered according to province or territory from west to east. Each section contains information specific to the region, followed by data on ski centres in that region.

Before making a long journey to a new ski destination, it is advisable to telephone ahead to ensure that the centre will be open, particularly if using this directory several years after it was published. The information was gathered during the 95-96 season.

Travel Information

Travel information can either be ordered or picked up at a provincial tourist information bureau in the region you are interested in. Tourist information packages can be ordered free of charge by calling a 1-800 number. The phone numbers and addresses of the tourist information bureaus for each province are listed at the beginning of the section for that province. Allow two to three weeks for delivery.

Some tourist bureaus supply a partial listing of lodging available in their region. A few provinces also provide an accommodation reservation service. Other sources of travel and accommodation information are the Canadian Automobile Association and various guide books.

Hostelling International is an non-profit organization that provides dormitory-style accommodation at budget prices in many locations across Canada.
1600 James Naismith Drive, Suite 608, Gloucester, ON K1B 5N4; (613) 748-5638, 1-800-663-5777

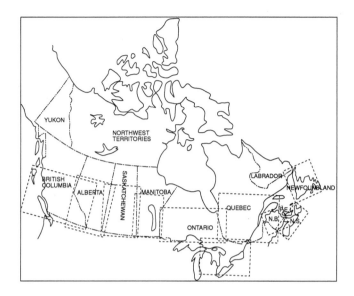

Figure 10.1 *Orientation of regional maps.*

Explanation of Listings

The directory is divided into twelve sections, one for each province and territory in Canada and is arranged in a west-to-east fashion. The section on each region begins with information about travel, cross-country organizations, winter climate and events in the region. A listing of the region's cross-country ski centres then follows. Centres are numbered and appear on the map and in the alphabetical index at the front of the section.

Entries for each ski centre in the directory contain information about trails, services and other winter activities that the centre offers and are explained below. Directory sections for British Columbia, Alberta and Quebec also include a listing of backcountry huts and lodges.

1. Centre Number: corresponds to the number shown on the map of the region at the front of each section. Centres are numbered consecutively in a general west-to-east pattern.

2. Centre Name: the name of the cross-country ski centre, park or municipality that offers skiing. Some large parks have trailheads at several different locations. In such a case, each section of the park has a separate listing.

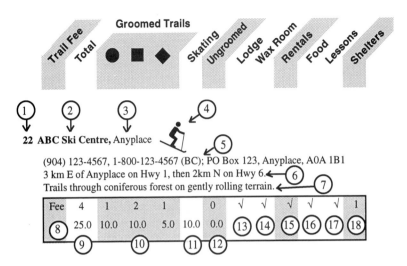

Figure 10.2 *Sample of a directory listing.*

3. Town: the name of the town nearest the ski centre that appears on the map published by the tourist information bureau.

4. Winter Activity: winter activities (other than cross-country skiing) that are offered at the centre are indicated by a symbol. Refer to Figure 10.3 for a key to the symbols.

5. Telephone and address: the phone number at the ski centre to obtain more information. If the telephone number is a tape recording, it is indicated as such. Some commercial ski centres have toll-free long-distance numbers. The toll-free number, in most cases, is followed by the regions that have access to the toll-free number.

6. Directions: route to follow to get from the nearest main highway or town to the ski centre. In some cases, there may be several different ways to get to the centre or there may be several access points to the trails.

7. Description: terrain, vegetation and configuration of the trail system. Most trail systems are laid out in some configuration of loops. The term "stacked loops" refers to a series of loops that, at various points, offer the choice of either continuing further on the trail or taking a cut-off to return to the start. Trail maps are provided free of charge with the purchase of a trail pass, unless otherwise noted.

Figure 10.3 *Winter Activity Symbol Key*

8. Trail Fee: cost of a pass for use of the trails. Fee is for one adult, unless otherwise indicated. The following abbreviations are used:

Car: fee for an entire carload

C: children rate   Y: youth (student) rate

F: family rate   S: senior rate

DA: no charge, but donations accepted

Entry Fee: most national parks charge an entrance fee if you are stopping in the park, whether for skiing or any other reason

GO: only guests of the resort have access to the trails

NC: no charge (donations may be accepted by some centres)

NA: information is not available.

9. Total Groomed: number and total length of the groomed trails in kilometres. Lengths of trails are as reported by the centre and may include overlap. The top number is the number of trails, the bottom number is the total length of trails.

10. ● ■ ◆ (Easy, Intermediate, Difficult): number and cumulative length in kilometres of groomed trails for each level of ability. Standard rating specifcations are not always followed, so there may be variations from one centre to the next.

11. Skating: cumulative length in kilometres of mechanically-packed trails suitable for the skating technique. Skating trails almost always run parallel to classic trails. Their length is therefore not included in the total length of groomed trails.

12. Ungroomed Trails: number and total length of ungroomed marked trails.

Note: The next five services are indicated by a check mark, "√," if they are offered at a centre.
E: service is offered on weekends only
C: service is available close by
R: reservations must be made

13. Lodge: shelter at start of trails. "T" signifies that there is no lodge but toilet facilities are available.

14. Waxing Room: heated room for waxing skis.

15. Rentals: rental of ski equipment. Call ahead to ensure that equipment will be available.

16. Food: restaurant or snack bar.

17. Lessons: ski instruction. Call ahead to reserve a lesson a day in advance. Many clubs offer child and adult ski instruction programs.

18. Shelters: the number of trailside shelters other than the main lodge.

Backcountry Lodges and Huts

Directory sections on British Columbia, Alberta and Quebec contain listings of lodges and huts that can only be accessed on skis, by snowcat or by helicopter. Accommodations range from full-service commercial lodges to primitive do-it-yourself huts.

Skiing terrain varies from track-set trails at some areas to alpine touring at others. Alpine touring requires knowledge of avalanche safety and rescue procedures, glacier traversing, crevasse rescue and survival techniques. Touring in such alpine areas is best done with an experienced guide.

Some alpine lodge operators suggest the use of alpine skis and boots with special touring bindings that can lock the heel in place for descents. Backcountry or telemark equipment and familiarity with telemark technique would be a viable alternative.

Most of the huts in BC and Alberta are operated by the Alpine Club of Canada, a non-profit organization. ACC also offers hostel-type accommodations at its clubhouse in Canmore and at the Alpine Centre at Lake Louise which is operated in conjunction with Hostelling International.

All ACC huts accessible on skis or by helicopter are listed here, but the access to some of them is hazardous or difficult. ACC publishes a guide describing the huts in detail. Chic Scott's *Ski Trails in the Canadian Rockies* offers an excellent description of ski tours in the vicinity of most of the huts and lodges in the Rockies. *Summits and Icefields,* by the same author, describes tours in the Selkirks, Purcells and Rockies.

ACC huts are rated as either Class A (heated) or Class B (unheated). All huts are equipped with foam mattresses, gas lanterns, cooking stoves and utensils. There is no indoor plumbing. Reservations must be made well in advance.

	Class A	Class B
ACC members	$14	$8
Nonmembers	$21	$11
Children under 13	Half price	

Alpine Club of Canada, PO Box 8040, Canmore, AB T1W 2T8; (403) 678-3200; fax: (403) 678-3224

Backcountry huts are available through concessionaires in several parks and reserves in Quebec. Most areas have numerous huts so therefore offer opportunities for hut-to-hut trips of several days. A few of the areas provide a baggage transfer service to the huts. Trails in Quebec, for the most part, are well-marked and can be navigated using the trail map provided by the concessionaire.

Before booking a hut in any region, ask whether it is heated. If it isn't, you will need a four-season sleeping bag. Reservations must be made well in advance, especially for weekends, when they are often booked solid months ahead.

11 British Columbia

Winter in British Columbia is a skier's paradise with dozens of alpine and cross-country skiing centres and limitless backcountry touring. Vancouver is one of those rare nirvanas where you can sail in the morning, then drive less than an hour and ski in the afternoon—provided you've got the energy.

Most of BC's ski centres are located in the interior where the colder temperatures produce light powdery snow. The Rocky Mountains and the adjacent Selkirk and Purcell ranges offer some fine backcountry lodges located amid spectacular scenery. A unique feature of Alberta and BC is that, in addition to the usual types of ski centres, there are several guest ranches that cater to skiers.

Skiers who prefer their trails groomed will have plenty to choose from. One of the largest networks of trails in Canada can be found at 100 Mile House. Many of the smaller ski centres in the province are operated by ski clubs.

Silver Star Resort offers an early-season training camp for skiers who are interested in competing, or just improving their technique.

Travel Information

Airport: Vancouver airport services many major airlines from outside BC and many regional airlines within BC.

Bus service: Greyhound Lines, 1150 Station St. ,Vancouver; (604) 662-3222, 1-800-661-8747 (Canada outside BC)

Ferry service: from Vancouver to Victoria or Nanaimo (604) 277-0277

B.C.

Highway information: road conditions, closures and delays for eight corridor routes. (604) 525-4997 (Vancouver) 1-800-663-4997 (throughout BC).

Rail service: Via Rail's transcontinental service connects Vancouver, Kamloops, Jasper and east. 1-800-561-8630 (western Canada). BC Rail runs from Vancouver to Whistler and other destinations. (604) 631-3500.

Ski report: Talking Yellow Pages (604) 299-9000 (Vancouver).

Tourist Information Bureau
Tourism British Columbia publishes an annual winter guide operates an accommodation reservation service. Parliament Buildings, Victoria, BC V8V 1X4; (604) 685-0032 (Vancouver), 1-800-663-6000 (Canada and USA)

Weather report: Environment Canada's weather forecast (604) 664-9021.

Cross Country Skiing Resources

Canadian Association of Nordic Ski Instructors (CANSI), 334-1367 West Broadway, Vancouver, BC V6H 4A9; (604) 733-7547

Cross Country BC - BC Division of Cross Country Canada publishes an annual ski guide in addition to its CCC functions. #106 - 3003 - 30th Street, Vernon, BC V1T 9J5 (604) 545-9600; fax: (604) 545-9614

Federation of Mountain Clubs of BC is an umbrella organization for BC climbing and ski touring clubs. Also offers wilderness and avalanche awareness courses, guided trips and backcountry hut rentals. #336 - 1367 West Broadway, Vancouver, BC V6H 4A9; (604) 737-3053.

Avalanche Bulletin: snow pack conditions in BC and Alberta from December to April. Canadian Avalanche Association (604) 290-9333 (Vancouver), 1-800-667-1105 (BC and Alberta)

Winter Climate

Due to the localization of climate patterns, ski seasons vary greatly from one region to another. Generally, the more south-westerly ski centres open around mid to early December and close mid-March. Ski centres located in central, eastern and northern BC operate from mid-November to about mid-April.

B.C.

Average Temperatures

Average Snowfall

100 Mile House

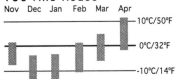

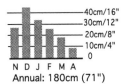

Annual: 180cm (71")

Kitimat

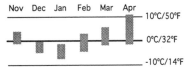

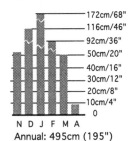

Annual: 495cm (195")

Salmon Arm

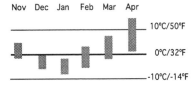

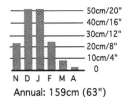

Annual: 159cm (63")

Rogers Pass

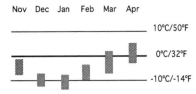

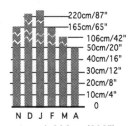

Annual: 996cm (392")

Fernie

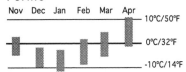

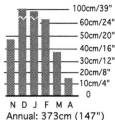

Annual: 373cm (147")

British Columbia

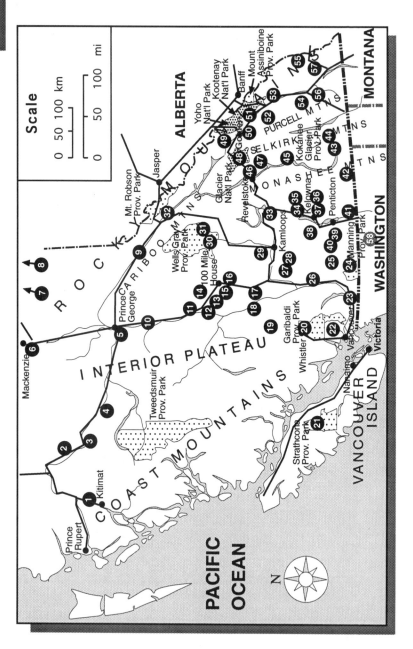

Cross Country Ski Areas

B.C.

BC Loppet Series

A CCC sponsored series requiring a CCBC licence ($5.00).
Entry fees vary from $20 to $30 for early registration. C=classic,
F=free technique

Date	Event, Distance, Technique	Location
mid-Dec	Sovereign Lake Loppet 30k C	Vernon
early Jan	Kelowna Loppet 30k F	Kelowna
early Jan	Highland Valley Classic 33k C	Logan Lake
mid-Jan	*Reino Keski-Salmi Loppet 36k C	Salmon Arm
late Jan	Black Jack Loppet 40k C	Rossland
late Jan	Caledonia Loppet 30k C	Prince George
early Feb	Cariboo Marathon 50k C	100 Mile House
early Feb	Wells Gray Loppet 30k C	Clearwater
mid-Feb	Chateau Whistler Cup 30k C	Whistler
mid-Feb	Yellowhead Loppet 36k C	McBride
mid-Feb	Nickel Plate Loppet 30k C	Penticton
early Mar	Cascade Cup Loppet 30k C	Manning Park
early Mar	Mt. Washington Marathon 35k C	Mt. Washington

* Canadian Ski Odyssey event

Groomed Trails

Legend columns: Trail Fee · Total · ● · ■ · ◆ · Skating · Ungroomed · Lodge · Wax Room · Rentals · Food · Lesons · Shelters

1 Kitimat Cross Country Ski Club, Kitimat PO Box 404, Kitimat, BC V8C 2M4

At Onion Lake (halfway to Terrace) and at Kitimat golf course.
Onion Lk trails are easy to intermediate. 1.6 km lit trail at golf club.

Trail Fee	Total	●	■	◆	Skating	Ungroomed	Lodge	Wax Room	Rentals	Food	Lesons	Shelters
6^{00}		-	-	-	-	0	√					1
3^{00} C	35.0					0.0						

2 Bulkley Valley Cross Country Ski Club, Smithers PO Box 4412,Smithers,V0J 2N0

10 minutes from Smithers on Hudson Bay Mountain.
High elevation permits a long ski season.

Trail Fee	Total	●	■	◆	Skating	Ungroomed	Lodge	Wax Room	Rentals	Food	Lesons	Shelters
Yes		-	-	-	-	0						1
	30.0					0.0						

3 Morice Mountain Nordic Ski Club, Houston PO Box 1573,Houston,V0J1Z0

8 km S of Hwy 16 on Buck Flats Rd.
Varied terrain, large lodge and a BC cabin for overnight

Trail Fee	Total	●	■	◆	Skating	Ungroomed	Lodge	Wax Room	Rentals	Food	Lesons	Shelters
5^{00}		-	-	-	-	-						2
2^{00} S	25.0	8.0	8.0	9.0	25.0	15.0						

4 Omineca Ski Club, Burns Lake PO Box 1008, Burns Lake, V0J 1E0

6 km S of Burns Lake on Hwy 35.
2 km trail lit for night skiing.

Trail Fee	Total	●	■	◆	Skating	Ungroomed	Lodge	Wax Room	Rentals	Food	Lesons	Shelters
5^{00}		-	-	-	-	0	√					0
	35.0	5.0	20.0	10.0	35.0	0.0						

5 Caledonia Nordic Ski Club, Prince George P.O. Box 1243, Prince George,V2L 4V3

7 km from Prince George on Otaway Road.
Varied terrain, large log cabin, 3 km lit trail.

Trail Fee	Total	●	■	◆	Skating	Ungroomed	Lodge	Wax Room	Rentals	Food	Lesons	Shelters
5^{00}		-	-	-	-	0	√	√		E		0
NCC	30.0	14.0	12.0	4.0	20.0	0.0						

6 Mackenzie Nordiques Cross Country Ski Club, Mackenzie PO Box 747,Mackenzie,V0J 2C0

2 hours N of Prince George in S Mackenzie near forestry office.
Rolling hills of spruce and pine, swamp and lakes.

Trail Fee	Total	●	■	◆	Skating	Ungroomed	Lodge	Wax Room	Rentals	Food	Lesons	Shelters
NC		5	1	3	1	0						3
	40.0					0.0						

7 Beatton Provincial Park, Fort St. John

(250) 787-3407 Beatton Provincial Park,10003 - 110 Avenue, Fort St. John,V1J 6M7
13 km N of Fort St John on N shore of Charlie Lake
Trails are groomed and maintained by Fort St. John ski club.

Trail Fee	Total	●	■	◆	Skating	Ungroomed	Lodge	Wax Room	Rentals	Food	Lesons	Shelters
NC		-	-	-	-	0	T					0
	12.0	2.0	8.0	2.0		0.0						

Groomed Trails

Trail Fee	Total	●	■	◆	Skating	Ungroomed	Lodge	Wax Room	Rentals	Food	Lessons	Shelters

8 Bear Mountain Cross-Country Ski Trails, Dawson Creek
SW of Dawson Creek on Bear Mountain.
Variety of terrain. Spruce, pine, poplar and willow trees.

Trail Fee	Total	●	■	◆	Skating	Ungroomed	Lodge	Wax Room	Rentals	Food	Lessons	Shelters
5^{00}	20	-	-	-	0						√	4
	35.0	10.0	10.0	15.0	0.0							

9 Yellowhead Ski Club, McBride; Yellowhead Ski Club, PO Box 258, McBride, V0J 2E0
2 sites - Dore R. 4 km W & Belle Mtn 7 km W of McBride
Dore River has 7 k family-oriented linear trail. Belle Mtn has 10 km loop.

Trail Fee	Total	●	■	◆	Skating	Ungroomed	Lodge	Wax Room	Rentals	Food	Lessons	Shelters
NA	-	-	-	-	0					√	√	2
	17.0				0.0							

10 Cariboo Ski Touring Club, PO Box 4611, Quesnel, BC V2J 3J8
2 areas with 10 km each–Ten Mile Lake & Hallis Lake.

Trail Fee	Total	●	■	◆	Skating	Ungroomed	Lodge	Wax Room	Rentals	Food	Lessons	Shelters
Yes	-	-	-	-	0							0
	20.0				0.0							

11 Williams Lake Cross Country Ski Club, Williams Lake
18 km N of Williams Lake. 3.5 km lit for night skiing.

Trail Fee	Total	●	■	◆	Skating	Ungroomed	Lodge	Wax Room	Rentals	Food	Lessons	Shelters
DA	4	-	-	-	0	√						0
	28.0	9.0	10.0	9.0	28.0	0.0						

12 108 Resort (Best Western), 108 Mile Ranch

(250) 791-5211, 1-800-667-5233; PO Box 2, 108 Mile Ranch, BC V0K 2Z0
8 miles N of 100 Mile House on Hwy 97.
Part of 150 km trail network, 4 km trail lit for night skiing, 62 rooms

Trail Fee	Total	●	■	◆	Skating	Ungroomed	Lodge	Wax Room	Rentals	Food	Lessons	Shelters
7^{00}	18	9	3	30			√		√	√	√	0
5^{00} C	56.4	26.3	10.7	7.4	0.0							

13 Hills Health & Guest Ranch, 108 Mile Ranch

(250) 791-5225; C-26, 108 Mile Ranch, BC V0K 2Z0
14 km N of 100 Mile House on Hwy 97.
Rolling ranchland, lakes, fir & aspen. Part of 150 km network.
Daycare, health spa, bar, 20 condos, 26 rooms

Trail Fee	Total	●	■	◆	Skating	Ungroomed	Lodge	Wax Room	Rentals	Food	Lessons	Shelters
7^{00}	18	18	0	0	0		√		√	√	√	2
5^{00} C	20.0	20.0			0.0							

B.C.

Columns: Trail Fee | Total | Groomed Trails (● ■ ◆) | Skating | Ungroomed | Lodge | Wax Room | Rentals | Food | Lesons | Shelters

14 Ruth Lake Lodge, Forest Grove PO Box 315,Forest Grove,V0K 1M0
(250) 397-2727
15 km loop around lake. No trail map. Trails for Guests Only.

Trail Fee	Total	●	■	◆	Skating	Ungroomed	Lodge	Wax Room	Rentals	Food	Lesons	Shelters
Guests	3	-	-	-		0	√					0
Only	27.0					0.0						

15 One Hundred Mile Nordic Ski Society, 100 Mile House PO Box 1888,100 Mile House,V0K 2E0
3.5 km lit trail. Links with 108 Mile trails to form 150 km network. Hotels

Trail Fee	Total	●	■	◆	Skating	Ungroomed	Lodge	Wax Room	Rentals	Food	Lesons	Shelters
6^{00}	-	-	-	-		0		√				0
	50.0				50.0	0.0						

16 Red Coach Inn, 100 Mile House
(250) 395-2266,1-800-663-8422 (Canada) PO Box 760,100 Mile House,V0K 2E0
On Hwy 97 in 100 Mile House. Bus & train depots in town.
Trails connect to 108 Resort & Hills Health Ranch trails. Bar, 46-room inn

Trail Fee	Total	●	■	◆	Skating	Ungroomed	Lodge	Wax Room	Rentals	Food	Lesons	Shelters
7^{00}	1	0	1	0		0	√	Y	C	√	C	0
5^{00} C	11.0		11.0			0.0						

17 Clinton Snow Jockey Club, Clinton
(250) 459-7751 PO Box 242,Clinton,V0K 1K0
Spectacular views.

Trail Fee	Total	●	■	◆	Skating	Ungroomed	Lodge	Wax Room	Rentals	Food	Lesons	Shelters
DA	-	-	-	-		0						4
	50.0					0.0						

18 Big Bar Guest Ranch, Clinton PO Box 27,Jesmond,Clinton,V0K 1K0
(250) 459-2333 55 km NW of Clinton.
Good variety of trails for all levels. 12 rooms, 4 cabins. Trails for Guests Only.

Trail Fee	Total	●	■	◆	Skating	Ungroomed	Lodge	Wax Room	Rentals	Food	Lesons	Shelters
Guests	8	-	-	-		0	√		√	√		0
Only	30.0					0.0						

19 Tyax Mountain Lake Resort, Gold Bridge (250) 238-2221,1-800-663-4431 Tyaughton Lake Rd,Gold Bridge,V0K 1P0
100 km W of Lillooet Remote wilderness resort in Chilcotin Mountains.
Huge log lodge. Bar, 28 suites, 4 chalets.

Trail Fee	Total	●	■	◆	Skating	Ungroomed	Lodge	Wax Room	Rentals	Food	Lesons	Shelters
NC	3	2	1	0		3	√	√	√	√	√	0
	17.0	10.0	7.0			20.0						

B.C.

Groomed Trails

Trail Fee	Total	●	■	◆	Skating	Ungroomed	Lodge	Wax Room	Rentals	Food	Lessons	Shelters

20 Whistler XC Ski Trails, Whistler

(250) 932-6436, (250) 932-4191(tape), 1-800-944-7853 (Canada & USA)
5 min. walk from Whistler Village. 4325 Blackcomb Way,Whistler,V0N 1B0
Rolling terrain with some steep hills. Many hotels and condos.

Trail Fee	Total	●	■	◆	Skating	Ungroomed	Lodge	Wax Room	Rentals	Food	Lessons	Shelters
9⁰⁰	17	8	7	3		0	C	√		√		0
5⁰⁰ C	30.0	12.7	11.2	6.3	30	0.0						

21 Mt Washington Resort, Courtenay

(250) 338-1386, (250) 334-5705(tape) PO Box 3069,Courtenay,V9N 5N3
30 km from Courtenay on Vancouver Island
Double track-set trails in Strathcona Prov. Park   Daycare, bar, 250 condos.

Trail Fee	Total	●	■	◆	Skating	Ungroomed	Lodge	Wax Room	Rentals	Food	Lessons	Shelters
9⁰⁰	7	2	3	2		0	√		√	√	√	0
4⁵⁰ C	46.5	6.0	18.5	22.0	42.0	0.0						

22 Cypress Bowl Cross Country Ski Area, West Vancouver

(604) 922-0825, (604) 926-6007 PO Box 91252,West Vancouver,V7V 3N9
Hwy 1 W of Vancouver exit #8, then 15 km to ski area parking.
Interconnected network, 3.7 km lit for night skiing.

Trail Fee	Total	●	■	◆	Skating	Ungroomed	Lodge	Wax Room	Rentals	Food	Lessons	Shelters
10⁵⁰	23	8	10	5		0	√	√	√	√	√	0
6⁵⁰ C	16.0	4.7	7.2	4.1	16.0	0.0						

23 Hemlock Valley Ski Resort, Agassiz

(604) 797-4411, (604) 520-6222(tape), 1-800-665-7080 (toll-free in 604)
30 km E of Mission on Hwy 7. Comp. 7,Hemlock Valley Site RR 1,Agassiz,V0M 1A0
Experts can take 1 ride on lift to top of ridge. Bar, condos & cabins.

Trail Fee	Total	●	■	◆	Skating	Ungroomed	Lodge	Wax Room	Rentals	Food	Lessons	Shelters
8⁰⁰	1	0	1	0		1	√		√	√	√	0
	7.0		7.0			6.0						

24 Manning Park Resort, Hope

(250) 840-8822 PO Box 1480,Hope,V0X 1L0
66 km E of Hope or 66 km W of Princeton on Hwy 3.
Located in Manning Park. Coniferous forest, beautiful views of lake. Bar, 78 rooms

Trail Fee	Total	●	■	◆	Skating	Ungroomed	Lodge	Wax Room	Rentals	Food	Lessons	Shelters
9⁵⁰	10	6	2	2		-	√	√	√	√	√	1
6⁵⁰ C	30.0	8.7	4.2	3.6	17	160.0						

Groomed Trails

Legend columns: Trail Fee · Total · ● · ■ · ◆ · Skating · Ungroomed · Lodge · Wax Room · Rentals · Food · Lesons · Shelters

B.C.

25 China Ridge Cross Country Ski Association, Princeton

(250) 295-7154 PO Box 2118,Princeton,V0X 1W0
Follow signs to Snowpatch Ski Hill, 7 km from Princeton.
Ridge trails with views, coniferous trees, deer & elk, low avalanche danger.

Trail Fee	Total	●	■	◆	Skating	Ungroomed	Lodge	Wax Room	Rentals	Food	Lesons	Shelters
DA	6	4	2			6	E	√	N	E		3
	35.0	30.0	5.0		10	45.0						

26 Kane Valley Ski Trails (Nicola Nordic Ski Club), Merritt

(250) 378-8400, (250) 378-5429 Nicola Nordic Ski Club, PO Box1499, Merritt,V0K 2B0
18 km S of Merritt on Hwy 97C/5A.
Varied terrain, riparian, lakeshore, gullies, swamp forested & open areas.

Trail Fee	Total	●	■	◆	Skating	Ungroomed	Lodge	Wax Room	Rentals	Food	Lesons	Shelters
5⁰⁰	20	-	-	-		0						0
	40.0					0.0						

27 Logan Lake Ski Trails (Highland Valley Outdoor Ass'n), Logan Lake

(250) 523-6791, (250) 523-6322 Highland Valley Outdoor Ass'n, PO Box 802 ,Logan Lake,V0K
Trails start in town of Logan Lake.
Mostly rolling hills in a pine & fir forest. 2km lit trail. Bar, 32 hotel rooms.

Trail Fee	Total	●	■	◆	Skating	Ungroomed	Lodge	Wax Room	Rentals	Food	Lesons	Shelters
NC	25	7	11	7		0				√		0
	36.0	10.0	16.0	10.0	36	0.0						

28 Stake Lake Trails (Overlander Ski Club), Kamloops

(250) 372-5514 Overlander Ski Club,PO Box 1191,Kamloops,V2C 6H3
20 minutes from Kamloops on Lac la Jeune Rd.
Rolling forested terrain.

Trail Fee	Total	●	■	◆	Skating	Ungroomed	Lodge	Wax Room	Rentals	Food	Lesons	Shelters
6⁵⁰	-	-	-	-		0	√			√		0
	40.0	24.0	8.0	8.0	40.0	0.0						

29 Sun Peaks Resort, Kamloops

(250) 572-7222, (250) 578-7232(tape), 1-800-663-2838 PO Box 869,Kamloops,V2C 5MB
40 minutes N of Kamloops. Trails are adjacent to Sun Peaks alpine resort.
Groomed trails are on golf course. BC loop trail to lake. Hotel, condos.

Trail Fee	Total	●	■	◆	Skating	Ungroomed	Lodge	Wax Room	Rentals	Food	Lesons	Shelters
NC	1	1	0	0		1	√			√	√	
	5.0					40.0						

30 Wells Gray Outdoor Club, Clearwater

(250) 674-2214 PO Box 404,Clearwater,V0E 1N0
In Wells Gray Provincial Park.

Trail Fee	Total	●	■	◆	Skating	Ungroomed	Lodge	Wax Room	Rentals	Food	Lesons	Shelters
NA	-	-	-	-		-						0
	50.0					Yes						

B.C.

Groomed Trails

Trail Fee	Total	●	■	◆	Skating	Ungroomed	Lodge	Wax Room	Rentals	Food	Lessons	Shelters

31 Helmcken Falls Lodge, Clearwater

(250) 674-3657; PO Box 239, Clearwater, V0E 1N0
35 km N of Clearwater on Wells Gray Park Rd. Lodge is 1 1/2 km before park.
Variety of terrain. Deciduous and coniferous trees. Bar, 19 rooms.

Trail Fee	Total	●	■	◆	Skating	Ungroomed	Lodge	Wax Room	Rentals	Food	Lessons	Shelters
NA	-	-	-	-	0			√	√	√		2
	32.0				0.0							

32 Jackman Flats (Yellowhead Outdoor Rec. Ass'n), Valemount

10 min. N on Hwy 5, look for sign. Yellowhead Outdoor Rec Ass'n, Box 448, Valemount, V0E 2Z0
Rolling terrain, pine forest.

Trail Fee	Total	●	■	◆	Skating	Ungroomed	Lodge	Wax Room	Rentals	Food	Lessons	Shelters
NA	4	-	-	-	0					√		0
	20.0				0.0							

33 Larch Hills Ski Area, Salmon Arm

1-800-661-4800 (Tourism Schuswap, PO Box 218, Salmon Arm, V1E 4M3)
12km S of Salmon Arm on Hwy 97B, 5 km E on Grand Bench Rd, 6 km N on Edgar.

Trail Fee	Total	●	■	◆	Skating	Ungroomed	Lodge	Wax Room	Rentals	Food	Lessons	Shelters
NC	12	6	5	1	-	√						1
	30.0				120.0							

34 Sovereign Lake Ski Area (Okanagan CC Ski Club), Vernon

(250) 542-3164; Okanagan CC Ski Club, PO Box 1231, Vernon, V1T 6N6
25 km NE of Vernon on Silver Star Road.
Links with Silver Star trails. View from top of Silver Star Mountain.

Trail Fee	Total	●	■	◆	Skating	Ungroomed	Lodge	Wax Room	Rentals	Food	Lessons	Shelters
6⁵⁰	15	3	4	8	1	√	√	C	C	C		3
3²⁵ C	42.0	2.0	11.0	27.0	42.0	1.2						

35 Silver Star Mountain Resort, Silver Star Mtn

(250) 542-0224, (250) 542-1745(tape), 1-800-663-4431 (Canada & USA)
20 km E of Vernon on Silver Star Rd. PO Box 2, Silver Star Mtn, V0E 1G0
Double tracked & skate on all trails. Varied terrain. Link with Sovereign Lake.
Daycare, bar, 136 rooms, 60 condos. Early season training camps.

Trail Fee	Total	●	■	◆	Skating	Ungroomed	Lodge	Wax Room	Rentals	Food	Lessons	Shelters
8⁵⁰	28	14	7	7	0			√	√	√		0
4⁵⁰ C	35.0	17.8	8.9	8.2	35.0	0.0						

36 Big White Ski Resort, Kelowna

(250) 765-3101, (250) 765-SNOW (tape), 1-800-663-2772 (Canada & USA)
On Hwy 33, 57 km E of Kelowna. PO Box 2039, Station R, Kelowna, V1X 4K5
Rolling mountainside trails, excellent views of Monashees, forested trails.
Daycare, bar, hotels, B&Bs, condos.

Trail Fee	Total	●	■	◆	Skating	Ungroomed	Lodge	Wax Room	Rentals	Food	Lessons	Shelters
NC	9	4	3	2	5	√	√	√	√	√		1
	18.0	7.0	7.0	4.0	7.0							

B.C.

Groomed Trails

Trail Fee / Total	●	■	◆	Skating	Ungroomed	Lodge	Wax Room	Rentals	Food	Lessons	Shelters

37 McCulloch Lakes Ski Center (Nordic XC Ski Club), Kelowna

(250) 862-8254; Isabel Lake Resort: (250) 868-2722 Nordic Ski Club, Box 105,Kelowna,V1Y 7N3
39 km E of Kelowna on Hwy 33 near Idabel Lake Resort.
BC country trails shared with snowmobiles go along Kettle Valley Trailway.

Trail Fee / Total	●	■	◆	Skating	Ungroomed	Lodge	Wax Room	Rentals	Food	Lessons	Shelters
DA	-	-	-	-							0
28.0				Yes							

38 Telemark Cross Country Ski Club, Westbank

(250) 768-1494; PO Box 26072,Westbank,V4T 2G3
9 km NW of Westbank on Glenrosa Road towards Crystal Mtn alpine center.
Varied terrain, 2.5 km lit trail.

Trail Fee / Total	●	■	◆	Skating	Ungroomed	Lodge	Wax Room	Rentals	Food	Lessons	Shelters
7⁰⁰	7	-	-	-	-	√		√			0
4⁰⁰ C	32.0	6.0	20.0	6.0	9.0						

39 Apex Resort, Penticton

(250) 492-2880; PO Box 1060, Penticton,V2A 7N7
35 km W of Penticton on Green Mtn Rd.
Trails around village. 1k lit for night skiing. 6k from Nickel Plate. Bar, condos.

Trail Fee / Total	●	■	◆	Skating	Ungroomed	Lodge	Wax Room	Rentals	Food	Lessons	Shelters
NC	-	-	-	0	√			√			0
12.0				0.0							

40 Nickel Plate Cross Country Ski Club, Penticton

(250) 492-0257   PO Box 20166, Penticton,V2A 8K3
35k W of Penticton on Green Mtn Rd to Apex alpine ski center then 6k.
Interlinked trails, high elevation for long season. Alpine touring available.

Trail Fee / Total	●	■	◆	Skating	Ungroomed	Lodge	Wax Room	Rentals	Food	Lessons	Shelters
7⁰⁰	10	-	-	-	√			√			0
30.0				30.0	20.0						

41 Mt Baldy Cross Country Area, Oliver

(250) 498-4086; tape: (250) 2262; PO Box 1528, Oliver,V0H 1T0
35 km E of Osoyoos

Trail Fee / Total	●	■	◆	Skating	Ungroomed	Lodge	Wax Room	Rentals	Food	Lessons	Shelters
NC	0			0	C						0
0.0				15.0							

42 Black Jack Cross Country Ski Club, Rossland

(250) 362-9465; PO Box1754, Rossland,V0G 1Y0
3 km N of Rossland on Hwy 3B. Facing Red Mountain Ski Resort.
Equal parts flat, up and downhills. Mixed forest, open meadows.

Trail Fee / Total	●	■	◆	Skating	Ungroomed	Lodge	Wax Room	Rentals	Food	Lessons	Shelters
5⁰⁰	-	-	-	0	√		C	C	√		2
10⁰⁰F	30.0	11.5	5.0	13.5	30.0	6.5					

B.C.

Groomed Trails

Table column headers: Trail Fee · Total · ● · ■ · ◆ · Skating · Ungroomed · Lodge · Wax Room · Rentals · Food · Lessons · Shelters

43 Paulson Cross Country Ski Trails (Castlegar Nordic Ski Club), Castlegar
(250) 365-3527; Castlegar Nordic Ski Club, PO Box 3213, Castlegar,V1N 3H5
Three access points along Hwy 3 about 30 km W of Castlegar.
Rolling terrain thru fields and forests. High elev allows long season.

Trail Fee	Total	●	■	◆	Skating	Ungroomed	Lodge	Wax Room	Rentals	Food	Lessons	Shelters
DA	-	-	-	-	0							3
	45.0				0.0							

44 Nelson Nordic Ski Club, Nelson
(250) 352-7025; PO Box 486, Nelson,V1L 5R3
Apex-Busk Ski Area is 10 minutes from Nelson.
Scenic trail along the Salmo River.

Trail Fee	Total	●	■	◆	Skating	Ungroomed	Lodge	Wax Room	Rentals	Food	Lessons	Shelters
Yes	-	-	-	-	0							1
	25.0				0.0							

45 Wensley Creek Ski Trails (Arrow Lakes CC Ski Club), Naksup
Figure 8 trail layout in scenic stand of timber. Arrow Lakes CC Ski Club,PO Box 733,Naksup,V0G 1R0

Trail Fee	Total	●	■	◆	Skating	Ungroomed	Lodge	Wax Room	Rentals	Food	Lessons	Shelters
Yes	-	0	-	0	0							1
	9.6	9.6			0.0							

46 Mount Revelstoke National Park, Revelstoke
(250) 837-7500; PO Box 350, Revelstoke, V0E 2S0
1 km E of Revelstoke on Trans-Canada Hwy. Possible avalanche danger.

Trail Fee	Total	●	■	◆	Skating	Ungroomed	Lodge	Wax Room	Rentals	Food	Lessons	Shelters
Entry	2	2	0	0	-							0
Fee	10.0	10.0			Yes							

47 Mt MacPherson XC Ski Trails (Revelstoke Cross Country Ski Club), Revelstoke
7.2 km S of junction of Hwys 1 & 23. Revelstoke CC Ski Club, PO Box 1618, Revelstoke, V0E 2S0
Rolling hills, mature evergreens, some regrown clearcuts, lakes, creeks.

Trail Fee	Total	●	■	◆	Skating	Ungroomed	Lodge	Wax Room	Rentals	Food	Lessons	Shelters
NC	28	10	8	10	0	√						1
	28.0	10.0	8.0	10.0	5.0							

48 Glacier National Park, Revelstoke
(250) 837-6274; PO Box 350, Revelstoke,V0E 2S0
50 km W of Golden OR 50 km E of Revelstoke on Hwy 1.
BC skiing on steep trails, excellent telemarking. Avalanche danger. 50 rooms

Trail Fee	Total	●	■	◆	Skating	Ungroomed	Lodge	Wax Room	Rentals	Food	Lessons	Shelters
Entry	0	0	0	0	-							0
Fee	0.0				140.0							

Groomed Trails

Trail Fee / Total ● ■ ◆ Skating Ungroomed Lodge Wax Room Rentals Food Lessons Shelters

49 Yoho National Park, Field

(250) 343-6324; PO Box 99, Field, V0A 1G0
Adjacent to Banff Nat'l Park on the Trans-Canada Hwy.
Backcountry: 4 novice (18k), 6 inter (65k), 4 expert (70 k) trails plus Wapta Icefield.

Trail Fee	Total	●	■	◆	Skating	Ungroomed	Lodge	Wax Room	Rentals	Food	Lessons	Shelters
Entry	1	1	0	0		15						0
Fee	5.2	5.2				150.0						

50 Whitetooth Ski Center, Golden

(250) 344-6114; PO Box 1925, Golden, V0A 1H0

Trail Fee	Total	●	■	◆	Skating	Ungroomed	Lodge	Wax Room	Rentals	Food	Lessons	Shelters
NA	-	-	-	-		0						0
	17.0					0.0						

51 Kootenay National Park, Radium Hot Springs

(250) 347-9615; PO Box 220, Radium Hot Springs, BC V0A 1M0
Ten trailheads on Hwy 93 between Radium and Castle Junction.
Trails are mainly easy and lightly used.

Trail Fee	Total	●	■	◆	Skating	Ungroomed	Lodge	Wax Room	Rentals	Food	Lessons	Shelters
Entry	0	0	0	0		10						0
Fee	0.0					100.0						

52 Panorama Resort, Panorama

(250) 342-6941, 1-800-663-2929 (Canada & USA) Panorama Resort, Panorama, V0A 1T0
18 km W of Invermere on Toby Creek Rd.
Trails are easy to intermediate. Bar, hotels, condos.

Trail Fee	Total	●	■	◆	Skating	Ungroomed	Lodge	Wax Room	Rentals	Food	Lessons	Shelters
5⁰⁰	-	-	-	-		0	√			√		0
	22.0					0.0						

53 Fairmont Hot Springs Resort, Fairmont

(250) 345-6311, 1-800-663-4979 (Canada); PO Box 10, Fairmont, V0B 1L0
At ski center and on golf course.

Trail Fee	Total	●	■	◆	Skating	Ungroomed	Lodge	Wax Room	Rentals	Food	Lessons	Shelters
NC	-	-	-	-		0						0
	5.0					0.0						

54 Kimberley Ski Resort, Kimberley

(250) 427-4881, (250) 427-4881, 1-800-667-0808; PO Box 40, Kimberley, V1A 2Y5
At foot of Kimberly alpine center. 3 km of lit trails. Bar, condos, chalets.

Trail Fee	Total	●	■	◆	Skating	Ungroomed	Lodge	Wax Room	Rentals	Food	Lessons	Shelters
NA	-	-	-	-		0	√		√	√		0
	26.0					0.0						

B.C.

Groomed Trails

Trail Fee / Total	●	■	◆	Skating / Ungroomed	Lodge	Wax Room	Rentals	Food	Lesons	Shelters

55 Elkford Nordic Ski Club, Elkford

(250) 865-2376; PO Box 563, Elkford,V0B 1H0
Located next to Elkford Alpine Center.

NA	-	-	-	0						0
15.0				0.0						

56 South Star Ski Trails, Cranbrook

(250) 426-5914; Cranbrook Chamber of Commerce,2279 Cranbrook St. N.,Cranbrook,V1C 4H6
At base of Cranbrook Mtn S of Cranbrook. Park at the end of 38th Ave.

N.C. 8	1	4	3	0						0
30.0				0.0						

57 Fernie Snow Valley Resort, Fernie

(250) 423-4655, (250) 423-3555; Fernie Snow Valley Resort, Ski Area Road,Fernie,V0B 1M1
5 km SW of Fernie, 1 km off Crowsnest Hwy 3.
Wooded benchland at foot of mountain. 750 cm avg annual snowfall. BC touring
& tele terrain accessible from chairlifts. Daycare, bar, 44 rooms, 96 condos, B&B.

2⁰⁰	3	0	3	0	-	√		√	√	√	0
1⁰⁰C 14.0			14.0		Yes						

58 Methow Valley Sports Trail Association, Winthrop,Wash.

(509) 996-3287, (509) 996-1815(tape), 1-800-682-5787(WA, ORE,ID)
NE Washington state 150 k SW of Osoyoos. PO Box 147, Winthrop,98862
Second largest centre in USA. Trails run from Winthrop to Mazama.
Varied terrain, dry powder. Bar, backcountry huts, inns, B&Bs.

12⁰⁰	48	-	-	-	-	√	√	√	√	√	0
NCC 175.0	75.0	63.0	37.0	175.0	Yes						

B.C.

Backcountry Huts and Lodges

Note: most backcountry lodges and huts are located in alpine areas which can be subject to white-out conditions. Danger due to avalanches and crevasses is also possible so it is essential to be prepared for these hazards. An experienced guide is the best insurance against injury or death. Most of these areas require heavy-duty backcountry, telemark or alpine touring equipment with metal-edged skis. Rates are approximate cost per person and include 7% Goods and Service Tax.

Flight Meadows Chalet, Wells Gray

Wells Gray Backcountry Chalets, Wells Gray Park

PO Box 188, Clearwater BC V0E 1N0
(250) 587-6444; fax: (250) 587-6446
Avalanche awareness courses: $203 with 1 night accom.
Full service rate is $118 p.p., p.n. including meals, guide and safety equipment. Self-sufficient: $36 p.p., p.n. (minimum 6 people).
Hut-to-hut touring for strong int. to advanced skiers at Trophy Chalet and Table Cabin. Gentler terrain at Flight Chalet (helicopter access $107).
Varied terrain-open bowls, meadows and trees for touring/telemarking.
Open early Dec to late April
Capacity: 12 in chalets, 8 in cabin
Amenities: propane stove, heat and lights, blankets (bring linen), sauna.

Dave Henry Lodge, Valemount

Headwaters Outfitting Ltd, P.O. Box 818, Valemount, BC V0E 2Z0
(250) 566-4718
$80/night (catered), $38/night (uncatered), $950/week incl. meals, guide and flight in (ski out is 27km).

Alpine and subalpine touring and telemarking. Swift Creek cabins are a further 15 km ski away and can accommodate 8 people.
Open late Dec to mid-April
Capacity: 10 (dormitory)
Amenities: mattresses and pillows (bring linen and blankets), sauna, propane stove

Monashee Chalet, Blue River

Interior Recreation Ltd., 1408-8th Ave., New Westminster, BC V3M 2S4
Tel./fax: (250) 522-1239
Lodge is at 6000 foot elevation in the Monashee range SE of Blue River. Opportunities abound for backcountry touring or telemarking at all levels of ability.
Access is a 14-km ski or 75-minute snowcat ride ($50).
$33/night (uncatered)
Open early Dec to mid-May
Capacity: 14
Amenities: showers, electric lights

Blanket Glacier Chalet, Revelstoke

Nordic Institute, PO Box 1050, Canmore, AB T0L 0M0
Tel./fax: (403) 678-4102
Limitless number of treed or glacier runs. 25-foot annual snowfall.
Telemark instructional camps are $700/week including meals and return helicopter flight.
Self-sufficient rate is $43/night.
Open mid-Dec to mid-May
Capacity: 16
Amenities: propane, sauna, shower

B.C.

Blanket Glacier

Golden Alpine

Golden Alpine Holidays, Golden
PO Box 1050, Golden B.C. V0A 1H0
Tel./fax: (250) 344-7273
Three lodges are located about 8 km apart in the Selkirk Mountains 60 km NW of Golden.
From $598/3 nights to $998/week including meals and guide. From $355/3 nights to $570/week no meals or guide (minimum 8 people). Prices include return flight in helicopter. Intermediate to expert alpine touring or telemark skiing ability required.
Open early Dec to late April
Capacity: 10 to 12 in double rooms
Amenities: sauna, chemical toilet, propane stove and lanterns

Mistaya Lodge & Alpine Tours, Golden
PO Box 809, Golden, BC V0A 1H0
Tel./fax: (250) 344-6689
Lodge is located N of Golden.
Rates range from $680 for 3 nights to $1380/week catered and guided.
Open early Dec to mid-May.
Capacity: 12 Amenities: sauna

A.O. Wheeler Hut, Glacier National Park
A.C.C. Class A
Access to log cabin is via a plowed road to 3 km S of Rogers Pass, then a short ski in. Lots of backcountry skiing in the area.
Capacity: 24
Cabin is equipped with a gas stove and lanterns and cooking and eating utensils.

Purcell Lodge, Golden
PO Box 1829, Golden, BC V0A 1H0
(250) 344-2639; fax: (250) 344-5520
Prices range from $145 to $197 p.p., p.n., d.o. including meals and guide. Alpine meadows, glades and bowls for downhill and touring. Access is a 15-minute helicopter flight ($193 return).
Open early Nov to late April
Capacity: 24 in 10 rooms
Amenities: bedding, showers, sauna, electricity, bar

Selkirk Lodge, Glacier Nat'l Park
PO Box 1409, Golden, BC V0A 1H0
(250) 344-5016, 1-800-663-7080
Powder skiing and touring on glacier, bowl & tree terrain in SW Glacier N.P.
$975/week includes return helicopter flight, meals, guide and beacons.
Open late Jan to mid-April
Capacity: 12 in 4 bedrooms
Amenities: showers, sauna, indoor plumbing, solar powered lights.

Selkirk Mountain Experience, Revelstoke
Ruedi Beglinger, PO Box 2998, Revelstoke, BC V0E 2S0
(250) 837-2381; fax: (250) 837-4685
Located 45 km NE of Revelstoke on the Durrand Glacier in the Columbia Mountains. A second chalet is a one-day ski away at Mt. Moloch.
$995/week including meals, guide, round-trip helicopter flight and beacons.
Open late Dec to early May
Capacity: 18 (2 to 4 per room)
Amenities: shower, sauna, electricity

Selkirk Mountain Experience

Fairy Meadow Hut, Northern Selkirk Mountains
A.C.C. Class A
High season: $20 mbrs/$25 non-mbrs
Accessible only by helicopter.
Due to high demand caused by excellent powder skiing opportunities reservations are difficult to obtain from mid-Feb to mid-April.
Capacity: 20
Amenities: gas stove,cooking utensils.

Great Cairn Hut, Northern Selkirk Mountains
A.C.C. Class B (there is a wood-burning stove, but no wood)
Best accessed by helicopter from Golden. Good touring and tele-marking area.
Capacity: 6 Equipped with gas stove and cooking and eating utensils.

Sorcerer Lake Lodge, Glacier National Park
PO Box 175, Golden BC V0A 1H0
(250) 344-2805; fax: (250) 344-2316
Located in the Selkirk Mountains just north of Glacier National Park.
$960/week includes return helicopter flight, meals and guide. Self-sufficient: $3425/week for lodge plus $214 p.p. for helicopter.
A variety of glacier, bowl and glade terrain for alpine or telemarking.
Open Dec 25 to late April
Capacity: 16 in 4 bedrooms
Amenities: bedding, sauna, lights.

Lake O'Hara Lodge, Yoho National Park
PO Box 55, Lake Louise, AB T0L 1E0
(250) 343-6418
An easy 11 km ski on packed trails to the lodge in Yoho National Park.
$175 p.p., p.n. for a minimum of 2 nights including meals, guides and use of avalanche beacons.
Lodge is set amidst intermediate to expert touring and telemark terrain.
Open mid-Jan to mid-April
Capacity: 16 in double rooms.
Amenities: bedding, showers, indoor toilets, propane stove, cooking utensils.

Elizabeth Parker Hut, Yoho National Park
A.C.C. Class A
A 11 km ski on a trail that usually packed by snowmobiles servicing the nearby Lake O'Hara Lodge.
Capacity: 20 in two cabins.
Cabins are equipped with gas stove and lanterns and cooking utensils.

Fay Hut, Kootenay National Park
A.C.C. Class A
Hut is located in northern end of park about 14 km ski on a scenic trail with a 650-metre climb from Hwy 93. Possibility of continuing through to Lake O'Hara.
Capacity: 12
Equipped with gas stove and lanterns, cooking and eating utensils.

Stanley Mitchell Hut, Yoho National Park
A.C.C. Class A
Located just west of the Wapta Traverse, this log cabin lies on a demanding alternative southern route about 20 km SW of the Bow Hut and 25 km N of the Trans-Canada.
Capacity: 22
Cabin is equipped with gas stove and lanterns and cooking utensils.

B.C.

Amiskwi Lodge

Amiskwi Lodge, Yoho National Park
Box 1747, Canmore AB T0L 0M0
(403) 678-1800; fax: (403) 678-4039
This newly-opened lodge is located
just north of Yoho National Park.
There is a mix of bowls and treed
slopes for touring or telemarking.
Self-sufficient rate is $535/week
including round-trip helicopter flight.
Open Dec to May
Capacity: 16 in 4 bedrooms
Amenities: propane lights and cooking
stove, wood stove, sauna.

Ptarmigan Tours, Kimberley
Margie Jamieson, P.O. Box 11,
Kimberley B.C. V1A 2Y5
(250) 422-3270; fax: (250) 422-3566
Boulder Lodge and Ptarmigan huts are
about 10 km apart in the Purcell
Mountains. Part-way through the week
skiers move to the huts then fly out.
A return helicopter flight is included
in the $895/week all-inclusive cost.
Open mid-Dec to mid-April
Capacity: 12
Amenities: bedding, sauna (at Ptarmi-
gan), hot tub (at Boulder), ski rentals

Vahalla Lodge, Kaslo
PO Box 1073, Kaslo BC V0G 1M0
(250) 353-7179; fax: (250) 353-2317
Lodge is at 6900 foot elevation in the
Valhalla Mountains. Rates are $1030
per week catered and guided, $749
uncatered or $675 self-sufficient.
Prices include flight in.
Telemark or alpine touring terrain.
Open from late Dec to mid-May
Capacity: 10 in 4 bedrooms
Amenities: bedding, propane stove
and lanterns, sauna.

Vahalla Mountain Touring,
New Denver
PO Box 43, RR#1, New Denver, BC
V0G 1S0 (250) 358-7905
Cabin is located just N of Valhalla
Provincial Park.
$775/5 days or $910/week including
snowcat transportation to cabin,
meals and guide. $450/week self-
sufficient. Avalanche awareness
course $415/3 days including meals
& instruction. Powder bowls, trees,
backcountry touring & telemarking.
Open mid-Dec to late March
Capacity: 10 in dormitory
Amenities: sauna

Silver Spray and Slocan Chief
Cabins, Kokanee Glacier Park
Kokanee Glacier Mountaineering,
Nelson (250) 354-4092
RR #1, Site 3, Comp. 32, Nelson, BC
V1L 5P4
Access is usually fly in and ski out.
Reservation is by lottery for groups
due to excessive demand for the great
powder skiing. Two cabins - Slocan
Chief & Silver Spray.
Cost is about $200 per week on a self-
sufficient basis.
Open Dec to May Capacity: 12
(Slocan) and 8 (Silver Spray)
Slocan Chief cabin has a gas stove.

Island Lake Mountain Tours,
Fernie
PO Box 1229, Fernie, BC V0B 1M1
(250) 423-3700; fax: (250) 423-4055
10 km ski-in or a 45 minute Snowcat
ride ($20) to lodge
Rates are $157/night (uncatered) to
$2155 for 5 days including meals,
guide and Snowcat transportation up
10,000 to 18,000 vertical feet per day.
Powder skiing, open bowls and treed
slopes plus touring terrain.
Open early Dec to mid-April
Capacity: 24 in 12 bedrooms
Amenities: bedding, showers, hot tub,
electricity, bar.

B.C.

12 Yukon Territory

At the turn of the century, the Yukon was the site of the fabled Klondike gold rush, drawing prospectors from all over the world. Nowadays, instead of trekking over the Chilkoot Pass, visitors can fly in or drive up the Alaska Highway.

Some of Canada's most spectacular mountains can be found in the St. Elias Range in Kluane National Park. Among them is Mount Logan, the highest peak in Canada, at 5959 m (19,550 ft.). Day-trippers have easy access to the fringes of the Kluane National Park while the more adventurous can fly into the interior on guided trips for backcountry and telemark skiing.

Travel Information

Tourist Information Bureau
Tourism Yukon, PO Box 2703, Whitehorse, Yukon Y1A 2C6; (403) 667-5340, 1-800-78-YUKON; fax: (403) 667-2634

Road Report: (403) 667-8215

Cross Country Organizations

Cross Country Canada - Yukon division, PO Box 4507, Whitehorse, Yukon Y1A 2R8; (403) 633-8420; fax: 667-4237

Yukon

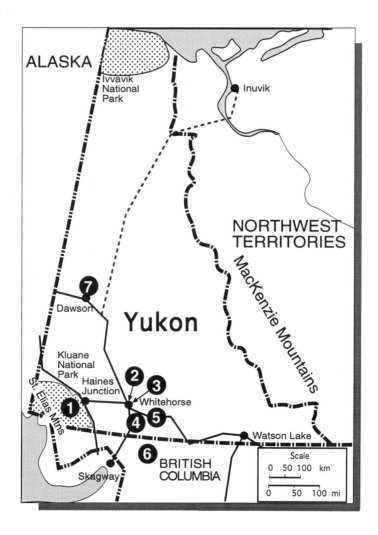

Cross Country Ski Areas

Winter Climate

Winter starts early in the Yukon with enough snow for skiing by late October to early November. Ski tourists should schedule their visits for the early or late season to avoid the colder months.

Average Temperatures   ## Average Snowfall

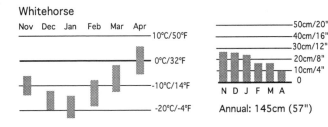

Whitehorse

Annual: 145cm (57")

Loppets

Date	Event	Location
Late Jan	"Not So Serious" Race	Whitehorse
Early Feb	Whitehorse Ski Club Loppet	Whitehorse
Early Mar	Yukon Gold Loppet	Whitehorse

Groomed Trails

Column headers: Trail Fee · Total · ● · ■ · ◆ · Skating · Ungroomed · Lodge · Wax Room · Rentals · Food · Lessons · Shelters

Yukon

1 Kluane National Park ▲ 🎿
PO Box 5495, Haines Junction, YT Y0B 1L0
(403) 634-2251, (403) 634-2686
7 trailheads are scattered along Haines Road near Haines Junction.

Trail Fee	Total	●	■	◆	Skating	Ungroomed	Lodge	Wax Room	Rentals	Food	Lessons	Shelters
NC	0	0	0	0		8						
						152.0						

2 Whitehorse Cross Country Ski Club, Whitehorse
(403) 668-4477, (403) 667-2774   PO Box 4639, Whitehorse, YT Y1A 2R8
At Mt MacIntyre Recreation Center in Whitehorse.
5 km lit trail. Trail for skiing with your dog. Hosts several loppets. Bar

Trail Fee	Total	●	■	◆	Skating	Ungroomed	Lodge	Wax Room	Rentals	Food	Lessons	Shelters
7⁰⁰	-	-	-	-			√	√		√		
	70.0	25.0	25.0	20.0	50.0							

3 Gray Mountain Biathlon Trails, Whitehorse
(403) 668-5017
On Gray Mountain Road 5 km from downtown.
Biathlon loops plus Magnusson Trail (20 km). 1 km lighted trail.

Trail Fee	Total	●	■	◆	Skating	Ungroomed	Lodge	Wax Room	Rentals	Food	Lessons	Shelters
3⁰⁰	8	-	-	-		0	√	√				
	45.0					25.0	0.0					

4 Carcross Community Ski Club, Carcross
Trail starts behind school in Carcross. PO Box 5964, Carcross, YT Y0B 1B0
Very scenic trails. Annual Carcross Classic race is very popular.

Trail Fee	Total	●	■	◆	Skating	Ungroomed	Lodge	Wax Room	Rentals	Food	Lessons	Shelters
NC	4	2	1	1								
	25.0	5.0	5.0	10.0	25.0							

5 Marsh Lake Trails, Marsh Lake

Trail Fee	Total	●	■	◆	Skating	Ungroomed	Lodge	Wax Room	Rentals	Food	Lessons	Shelters
NA												
	20.0											

6 Ruffner Bay Lodge, Aitlin B.C.
(403) 668-6999   PO Box 5480, Whitehorse, YT Y1A 5H4
Guided backcountry trips, fly-in telemark skiing. Lodge accommodates 8 guests.

Trail Fee	Total	●	■	◆	Skating	Ungroomed	Lodge	Wax Room	Rentals	Food	Lessons	Shelters
NA	-	-	-	-			√			√		
	45.0					Yes						

7 Dawson City Jackrabbit Cross Country Ski Club, Dawson City
On the Dome near Dawson City. PO Box 135, Dawson City, Y0B 1G0

Trail Fee	Total	●	■	◆	Skating	Ungroomed	Lodge	Wax Room	Rentals	Food	Lessons	Shelters
NC	2	1	1	0								
	7.0	2.0	5.0									

13 Northwest Territories

Encompassing one-third of the area of Canada but with a population of about 65,000, the Northwest Territories are the last great wilderness area remaining in North America. Access to much of the region is by air only, a factor that helps it remain relatively pristine.

Several national parks have been created to preserve this heritage for future generations. Auyuttuq National Park on Baffin Island is becoming a popular destination for expeditions. Ski touring in remote wilderness regions is best done with an experienced tour operator–several are listed in the tourist guide available from the NWT tourism bureau.

Except for the band of boreal forest running across the southwest corner, most of the territory is tundra. Winter is prime time for viewing the *aurora borealis*. Unfortunately, winters are quite harsh and daylight hours are short, so skiing is best left to early or late in the season.

Travel Information

NWT Tourism Information, PO Box 2107, Yellowknife, NT X1A 2P6; (403) 873-7200, 1-800-661-0788 (Canada and USA); fax: (403) 920-2801

Cross Country Skiing Organizations

Cross Country Canada - NWT Division,
PO Box 2098, Hay River, NT X0E 0R0;
(403) 874-6857; fax: (403) 874-6857

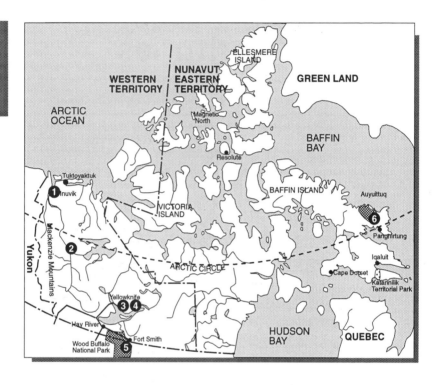

Cross Country Ski Areas

Auyuittuq National Park	6
Blanchford Lake Lodge	4
Inuvik Ski Club	1
Norman Wells Cross Country Ski Club	2
Wood Buffalo National Park	5
Yellowknife Ski Club	3

Winter Climate

As in the Yukon, the best time for cross-country skiing is during the milder months of March and April.

Average Temperatures

Average Snowfall

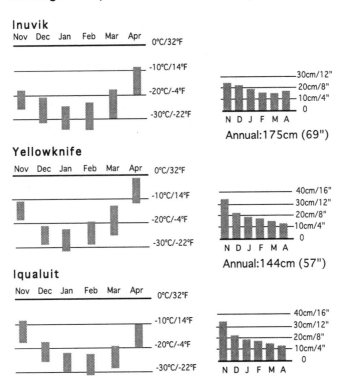

Inuvik

Annual:175cm (69")

Yellowknife

Annual:144cm (57")

Iqualuit

Annual: 257cm (101")

NWT

1   Inuvik Ski Club
Tourist Centre: (403) 979-4727
Trail starts on Loucheux Road behind Grollier Hall.
3 and 5 km loops, cabin at start of trail, 3 km lighted trail.

2   Norman Wells Cross Country Ski Club, Norman Wells
PO Box 102, Norman Wells, NWT X0E 0V0
Trail starts just outside of town and leads 3 km to a cabin.
Total length groomed is 4 km. Each year some club members fly by
helicopter into the Mackenzie Mountains for touring & telemarking.

3   Yellowknife Ski Club
PO Box 1598, Yellowknife, NWT X1A 2P2
Traihead is about 1 km outside of town near turnoff to airport.
Club has active Jackrabbit and youth skier development programs.
Trail fee is $5 in lieu of membership. Six looped trails (1,2,3,5,7.5,10 km)
are groomed for a total of 25 km with about 15 km groomed for skating.
Canteen in chalet is open weekends. Skis can be rented in town.

4   Blanchford Lake Lodge
(403) 873-3303 PO Box 1568, Yellowknife, NWT X1A 2P2
100 km SE of Yellowknife, access by ski-plane only.
20 km of groomed trails and unlimited backcountry skiing. 5 log cabins.

5   Wood Buffalo National Park
P.O. Box 750, Fort Smith, NWT X0E 0P0
(403) 872-2349, (403) 872-2878 (24-hrs)
Home to the world's largest free-roaming bison herd.
Bogs, forests, lakes and meadows offer a variety of backcountry skiing.

6   Auyuittuq National Park, Baffin Island
P.O. Box 353, Pangnirtung, NWT X0A 0R0
(819) 473-8828, (819) 473-8612
Park entrance is 31 km N of Pangnirtung on Baffin Island.
April, May and June are best months for skiing the spectacular
Pangnirtung Pass 110 km north to Broughton Island.
User fees are $15.00 per day or $100 for long-term stays.

14 Alberta

Nestled up against the Alberta-BC border, the world-famous Banff and Jasper National Parks are criss-crossed with dozens of hiking trails, some of which are groomed for cross-country skiing in winter. The backcountry trails and wide open spaces of the Rockies offer boundless opportunities for touring and telemark skiing.

Just a short ski south of Banff lies Kananaskis Country. Scattered throughout K-Country are seven cross-country ski areas totalling over 300 km of groomed trails, the highest concentration of any region in Canada. Foremost among them is the Canmore Nordic Centre, site of the 1988 Winter Olympic cross-country skiing races and home of the National Ski Team.

Central Alberta also has plenty to offer. Cooking Lake-Blackfoot Recreation Park east of Edmonton has one of the largest trail networks in the province and hosts up to 2,000 skiers at the Canadian Birkebeiner in February each year.

Travel Information

Bus Service: Greyhound 1-800-661-8747

Rail Service: VIA Rail runs a transcontinental service through Edmonton and Jasper three times a week.

Tourist Information Bureau
Travel Alberta publishes an annual winter guide and also provides road and weather reports and ski conditions. Alberta Economic Development & Tourism, 10155 - 102 Street, Edmonton, AB T5J 4L6; 1-800-661-8888 (North America)

Cross Country Skiing Resources

Cross Country Alberta
11759 Groat Road, Edmonton, Alberta T5M 3K6
(403) 453-8620; fax: (403) 453-8553

CANSI Alberta/NWT, PO Box 1365 Main, Edmonton, Alberta
T5L 2N2; (403) 678-6764

Avalanche bulletin: Canadian Avalanche Association
(403) 243-7253 ext 7669 (Calgary),
1-800-667-1105 (BC and Alberta)

Banff Avalanche Report (tape) (403) 762-2088

Winter Climate

Southern and central Alberta east of the foothills has a cross-country ski season that extends from approximately mid-December to mid-March. Northern Alberta and areas at higher altitudes have seasons one or two months longer.

Average Temperatures   Average Snowfall

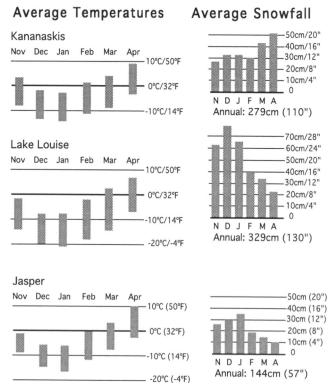

Kananaskis
Annual: 279cm (110")

Lake Louise
Annual: 329cm (130")

Jasper
Annual: 144cm (57")

Alberta

Edmonton

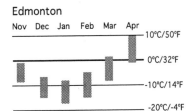

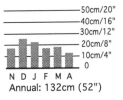

Annual: 132cm (52")

Alberta Loppet Series

Entry fees vary from $5 for children to $10 to $20 for adults' advance registration. Distances for each event vary from 30 to 40 km with the exceptions of the 10-km Suntasia and the 55-km Canadian Birkebeiner. Most events offer several shorter length courses starting at one or two km for youngsters and ranging to up to half the regular length for those who want less of a challenge.

Date	Event	Location
mid Dec	Drayton Valley Loppet	Drayton Valley
late Dec	Troll in the Park	Edmonton
early Jan	Jasper Park Loppet	Jasper Park Lodge
early Jan	Suntasia Invitational	Alberta Assoc. for Disabled Skiers
mid Jan	Athabasca Loppet	Muskeg Creek Trails
mid Jan	Ole Uffda Ski Gallop	Camrose Ski Club Trails
late Jan	Freddy the Fox Loppet	Vermilion Nordic Ski Club
late Jan	The Ramblin' Rose	Rose Creek Trails
early Feb	Red Deer Loppet	Riverbend Golf & Rec. Area
early Feb	St. Albert Family Fun	St. Albert Nordic Ski Club
early Feb	Canadian Birkebeiner*	Cooking Lake-Blackfoot
mid Feb	Kananaskis Marathon	Peter Lougheed Prov. Park host: Foothills Nordic Ski Club (403)284-1190
mid Feb	Hinton Marathon	Hinton Nordic Skiers
late Feb	Mooseheart Loppet	Edson Muskeg Flyers
early Mar	Lac La Loppet	Shaw Lake
early Mar	Grizzly Ridge Loppet	Grizzly Ridge
early Mar	Lake Louise Loppet	host: Calgary Ski Club 901, 11 Ave. NW, Calgary
early Mar	Sveinungsgaard Loppet	Wapiti Nordic Ski Club

*Canadian Ski Odyssey

Alberta

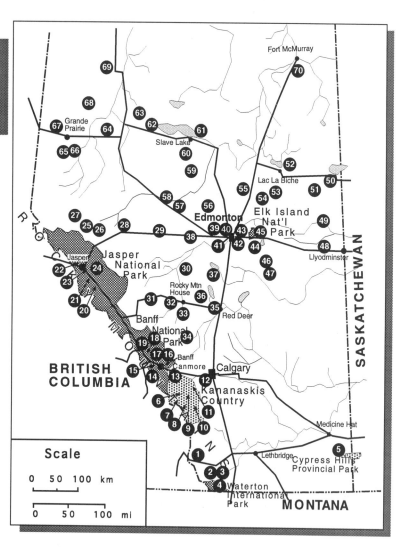

Cross-Country Ski Areas

Groomed Trails — Trail Fee | Total | ● ■ ◆ | Skating | Ungroomed | Lodge | Wax Room | Rentals | Food | Lessons | Shelters

Alberta

1 Allison - Chinook, Blairmore ⚡

(403) 562-7331 c/o Bow/Crow Forest Service, PO Box 540, Blairmore, AB T0K 0E0
3 km W of Coleman to Chinook Lake/Atlas Rd then 3 km N to ski area.
Interesting trails on old logging roads. 6 km trail leads to Deadman Pass.

Trail Fee	Total	●	■	◆	Skating	Ungroomed	Lodge	Wax Room	Rentals	Food	Lessons	Shelters
NC	7	3	4			0	√					0
	25.0	9.0	16.0			0.0						

2 Syncline, Blairmore c/o Bow/Crow Forest, PO Box 540, Blairmore,T0K 0E0
(403) 562-7331   15 km SW of Beaver Mines on Hwy 774.
Scenic trails with views of river and mountains on old logging trails.

Trail Fee	Total	●	■	◆	Skating	Ungroomed	Lodge	Wax Room	Rentals	Food	Lessons	Shelters
NC	8	6	2			0	T					0
	15.0	8.0	7.0			0.0						

3 Beauvais Lake Provincial Park, Pincher Creek

(403) 627-2021 PO Box 1810,PincherCreek,T0K 1W0
11 km W of Pincher Creek on Sec Hwy 507, then 8 km S on access road to park.
Foothills montaine, mixed forest and meadows, beaver pond.

Trail Fee	Total	●	■	◆	Skating	Ungroomed	Lodge	Wax Room	Rentals	Food	Lessons	Shelters
NC	7	3	3	1		0						0
	10.5	4.3	5.4	0.8		0.0						

4 Waterton Lakes National Park, Waterton Lake

(403) 859-2224 Waterton Lakes National Park, Waterton Lake, T0K 2M0
Two accesses - at end of Akamina Hwy, 3k from end (14/11 km from Waterton)
Easy trail connects parking lots, the other goes to Cameron Lake.

Trail Fee	Total	●	■	◆	Skating	Ungroomed	Lodge	Wax Room	Rentals	Food	Lessons	Shelters
Entry	2	1	1	0		0						0
Fee	6.0	3.0	3.0			0.0						

5 Cypress Hills Prov. Park, Elkwater

(403) 893-3777 PO Box 12, Elkwater,T0J 1C0
32 km E of Medicine Hat on Hwy 1, then 34 km S on Hwy 41.
Three trailheads. Mixed forest of logepole pine, spruce, aspen and grasslands.

Trail Fee	Total	●	■	◆	Skating	Ungroomed	Lodge	Wax Room	Rentals	Food	Lessons	Shelters
NC	4	1	2	1		5						2
	14.2	9.5	3.5	1.2		13.9						

Groomed Trails

6 Mount Shark, Kananaskis Country

#100, 1101 Glenmore Trail S.W., Calgary, T2V 4R6
(403) 591-7222
31 km S of Canmore on Smith-Dorrien/Spray Trail road, W on Mt. Shark Rd.
Challenging trails designed for training and racing. Near Mt. Engadine Lodge.

Trail Fee	Total	●	■	◆	Skating	Ungroomed	Lodge	Wax Room	Rentals	Food	Lessons	Shelters
NC	7	2	1	4	1							0
	20.0	6.7	5.0	13.0	10.0							

7 Smith-Dorrien, Kananaskis Country

(403) 591-7222
42 km S of Canmore on Smith-Dorrien/Spray Trail road.
Two accesses. Trails are not groomed regularly and are int to advanced.

Trail Fee	Total	●	■	◆	Skating	Ungroomed	Lodge	Wax Room	Rentals	Food	Lessons	Shelters
NC	6	0	5	1	5							0
	32.0		30.2	1.8	32.5							

8 Peter Lougheed Prov. Park, Kananaskis Country

(403) 591-7222
Hwy 40 S from TCH OR Smith-Dorrien/Spray Trail S from Canmore. 8 accesses.
Popular area due to long snow season and wide variety of trails.

Trail Fee	Total	●	■	◆	Skating	Ungroomed	Lodge	Wax Room	Rentals	Food	Lessons	Shelters
NC	26	5	15	6	1	√			√			0
	85.0	16.6	38.3	23.0	7.2							

9 Ribbon Creek, Kananaskis Country

(403) 673-3663, (403) 232-8477 (Calgary)
From TCH take Hwy 40 S to Nikiska Ski Area. Three access points.
Dramatic views of the valley and mountains from several points. Daycare, bar

Trail Fee	Total	●	■	◆	Skating	Ungroomed	Lodge	Wax Room	Rentals	Food	Lessons	Shelters
NC	18	6	10	2	0	√			√	√		0
	58.5	17.1	34.4	4.0	0.0							

10 Sandy McNabb, Kananaskis Country

(403) 949-3754
18/20 km W of Turner Valley on Hwy 546 at Sheep River OR Sandy McNabb.
Converted logging roads thru aspen groves and over ridges.

Trail Fee	Total	●	■	◆	Skating	Ungroomed	Lodge	Wax Room	Rentals	Food	Lessons	Shelters
NC	19	13	5	1	0							0
	37.0	27.1	9.6	0.3	0.0							

Groomed Trails — Trail Fee | Total | ● ■ ◆ | Skating | Ungroomed | Lodge | Wax Room | Rentals | Food | Lessons | Shelters

Alberta

11 Kananaskis Country, West Bragg Creek
(403) 949-3754
End of W Bragg Creek Road OR at Allen Bill Pond W of Bragg Creek on Hwy 66.
Hills, ridges, meadows, aspen and pine.

Trail Fee	Total	●	■	◆	Skating	Ungroomed	Lodge	Wax Room	Rentals	Food	Lessons	Shelters
NC	6	3	3	0		0						0
	45.0	13.6	31.4			0.0						

12 Canada Olympic Park, Calgary
(403) 286-2632, (403) 247-5452 88 Canada Olympic Park Rd S.W., Calgary,T3B 5R5
88 Canada Olympic Rd SW, Calgary
Site of the 88 Olympic ski jumping, bob sled and luge. Bar

Trail Fee	Total	●	■	◆	Skating	Ungroomed	Lodge	Wax Room	Rentals	Food	Lessons	Shelters
7⁰⁰	1	1	1	0		0	√		√	√	√	0
4⁰⁰	1.8	0.4	1.4		1.8	0.0						

13 Canmore Nordic Centre, Canmore
PO Box 1979, Canmore, T0M 0L0
(403) 678-2400 (tape)
2 miles S of Canmore on Spray Lakes Rd.
Mountainous and hilly, conifers. Novice and Olympic-calibre trails.

Trail Fee	Total	●	■	◆	Skating	Ungroomed	Lodge	Wax Room	Rentals	Food	Lessons	Shelters
10⁰⁰	6	-	-	-		0	√	√	√	√	√	0
	80.0	21.0	38.0	21.0	65.0	0.0						

14 Banff townsite, Banff National Park
(403) 762-1500 PO Box 900, Banff,T0L 0C0
Cave & Basin (5k trails), Spray River(18 k), golf course (10k) Banff Springs Hotel
Spray River trail continues thru to Canmore 18 km one way.

Trail Fee	Total	●	■	◆	Skating	Ungroomed	Lodge	Wax Room	Rentals	Food	Lessons	Shelters
Entry	3	-	-	-		2						0
Fee	33.0					40.0						

15 Sundance Trails, Banff National Park
(403) 762-1500
Two accesses - Cave & Basin or Sunshine Village parking lot.
Healy Creek trail leads 16km to Sundance Lodge.

Trail Fee	Total	●	■	◆	Skating	Ungroomed	Lodge	Wax Room	Rentals	Food	Lessons	Shelters
Entry	4	0	4	0		4						0
Fee	13.0	0	13.0	0		40.0						

16 Banff National Park, Lake Minnewanka/Cascade
(403) 762-1500
At end of Lake Minnewanka Road near parking lot.
A linear trail leads to Stony Creek. One of the most popular in Banff.

Trail Fee	Total	●	■	◆	Skating	Ungroomed	Lodge	Wax Room	Rentals	Food	Lessons	Shelters
Entry	1	1	0	0		0						0
Fee	15.0	15.0				0.0						

Groomed Trails — Trail Fee · Total · ● ■ ◆ · Skating · Ungroomed · Lodge · Wax Room · Rentals · Food · Lessons · Shelters

17 Castle Junction, Banff National Park
(403) 762-1500
Johnston Canyon, Redearth Creek (12 k), Boom Lake and Castle Mtn (9 k).
Boom Lake and Johnston Canyon are ungroomed. Hostel and hotel are nearby.

	Total	●	■	◆	Skating	Ungroomed	Lodge	Wax Room	Rentals	Food	Lessons	Shelters
Entry	4	4	0	0		2	C			C		0
Fee	21.0	21.0				10.0						

18 Baker Creek, Banff National Park
Baker Creek Chalets, PO Box 66, LakeLouise,T0L 1E0 (403) 522-3761
10 km E of Lake Louise on Hwy 1A in Banff National Park.
Log chalets with mountain and creek views. No trail map. Bar, lodge & 25 chalets

	Total	●	■	◆	Skating	Ungroomed	Lodge	Wax Room	Rentals	Food	Lessons	Shelters
Entry	2	1	1	0		2	√			√		0
Fee	17.0	10.0	7.0			25.0						

19 Lake Louise, Banff National Park

(403) 762-1500
4 areas - Bow River Loop in town, Chateau loops, Pipestone and Whitehorn.
Trails are scattered over both sides of valley. About half of the trails are loops.
Close to Chateau Lake Louise hotel accommodations: 1-800-441-1414

	Total	●	■	◆	Skating	Ungroomed	Lodge	Wax Room	Rentals	Food	Lessons	Shelters
Entry	12	5	6	1		0	C		C	C		0
Fee	70.6	23.3	48.0	9.3	28.0	0.0						

20 Athabasca Falls, Jasper National Park
(403) 852-6176 PO Box10, Jasper,T0E 1E0
30 km S of Jasper on Hwy 93A or Hwy 93 (Two accesses).
Trail along unplowed Hwy 93A plus 2 loops and 9 km trail to Moab Lake.

	Total	●	■	◆	Skating	Ungroomed	Lodge	Wax Room	Rentals	Food	Lessons	Shelters
Entry	4	4	0	0		0						0
Fee	31.0	31.0				0.0						

21 Whistlers Campground, Jasper National Park
3 km S of Jasper on Hwy 93 turn onto Whistlers Mtn Rd then left, go to end.
Campground trails lit for night skiing.

	Total	●	■	◆	Skating	Ungroomed	Lodge	Wax Room	Rentals	Food	Lessons	Shelters
Entry	1	1	0	0		0						0
Fee	4.0	4.0				0.0						

22 Pyramid Lake Rd, Jasper National Park
(403) 852-6176
N of town 3 trails - Mina Lake(7k), Pyramid Bench (5 km), Patricia Lk (6k).
Pyramid Bench trail provides beautiful view of the valley.

	Total	●	■	◆	Skating	Ungroomed	Lodge	Wax Room	Rentals	Food	Lessons	Shelters
Entry	3	0	3	0		0						0
Fee	17.3		17.3			0.0						

Groomed Trails

	Trail Fee	Total	●	■	◆	Skating	Ungroomed	Lodge	Wax Room	Rentals	Food	Lesons	Shelters

23 Jasper Park Lodge, Jasper National Park

Lodge: (403) 852-3301, 1-800-642-3817 (Alberta) PO Box 40, Jasper,T0E 1E0
5 km from town of Jasper via Hwy 16 and Lodge Road.
River, lakes, meadows, forest. Moderate to rolling terrain. Daycare, bar, 440 rooms

Entry	4	2	2	0		0	√	√	√	√	√	0	
Fee	29.0	15.0	14.0			0.0							

24 Maligne Road, Jasper National Park

Beaver-Summit Lakes trail is 27 km, Maligne Lake is 47 km on Maligne Rd.
Summit Lk trail is 5 km each way. Maligne Lk trails are loops except Bald Hill

Entry	7	4	1	2		0							0
Fee	45.0	19.0	7.3	18.5		0.0							

25 Blue Lake Adventure Lodge (William Switzer Prov. Park), Hinton

(403) 865-4741 1-800-582-3305 (Canada, USA) PO Box 6150, Hinton,T7V 1X5
25 km NW of Hinton on Hwy 40. Hills and boreal forest.
Courses in ski touring, XC, CANSI, avalanche safety, etc Bar, chalet & cabins

3⁰⁰	-	-	0	0		0	√	√	√	√	√	0	
	22.0	22.0				7.0	0.0						

26 Athabathsca Lookout Nordic Centre (Hinton Nordic Ski Club), Hinton

(403) 865-2400 c/o Hinton Nordic Ski Club, PO Box 6455, Hinton,T7V 1X7
From Hinton take Hwy 40 22 km N to Athabasca Tower turn-off.
Stacked loops. Views from some points. 1.5 km lit for night skiing. Luge.

5⁰⁰	8	2	3	2		0	√						2
	33.0	2.5	11.3	15.0	33.0	0.0							

27 Pierre Grey's Lakes, Grande Cache

(403) 845-2400 227 Kelly Road,Hinton,T7V 1H2
Approx 40 km E of Grande Cache on Hwy 40 OR 110 km NW of Hinton.
Caribou and other wildlife can often be spotted.

NC	3	1	2	0		0	√						2
	15.7	2.1	9.6			0.0							

Alberta

Groomed Trails legend: Trail Fee | Total | ● ■ ◆ | Skating | Ungroomed | Lodge | Wax Room | Rentals | Food | Lessons | Shelters

28 Hornbeck Cross-Country Ski Centre, Edson

(403) 723-8269 c/o Alberta Forest Service, #203 - 111 - 54 St., Edson,T7E 1T2
7 km W of Edson on Hwy 16 N on Schlick Rd 11 km.
Gently rolling terrain mixed forest of aspen and spruce and muskeg.
5 km from Aspenhill Lodge (403) 723-6019.

Trail Fee	Total	●	■	◆	Skating	Ungroomed	Lodge	Wax Room	Rentals	Food	Lessons	Shelters
NC	8	6	1	1		0	√	√	C		√	0
	37.4	28.9	3.5	5.0		0.0						

29 Pembina River Prov. Park, Evansburg

(403) 727-3643 PO Box 446,Evansburg,T0E 0T0
1 km N of Entwistle. (100 km W of Edmonton)
River valley, mostly flat.

Trail Fee	Total	●	■	◆	Skating	Ungroomed	Lodge	Wax Room	Rentals	Food	Lessons	Shelters
NC	1	1	0	0		0						1
	4.5	4.5				0.0						

30 Rose Creek Trails, Alder Flats

(403) 388-3927
5 km W of Alder Flats. Host of the Ramblin' Rose loppet.

Trail Fee	Total	●	■	◆	Skating	Ungroomed	Lodge	Wax Room	Rentals	Food	Lessons	Shelters
NC	7	-	-	0		0	√					0
	56.0	11.0	45.0		56.0	0.0						

31 Shunda Creek Hostel, Nordegg

(403) 721-2140 c/o Hostelling International, 10926 - 88th Avenue,Edmonton,T6G 0Z1
W of Nordegg, 3km N of Hwy 11 on the Shunda Creek Recreation Road.
Trails are mostly linear. Mainly hilly, conifers, muskeg and lakes. 48 bed hostel

Trail Fee	Total	●	■	◆	Skating	Ungroomed	Lodge	Wax Room	Rentals	Food	Lessons	Shelters
NC	6	2	4	0		0	√					6
	20.5	8.5	12.0			0.0						

32 Crimson Lake Prov. Park, Rocky Mountain House

(403) 845-2340 PO Box 2100, Rocky Mountain House,T0M 1T0
12 km W of Rocky Mtn House then 8 km N on Sec Hwy 756.
Rolling foothills in boreal forest. Several backcountry trails.

Trail Fee	Total	●	■	◆	Skating	Ungroomed	Lodge	Wax Room	Rentals	Food	Lessons	Shelters
NC	9	0	9	0		-						2
	17.0		17.0			Yes						

Groomed Trails

Trail Fee	Total	●	■	◆	Skating	Ungroomed	Lodge	Wax Room	Rentals	Food	Lessons	Shelters

33 Terratima Lodge, Rocky Mountain House

Box 1636, Rocky Mountain House (403) 845-6786
From Junc Hwy 11&22 SE of Rocky Mtn House, go 10 km S on 22, follow signs.
Mixed-wood forest, creeks , flats and hills. 2 km lit trail. Lodge & cabins

Trail Fee	Total	●	■	◆	Skating	Ungroomed	Lodge	Wax Room	Rentals	Food	Lessons	Shelters
Yes	-	-	-		-	√		√		√	√	0
	30.0					50.0						

34 Bearberry Nordic Centre, Bearberry
(403) 638-4153
35 km NW of Sundre in the Bow Crow Forest.
Pine and spruce forest. Two chalets, dorm and bunkhouse for overnighting.

Trail Fee	Total	●	■	◆	Skating	Ungroomed	Lodge	Wax Room	Rentals	Food	Lessons	Shelters
5⁰⁰	10	4	3	3		0	√	√				2
	35.0					35.0						

35 River Bend, Red Deer
(403) 343-6341
At River Bend Golf and Recreation Area.

Trail Fee	Total	●	■	◆	Skating	Ungroomed	Lodge	Wax Room	Rentals	Food	Lessons	Shelters
2⁰⁰	-	-	-			0						0
	11.0					0.0						

36 Pigeon Lake Prov. Park, Westerose

(403) 586-2645 RR 1,Site 4, Box 4,Westerose,T0C 2V0
33 km W of junction of Hwys 2 & 13 on Hwy 13 to Hwy 771, N on Hwy 771.
Campground and lakeshore. Varied terrain over aspen parkland.

Trail Fee	Total	●	■	◆	Skating	Ungroomed	Lodge	Wax Room	Rentals	Food	Lessons	Shelters
NC	2	1	1	0		0						0
	10.0	5.0	5.0			0.0						

37 Jarvis Bay Prov. Park, Sylvan Lake

(403) 887-5575 PO Box 239, Sylvan Lake,T0M 1Z0
5 km N of town of Sylvan Lake.
On campground in aspen parkland. Quite flat.

Trail Fee	Total	●	■	◆	Skating	Ungroomed	Lodge	Wax Room	Rentals	Food	Lessons	Shelters
NC	3	3	0	0		0						0
	7.0	7.0				0.0						

Alberta

Groomed Trails

Alberta

38 Wabamun Lake Prov. Park, Wabamun

(403) 892-2702 PO Box 30, Wabamun,T0E 2K0
63 km W of Edmonton on Hwy 16.
Rolling hills, mixed wood forest.

Trail Fee	Total	●	■	◆	Skating	Ungroomed	Lodge	Wax Room	Rentals	Food	Lessons	Shelters
NC	2	2	0	0		0						0
	7.3	7.3				0.0						

39 St. Albert Nordic Ski Club, St. Albert

(403) 459-2459
Near town of St. Albert. Host of St. Albert Family Fun loppet

Trail Fee	Total	●	■	◆	Skating	Ungroomed	Lodge	Wax Room	Rentals	Food	Lessons	Shelters
NA	-	-	-	-		0	√					0
	18.0				18.0	0.0						

40 Chickakoo Lake Recreation Area, Stony Plain

(403) 963-8448 c/o Parkland County, 4601 48 St., Stony Plain,T7Z 1R1
6 km N of Hwy 16 on Rte 779 turn W at sign, turn N after 4 km
Trails skirt several lakes. Aspen parkland w stands of birch & spruce.

Trail Fee	Total	●	■	◆	Skating	Ungroomed	Lodge	Wax Room	Rentals	Food	Lessons	Shelters
NA	4	1	2	1		0						0
	12.5	1.4	6.7	4.4		0.0						

41 River Valley Outdoor Centre, Edmonton 10125 - 9 Avenue,Edmonton,T5K 0B3

(403) 496-PARK; Lessons (AusCan Int'l): (403) 439-1883
6 parks - Gold Bar(10k), Terwilligar(8k), Kinsmen, Mill Creek, Wm Hawrelak(10)

Trail Fee	Total	●	■	◆	Skating	Ungroomed	Lodge	Wax Room	Rentals	Food	Lessons	Shelters
NC	-	√	√	-		0	√					0
	40.0					0.0						

42 Strathcona Wilderness, Sherwood Park

(403) 922-3939, tape: (403) 467-5800 2025 Oak St., Sherwood Park,T8A 0W9
16 km E of Sherwood Park on Baseline Rd at Range Rd 212.
Mix of flat, rolling and steep terrain thru aspen parkland and on lake.

Trail Fee	Total	●	■	◆	Skating	Ungroomed	Lodge	Wax Room	Rentals	Food	Lessons	Shelters
3⁰⁰	7	5	2			0	√		√	E	√	0
1⁰⁰C	14.1	10.5	4.6			0.0						

43 Strathcona Science Provincial Park, Sherwood Park

(403) 427-9488 2025 Oak St., Sherwood Park,T8A 0W9
Located E of Edmonton on 17th St. 1 km S of Hwy 16.
Trails wind along banks of N Sakatchewan River. Views of city and valley.

Trail Fee	Total	●	■	◆	Skating	Ungroomed	Lodge	Wax Room	Rentals	Food	Lessons	Shelters
NC	6	4	1	1		0	√			√		0
	8.0	5.8	1.5	0.5		0.0						

Groomed Trails

| Trail Fee | Total | ● | ■ | ◆ | Skating | Ungroomed | Lodge | Wax Room | Rentals | Food | Lessons | Shelters |

44 Cooking Lake -Blackfoot Provincial Recreation Area, Sherwood Park

(403) 922-3293, (403) 922-4676 (tape); PO Box 57104, Eastgate PO, Sherwood Park,T8A 5L7
30 km E of Sherwood Park on Hwy 16 then 7 km S on Range Rd 210. 3 accesses.
Knob and kettle terrain, rolling hills, lakes. Backcountry skiing.
Site of the Canadian Birkebeiner

Trail Fee	Total	●	■	◆	Skating	Ungroomed	Lodge	Wax Room	Rentals	Food	Lessons	Shelters
NC	21	10	11	1								7
	85.0	31.0	50.0	4.0	32.0	Yes						

45 Elk Island National Park, Fort Saskatchewan

(403) 992-6380 Site 4, RR 1,Fort Saskatchewan,T8L 2N7
About 50 km E of Edmonton.

Trail Fee	Total	●	■	◆	Skating	Ungroomed	Lodge	Wax Room	Rentals	Food	Lessons	Shelters
Entry	0	0	0	0		12						0
Fee	0.0					100.0						

46 Miquelon Lake Prov. Park, Camrose

(403) 672-7274; PO Box 1977, Camrose,T4V 1X8
22 km N of Camrose on Sec Hwy 833, then 9 km W on Sec Hwy 623.
Novice trails over camp ground. Intermediate trails over Knob & Kettle moraine.

Trail Fee	Total	●	■	◆	Skating	Ungroomed	Lodge	Wax Room	Rentals	Food	Lessons	Shelters
NC	8	5	3	0		0						2
	18.0	7.0	11.0			0.0						

47 Camrose Ski Club, Camrose PO Box 1973,Camrose,T4V 1X8

In town of Camrose on Stony Creek Valley. Follow signs to campground.
Ole Uffda Ski Gallop loppet

Trail Fee	Total	●	■	◆	Skating	Ungroomed	Lodge	Wax Room	Rentals	Food	Lessons	Shelters
2⁰⁰	6	0	3	3		0	√					0
5⁰⁰ F	30.0		15.0	15.0	25.0	0.0						

48 Vermilion Provincial Park, Vermilion

(403) 853-8159; PO Box 1140, Vermilion,T0B 4M0
NW corner of Vermilion. (177 km E of Edmonton)
Lakeside trails. Freddy the Fox Loppet

Trail Fee	Total	●	■	◆	Skating	Ungroomed	Lodge	Wax Room	Rentals	Food	Lessons	Shelters
NC	7	1	3	1		4						1
	14.8	7.4	5.4	2.0		4.9						

Groomed Trails

| Trail Fee | Total | ● | ■ | ◆ | Skating | Ungroomed | Lodge | Wax Room | Rentals | Food | Lesons | Shelters |

49 Whitney Lakes Prov. Park, Elk Point

(403) 943-3761; PO Box 39, Elk Point,T0A 1A0
30 km E of Elk Point on Hwy 646.
Rolling terrain in pine, spruce and aspen forest. Between 4 lakes.

NC	1	0	1	0	1						2
	8.6	8.6			4.9						

50 Cold Lake Provincial Park, Cold Lake

(403) 639-3341; PO Box 8208, Cold Lake,T0A 0V0
3 km E of town of Cold lake on S shores of Cold Lake.
Park is situated on peninsula. Old homesteads and views of lake.

NC	4	3	1	0	2	√					0
	13.3	10.3	3.0		1.5						

51 Moose Lake Prov. Park, Bonnyville

(403) 826-5853; PO Box 7157,Bonnyville,T0N 2H5
14 km W of Bonnyville on Hwy 660.
Gently rolling sheltered pine forest. Scenic views of Moose Lake.

NC	6	3	3	0	3	√					1
	10.0	3.0	6.5		3.0						

52 Shaw Lake Ski Trails (Lakeland Provincial Park), Lac La Biche

(403) 623-5434; Lakeland Provincial Park, PO Box 959, Lac La Biche, T0A 2C0
24 km E of Lac La Biche. Take Rte 881 E then Rte 663 to Lakeland Prov. Pk.
Linked loop trails around lake. N side is gently rolling, S is hilly. Lac La Loppet

NC	7	2	4	1	0	√				R	0
	26.0	5.0	14.8	6.2	0.0						

53 Long Lake Prov. Park, Boyle

(403) 576-3960; PO Box 270, Boyle,T0A 0M0
16 km S of Boyle on Route 831.
Loop on campground and linear trail along lakeshore. Mixed forest.

NC	2	2	0	0	0	√					0
	5.0	5.0			0.0						

Alberta

Groomed Trails

| Trail Fee | Total | ● | ■ | ◆ | Skating | Ungroomed | Lodge | Wax Room | Rentals | Food | Lesons | Shelters |

54 Tawatinaw (Westlock Ski Club), Athabasca

(403) 349-5955
3 km E of Hwy 2 on Tawatinaw Rd next to alpine center.

2⁰⁰	5	-	-	-		0	√			√		0
	35.0	17.0	11.0	7.0	15.0	0.0						

55 Muskeg Creek Ski Trails, Athabasca

(403) 675-4116; PO Box 66,Athabasca,T0G 0B0
In town of Athabasca on W boundary and on golf course.
1.5 km lit trail. Trail W of town is a 10 k figure eight. Site of Athabasca Loppet.

DA	-	-	-	0		0	√					1
	25.0	15.0	10.0		15.0	0.0						

56 Thunder Lake Prov. Park, Barrhead

(403) 674-6454; Site 19, Box 4, RR 2, Barrhead,T7N 1N3
18 km W of Barrhead on Hwy 18, then 3 km on access road to park.
Flat & hills. Mixed vegetation— spruce, aspen, heavy shrub.

NC	6	3	3	0		0						0
	11.9	3.6	8.3			0.0						

57 Carson-Pegasus Provincial Park, Whitecourt

(403) 778-6628; PO Box 10, Whitecourt,T7S 1N3
8 km NW of Whitecourt on Hwy 43 then about 10 Km N on Hwy 32 to access rd.
Mixed boreal forest, lake Some hills on intermediate trails

NC	3	1	2	0		0	√					0
	6.2	2.2	4.0			0.0						

58 Sandhills, Whitecourt

(403) 778-7153; c/o Whitecourt Forest, 4004 - 47 Street, Whitecourt, T7S 1M8
7 km E of Whitecourt on secondary road.
Stacked loops on varied terrain. Mixed forest and muskeg.

NC	7	4	2	1		0	√					0
	26.0	10.4	1.8	6.5		0.0						

59 Swan Hills Cross-Country Trails, Swan Hills

(403) 333-2811; c/o Alberta Forest Service, Bag 272, Swan Hills,T0G 2C0
On Hwy 33 at junction of Hwy 32 on S side of Swan Hills.
Stacked loops through mature timber stands, low lands, muskeg.

NC	2	2	0	0		0	√					0
	8.1	8.1				0.0						

Alberta

Groomed Trails

Trail Fee | Total | ● ■ ◆ | Skating | Ungroomed | Lodge | Wax Room | Rentals | Food | Lessons | Shelters

60 Grizzly Ridge, Slave Lake PO Box 1071,Slave Lake,T0G 2A0

17 km S of town of Slave Lake near alpine center. Grizzly Ridge Loppet

Trail Fee	Total	●	■	◆	Skating	Ungroomed	Lodge	Wax Room	Rentals	Food	Lessons	Shelters
2^{00}	-	-	-	-		0	√	√		C		0
5^{00} F	30.0				15.0	0.0						

61 Lesser Slave Lake Prov. Park, Slave Lake

(403) 849-7100; PO Box 730, Slave Lake, T0G 2A0
Two sites - North Shore & Marten River Trails, 10 & 34 km N of Slave Lake. Linear trails with loops at end. Mixed terain and forest.

Trail Fee	Total	●	■	◆	Skating	Ungroomed	Lodge	Wax Room	Rentals	Food	Lessons	Shelters
NC	2	2	0	0		0	√					0
	8.0	8.0				0.0						

62 Hilliard's Bay Prov. Park, Girouard

(403) 751-3789; PO Box 69, Girouard, T0G 1C0
17 km E of High Prairie on Hwy 2, 24 km N on Hwy 750, 1 km N of Girouard
Linear trails with loops at ends. Limited trail grooming

Trail Fee	Total	●	■	◆	Skating	Ungroomed	Lodge	Wax Room	Rentals	Food	Lessons	Shelters
NC	2	0	2	0		0	√					0
	10.0		10.0			0.0						

63 Winagami Lake Provincial Park, McLennan

(403) 523-2427; PO Box 20,McLennan,T0H 2L0
32 km NW of High Prairie on Hwys 749 and 679.
Mixed mature boreal forest. Fairly flat with gently rolling hills.

Trail Fee	Total	●	■	◆	Skating	Ungroomed	Lodge	Wax Room	Rentals	Food	Lessons	Shelters
NC	2	0	2	0		0	√					0
	17.0		17.0			0.0						

64 Young's Point Prov. Park, Valleyview

(403) 957-2699; PO Box 1140, Valleyview, T0H 3N0
38 km W of Valleyview on Hwy 34, N on access road to park.
Mixed aspen, spruce, birch. Flat with some hills.

Trail Fee	Total	●	■	◆	Skating	Ungroomed	Lodge	Wax Room	Rentals	Food	Lessons	Shelters
NC	5	3	2	0		0						0
	16.1	8.6	7.5			0.0						

65 O'Brien Prov. Park, Wembley

(403) 766-2636; POBox 146, Wembley, T0H 3S0
17 km S of Grande Prairie on Hwy 40.
Trails are infrequently groomed. Riverbank trails through aspen and alder.

Trail Fee	Total	●	■	◆	Skating	Ungroomed	Lodge	Wax Room	Rentals	Food	Lessons	Shelters
NC	4	2	1	1		0	√					0
	12.0	3.0	4.0	5.0		0.0						

Alberta

Groomed Trails

Trail Fee	Total	●	■	◆	Skating	Ungroomed	Lodge	Wax Room	Rentals	Food	Lesons	Shelters

Alberta

66 Wapiti Nordic Ski Club, Grande Prairie

(403) 539-9050; PO Box 1176, Grande Prairie, T8V 4B6
11 km S of Grande Prairie on Hwy 40 and 1 km W.
Site of the 1995 Canada Winter Games. Hosts Sveinungsgaard Loppet

Trail Fee	Total	●	■	◆	Ungroomed	Lodge	Wax Room	Rentals	Food	Lesons	Shelters
8⁰⁰	8	6	1	1	0	√	√	√	C	√	2
	30.0	22.0	4.0	5.0	0.0						

67 Saskatoon Island Prov. Park, Wembley

(403) 766-2636; PO Box 146, Wembley, T0H 3S0
20 km W of Grande Prairie on Hwy 2, then N on access road.
Fairly flat terrain with poplar trees and saskatoon bush.

Trail Fee	Total	●	■	◆	Ungroomed	Lodge	Wax Room	Rentals	Food	Lesons	Shelters
NC	4	3	0	1	0	√					0
	5.0	3.7		1.3	0.0						

68 Moonshine Provincial Park, Spirit River

(403) 864-2266; PO Box 716, Spirit River,T0H 3G0
27 km W of Spirit River on Hwy 49 then 7 km N on Hwy 725.
Fairly flat, some rolling hills. Spruce, aspen, birch, varied vegetation.

Trail Fee	Total	●	■	◆	Ungroomed	Lodge	Wax Room	Rentals	Food	Lesons	Shelters
NC	6	6	0	0	0	√					1
	22.0	22.0			0.0						

69 Queen Elizabeth Prov. Park, Grimshaw

(403) 332-4167; PO Box 617, Grimshaw,
4 km N of Grimshaw on Hwy 35 then 5 km W on access road.
Flat terrain with aspen, spruce, willows, mixed boreal forest.

Trail Fee	Total	●	■	◆	Ungroomed	Lodge	Wax Room	Rentals	Food	Lesons	Shelters
NC	1	1	0	0	0	√					0
	4.5	4.5			0.0						

70 Gregoire Lake Prov. Park, Fort McMurray

(403) 334-2222; PO Box 5240, Fort McMurray, T9H 3G3
16 km S of Fort McMurray on Hwy 63 to Rte 881, E on Rte 881 to park.
Trails on N side of lake. Scenic views and wildlife Aspen uplands - hilly.

Trail Fee	Total	●	■	◆	Ungroomed	Lodge	Wax Room	Rentals	Food	Lesons	Shelters
NC	0				1	√					1
	0.0				5.2						

Backcountry Huts and Lodges

Note: most backcountry lodges and huts are located in alpine areas where white-out conditions may occur. Danger due to avalanches and crevasses is also possible so it is essential to be prepared for these hazards. An experienced guide is the best insurance against injury or death. Rates are approximate cost per person and include 7% Goods and Service Tax.

Mount Assiniboine Lodge, Mt Assiniboine Prov. Park (B.C.)
PO Box 1829, Golden, BC V0A 1H0
(250) 344-2639; fax: (250) 344-5520
A challenging 28 km ski from Kananaskis (helicopter costs $125). Most people fly in and ski out.
Easy to advanced ski tours and telemarking in surrounding area.
Rates: $135 to $160 p.p., p.n., d.o. meals and guide included (min 3 nights).
Open mid-Feb to mid-April
Capacity: 30 in lodge and 6 log cabins.
Amenities: sauna, heating, bedding

R.C. Hind Hut, Mt Assiniboine Provincial Park
B.C. Parks, East Kootenay District
(604) 422-3212
No charge, first come/first served.
Unheated, no mattresses or cooking utensils.

Naiset Cabins, Mt Assiniboine Provincial Park
B.C. Parks, East Kootenay District
(604) 422-3212
Self-sufficient rate: $10 per night.
Reservations required.
Capacity: 6

Banff Sundance Lodge, Banff
PO Box 2280, Banff AB T0L 0C0
(403) 762-4551; fax: (403) 762-8130
A 10-km ski from Healy Creek on a groomed, intermediate trail.
$97 p.p., p.n., d.o. (meals included).
Open mid-Dec to mid-March
Capacity: 20 (10 rooms)
Amenities: bedding, hot showers, indoor toilets

Shadow Lake Lodge and Cabins, Banff
PO Box 2606, Banff AB T0L 0C0
(403) 762-0116; fax: (403) 760-2866
A 14 km ski on a groomed, intermediate-rated trail from Red Earth parking lot 20 km W of Banff.
$114 p.p., p.n., d.o. (meals included), $ 90 for extra person in room
Open mid-Dec to mid-April
Capacity: 24 (9 cabins)

Skoki Lodge, Lake Louise
PO Box 5, Lake Louise AB T0L 1E0
(403) 522-3555; fax: (403) 522-2095
An 11 km ski from Temple Lodge at Lake Louise alpine centre.
Choice of wooded trails, alpine touring or telemarking.
From $120 p.p., p.n. to $440/5 nights (meals included)
Open late Dec to mid-April
Capacity: 22 in lodge and cabins
Amenities: bedding, sauna, propane.

Peter and Catherine Whyte (Peyto) Hut, Banff National Park
A.C.C. Class B (unheated)
Northenmost hut on the Wapta Icefield Traverse about 10 km S of, and a 600-metre climb from Hwy 93 at Peyto Lake.
Capacity: 16

Alberta

Bow Hut, Banff National Park
A.C.C. Class A
On the Wapta Traverse about 8 km from Hwy 93 at Bow Lake (a 400-metre climb) or about 6 km S of and a 300-metre climb from the Whyte hut.
Capacity: 30

Balfour Hut, Lake Louise
A.C.C. Class B (unheated)
On the Wapta Traverse about 7 km S of Bow hut.
Capacity: 16

Scott Duncan Hut, Lake Louise
A.C.C. Class B (unheated)
Southernmost hut on the Wapta Traverse about 11 km N of and 1300 metres above the Trans-Canada Highway.
Capacity: 12

Sydney Vallance Hut, Jasper
A.C.C. Class A
A 12-km ski along the Fryatt Valley trail with a 800-metre net gain in altitude.
Capacity: 12

Wates-Gibson Memorial Hut, Jasper
A.C.C. Class A
A 25-km ski via the Astoria Valley from Edith Cavell Road. Note that the Edith Cavell hostel half-way in can be used for overnight if arranged with Whistler hostel.
Capacity: 30

Tonquin Valley Cross Country Ski Lodge, Jasper
PO Box 550, Jasper AB T0E 1E0
(403) 852-3909; fax: (403) 852-3763
Located 33 km SW of town of Jasper.
A 23-km ski on a gradually climbing trail.
$86/night or $595/week (meals included) Guides: $130/day
Open Feb 1 to March 31 Capacity: 20 in private rooms
Amenities: bedding

15 Saskatchewan

When people think of Saskatchewan, the image of the great plains of the southern region most often springs to mind. In reality, much of the province is mantled with parkland and boreal forest, providing attractive settings for the province's numerous parks.

In winter, many of Saskatchewan's parks groom their trails for cross-country skiing. Prince Albert National Park is the largest of these with about 150 km of groomed trails.

Travel Information

Airports: Regina and Saskatoon are the major air centers serviced by Air Canada and Canadian Airlines.

Bus Service: Interprovincial service is provided by Greyhound 1-800-661-8747 (Canada). Regional service is provided by the Saskatchewan Transportation Co.

Railway: Via Rail's triweekly transcontinental service connects Saskatoon with Edmonton and Winnipeg. 1-800-561-8630 (Western Canada)

Time Zone: Central Standard Time

Tourist Information
Tourism Saskatchewan publishes an annual winter guide and operates an accommodation reservation service.
500 - 1900 Albert Street, Regina, SK S4P 4L9;
(306) 787-2300 (Regina); 1-800-667-7191 (Canada and USA);
fax: (306) 787-5744

Saskatchewan

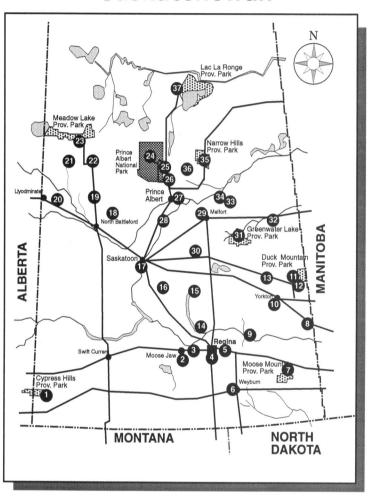

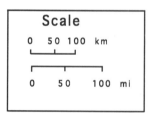

Scale

0 50 100 km

0 50 100 mi

Cross Country Ski Areas

Anglin Lake Ski Trails	25	Landrose Ski Trails	20
Battlefords Provincial Park	19	Little Red River Park	27
Blackstrap Provincial Park	16	Makwa Lake Provincial Park	21
Buffalo Pound Provincial Park	3	Manitou Beach	15
Candle Lake Provincial Park	36	Meadow Lake Area	22
Carlton Trail Regional Park	8	Meadow Lake Prov. Park	23
Carlton Trail Ski Club	30	Moose Jaw River Park	2
Cypress Hills Provincial Park	1	Moose Mountain Prov.l Park	7
Duck Mountain Prov. Park	11	Narrow Hills Provincial Park	35
Duck Mountain Regional Park	12	Nipawin Area Ski Trails	34
Eb's Trails	28	Nipawin Regional Park	33
Echo Valley Provincial Park	9	Prince Albert National Park	24
Emma Lake Recreation Site	26	Rowan's Ravine Prov.l Park	14
Good Spirit Provincial Park	13	Saskatoon	17
Greenwater Provincial Park	31	Wascana Centre	4
Gronlid Trails	29	Weyburn Cross-Country	6
Hudson Bay Ski Area	32	White Butte Trails	5
Lac La Ronge Prov. Park	37	White Tail Resort	18
		York Lake Regional Park	10

Sask

Cross Country Skiing Organizations

Cross Country Saskatchewan - Saskatchewan division of Cross Country Canada 1860 Lorne Street, Regina, SK S4P 2L7 (306) 780-9240; fax: (306) 781-6021

Climate

Despite low snowfalls, the cross-country ski season extends from approximately early December to late March.

Average Temperatures   ## Average Snowfall

Regina (Saskatoon is similar)

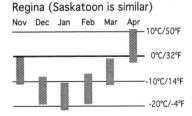

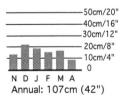

Annual: 107cm (42")

151

La Ronge

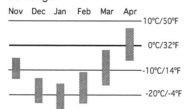

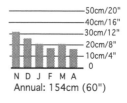

Annual: 154cm (60")

Saskatchewan Premium Loppet Series

Lily Plain trails are only used for the Liliy Plain Loppet.
In addition to the Premium Loppet Series there is the Great
Northern Ski Quest at about 10 northern communities.

Date	Event	Location
late Jan	Greenwater Loppet	Greenwater Provincial Park
early Feb	Borderglide	Lloydminster
early Feb	Carlton Trail	Humboldt
mid Feb	Lily Plain	Macdowall
late Feb	Duck Mountain	Duck Mountain Provincial Park
early Mar	*Saskaloppet	La Ronge

* Canadian Ski Odyssey event

		Groomed Trails										
Trail Fee	Total	●	■	◆	Skating	Ungroomed	Lodge	Wax Room	Rentals	Food	Lessons	Shelters

1 Cypress Hills Provincial Park, Maple Creek

(306) 662-4411; PO Box 850, Maple Creek, SK S0N 1N0
30 km S of Maple Creek on Hwy 21.
Two-way linked loops thru pine forest. Resort, condos.

Trail Fee	Total	●	■	◆	Skating	Ungroomed	Lodge	Wax Room	Rentals	Food	Lessons	Shelters
NC	9	5	4	0		0	√		√	√		0
	24.0	15.4	8.3			0.0						

2 Moose Jaw River Park, Moose Jaw

(306) 694-4447; Parks & Rec. Dept., 228 Main St., Moose Jaw, S6H 3J8
Kiwanis River Park in Wakamow Valley.

Trail Fee	Total	●	■	◆	Skating	Ungroomed	Lodge	Wax Room	Rentals	Food	Lessons	Shelters
NC	3	1	2	0		0	T					1
	14.0					0.0						

3 Buffalo Pound Provincial Park, Moose Jaw

(306) 694-3659; Mailing Adress: 206 - 110 Ominica St. W., Moose Jaw, S6H 6V2
27 km E of Moose Jaw via Hwys 2 and 202.
One main loop with short loops.

Trail Fee	Total	●	■	◆	Skating	Ungroomed	Lodge	Wax Room	Rentals	Food	Lessons	Shelters
NC	5	-	-	-		0	√		√	√		0
	5.0					0.0						

4 Wascana Centre, Regina

(306) 522-3661; Mailing Adress: 2900 Wascana St., Regina, S4S 2G8
In S end of Regina.
Some trails lit for night skiing.

Trail Fee	Total	●	■	◆	Skating	Ungroomed	Lodge	Wax Room	Rentals	Food	Lessons	Shelters
NC	-	-	-	-		0	T					1
	20.0					0.0						

5 White Butte Trails, Regina

(306) 787-2790; c/o Enviroment & Resource, 3211 Albert St., Regina S4S 5W6
4 km N of White City on grid rd W of junction of Hwys 1 and 48.

Trail Fee	Total	●	■	◆	Skating	Ungroomed	Lodge	Wax Room	Rentals	Food	Lessons	Shelters
NC	6	3	3	0		0						1
	10.0					0.0						

6 Weyburn Cross-Country Ski Trails, Weyburn

(306) 842-7978; c/o Weyburn Recreation Dept., Weyburn
3 locations - River Park, Tatagwa Parkway and on hospital grounds.

Trail Fee	Total	●	■	◆	Skating	Ungroomed	Lodge	Wax Room	Rentals	Food	Lessons	Shelters
NC	3	-	-	-		0						0
	12.5					0.0						

Trail Fee	Total	●	■	◆	Skating	Ungroomed	Lodge	Wax Room	Rentals	Food	Lessons	Shelters

Groomed Trails

7 Moose Mountain Provincial Park, Kenosee

(306) 577-2131; PO Box 220, Kenosee, S0C 2S0
25 km N of Carlyle on Hwy 9. Linked loops.
Two trails at Beaver Lake, remainder at Riding Academy.

Trail Fee	Total	●	■	◆	Skating	Ungroomed	Lodge	Wax Room	Rentals	Food	Lessons	Shelters
NC	9	2	4	3		0	√		√	√		6
	52.9	8.5	27.7	16.7		0.0						

8 Carlton Trail Regional Park, Langenburg

(306) 534-2132; Carlton Trail Ski Club, PO Box 1972, Humboldt, S0K 2A0
22km E of Langenburg on Hwy 8 then 8km N of Spy Hill.
Novice and intermediate trails.

Trail Fee	Total	●	■	◆	Skating	Ungroomed	Lodge	Wax Room	Rentals	Food	Lessons	Shelters
NA	4	-	-	-		0						0
	6.4					0.0						

9 Echo Valley Provincial Park, Fort Qu'Appelle

(306) 332-3215; PO Box 790, Fort Qu'Appelle, S0G 1S0
8 km W of Fort Qu'Appelle on Hwy 210, S side of Pasqua Lake.

Trail Fee	Total	●	■	◆	Skating	Ungroomed	Lodge	Wax Room	Rentals	Food	Lessons	Shelters
NC	4	2	1	1		0						1
	9.7	3.8	4.9	1.2		0.0						

10 York Lake Regional Park, Yorkton

(306) 782-7080; PO Box 1166, Yorkton, S3N 2X3
3 km S of Yorkton on Gladstone Ave.

Trail Fee	Total	●	■	◆	Skating	Ungroomed	Lodge	Wax Room	Rentals	Food	Lessons	Shelters
NA	1	1	0	0		2						0
	11.0	11.0				11.0						

11 Duck Mountain Provincial Park, Kamsack

(306) 542-3482; PO Box 37, Kamsack, S0A 1S0
21 km NE of Kamsack on Hwy 57.
Linked loop trails connect with Regional Park.

Trail Fee	Total	●	■	◆	Skating	Ungroomed	Lodge	Wax Room	Rentals	Food	Lessons	Shelters
NC	11	4	4	3		-	√	√	√	√		3
	57.6	7.6	30.4	19.6		15.0						

12 Duck Mountain Regional Park, Kamsack

(306) 542-4111; Duck Mountain Regional Park, Kamsack, S0A 1S0
8 km S of 25 E of Kamsack to Duck Mtn Prov. Park then 8 km S to alpine ctr.
Links with Duck Mtn Prov. Park.

Trail Fee	Total	●	■	◆	Skating	Ungroomed	Lodge	Wax Room	Rentals	Food	Lessons	Shelters
NA	6	3	0	3		0	√		√	√		0
	15.0					0.0						

Groomed Trails

Trail Fee	Total	●	■	◆	Skating	Ungroomed	Lodge	Wax Room	Rentals	Food	Lessons	Shelters

13 Good Spirit Provincial Park, Yorkton

(306) 792-4565; Mailing Adress: 120 Smith St. E., Yorkton, S3N 3V3
31 km N of Yorkton on Hwy 9 then 21 km W on Hwy 229.
5 km trail leads to stacked loops. 2 km to lodge

Trail Fee	Total	●	■	◆	Skating	Ungroomed	Lodge	Wax Room	Rentals	Food	Lessons	Shelters
NC	6	2	4	0		0				√		0
	18.9	4.8	14.1			0.0						

14 Rowan's Ravine Provincial Park, Strasbourg

(306) 725-4423; PO Box 30, Strasbourg, S0G 4V0
22 km W of Bulyea (90 km NW of Regina).

Trail Fee	Total	●	■	◆	Skating	Ungroomed	Lodge	Wax Room	Rentals	Food	Lessons	Shelters
NC	1	-	-	-		0						0
	6.2					0.0						

15 Manitou Beach (Watrous-Manitou Ski Club), Watrous

Watrous-Manitou Ski Club, PO Box 615, Watrous
SW side of Manitou Beach at golf course.

Trail Fee	Total	●	■	◆	Skating	Ungroomed	Lodge	Wax Room	Rentals	Food	Lessons	Shelters
NA	-	-	-	-		0						0
	9.0					0.0						

16 Blackstrap Provincial Park, Saskatoon

(306) 933-6240; Mailing Address:102 - 112 Research Drive, Saskatoon, S7K 2H6
10 km E of Dundurn.

Trail Fee	Total	●	■	◆	Skating	Ungroomed	Lodge	Wax Room	Rentals	Food	Lessons	Shelters
NC	1	-	-	-		0	√			√		0
	5.0					0.0						

17 Saskatoon municipal trails

(306) 975-3300; Parks Dept., 222 - 3rd Ave N., Saskatoon, S7K 0J5
At Ave R South and Dudley St in Saskatoon.

Trail Fee	Total	●	■	◆	Skating	Ungroomed	Lodge	Wax Room	Rentals	Food	Lessons	Shelters
NC	3	2	1	0		0	√			√		0
	14.0	10.0	4.0			1	0.0					

18 White Tail Resort, North Battleford

(306) 445-4941; White Tail Resort, RR 1, North Battleford, S9A 2X3
32 km NE of N Battleford via Hwy 4 and Hwy 378.
Interconnected network over rugged terrain - valley, ridges, forest. 2 cabins, hostel

Trail Fee	Total	●	■	◆	Skating	Ungroomed	Lodge	Wax Room	Rentals	Food	Lessons	Shelters
2⁰⁰	8	1	4	2		0	√	√	E	E	√	1
	31.6	6.4	15.2	10.0		0.0						

Trail Fee	Total	Groomed Trails ● ■ ◆			Skating	Ungroomed	Lodge	Wax Room	Rentals	Food	Lessons	Shelters

19 Battlefords Provincial Park, Cochin

(306) 386-2212; PO Box 100, Cochin, S0M 0L0
32 km N of North Battleford.
Stacked loops of one-way trails, lodge.

Trail Fee	Total	●	■	◆	Skating	Ungroomed	Lodge	Wax Room	Rentals	Food	Lessons	Shelters
NC	7	3	2	2	0	√			√			0
	18.7	6.9	3.9	5.8	0.0							

20 Landrose Ski Trails/Llyodminster Ski Club, Llyodminster

(306) 825-2795; Llyodminster Ski Club, PO Box 922, Llyodminster, S9V 1C4
16 km E of Lloydminster on Hwy 303, then 5 km N, follow signs.
Linked loops, separate skating trails.

Trail Fee	Total	●	■	◆	Skating	Ungroomed	Lodge	Wax Room	Rentals	Food	Lessons	Shelters
6⁰⁰	7	3	2	2	-	√	√	√	√	√		0
	35.0	15.0	10.0	10.0	21.0							

21 Makwa Lake Provincial Park, Loon Lake

(306) 837-2092; PO Box 39, Loon Lake, S0M 1L0
2 km W of town of Loon Lake. (60 km W of Meadow Lake).
Stacked loops, mixed wood forest in transition zone of boreal forest/parkland

Trail Fee	Total	●	■	◆	Skating	Ungroomed	Lodge	Wax Room	Rentals	Food	Lessons	Shelters
NC	4	0	4	0	0	√			√			0
	15.0		15.0		0.0							

22 Meadow Lake Ski Club, Meadow Lake

(306) 236-3421; Meadow Lake Ski Club, PO Box 937, Meadow Lake, S0M 1V0
14 km E of Meadow Lake on Hwy 55, 1.5 km N on Island Hill Rd.

Trail Fee	Total	●	■	◆	Skating	Ungroomed	Lodge	Wax Room	Rentals	Food	Lessons	Shelters
NA	6	3	1	2	0	√						1
	20.0	6.0	5.0	10.0	11.0	0.0						

23 Meadow Lake Provincial Park, Dorintosh

(306) 236-7680; PO Box 70, Dorintosh, S0M 0T0
7 km N of Dorintosh on Hwy 4, W on Hwy 224 to Greig Lake. Stacked loops.

Trail Fee	Total	●	■	◆	Skating	Ungroomed	Lodge	Wax Room	Rentals	Food	Lessons	Shelters
NC	4	2	1	1	0	√						0
	24.3	7.1	8.0	9.2	0.0							

24 Prince Albert National Park, Wakesiu Lake

(306) 663-5322; PO Box 100, Wakesiu Lake, S0J 2Y0
88 km N of Prince Albert on Hwy 2 and 264.
Rolling terrain, transition between aspen parkland and boreal forest.

Trail Fee	Total	●	■	◆	Skating	Ungroomed	Lodge	Wax Room	Rentals	Food	Lessons	Shelters
Entry Fee	9	4	4	1	-					C		0
	150.0	36.0	44.0	8.5	Yes							

Groomed Trails

Legend columns: Trail Fee | Total | ● | ■ | ◆ | Skating | Ungroomed | Lodge | Wax Room | Rentals | Food | Lessons | Shelters

25 Anglin Lake Ski Trails, Christopher Lake

(306) 982-2002; PO Box 66, Christopher Lake, S0J 0N0
32 km NW of Christopher Lake on Anglin Lake Rd.
Linked loops. Connects with Prince Albert Nat'l Park trails.

Trail Fee	Total	●	■	◆	Ungroomed	Rentals	Shelters
NC	5	2	1	3	0	√	0
	21.1	9.6	1.9	9.0	0.0		

26 Emma Lake Recreation Site, Christopher Lake

5 km W of Christopher Lake on Hwy 263, then 5 km N to Murray Point.
12 km linear trail plus 2 loops. PO Box 66, Christopher Lake, S0J 0N0

Trail Fee	Total	●	■	◆	Ungroomed	Lodge	Shelters
NC	2	1	1	0	0	√	0
	19.5	9.0	10.5		0.0		

27 Little Red River Park, Prince Albert

Prince Albert Lodge: (306) 953-4879
3 km E of Prince Albert on Hwy 55.
5 km lighted trail for night skiing.

Trail Fee	Total	●	■	◆	Ungroomed	Shelters
NA	10	3	3	4	0	0
	18.0	13.5	9.2	18.0	0.0	

28 Eb's Trails, Duck Lake

(306) 652-0385; c/o Eb's Sports, 1640 Saskatchewan Ave., Saskatoon, S7K 1P6
At Nibset Provincial Forest, 14km N of Duck Lake on Hwy 11.
Ski rentals in Saskatoon. Loop trails of various lengths.

Trail Fee	Total	●	■	◆	Ungroomed	Lodge	Wax Room	Shelters
NA	5	2	3	0	1	√	√	2
	30.0				10.0			

29 Gronlid Trails (Melfort CC Ski Club), Melfort

(306) 752-4361; Melfort CC Ski Club, PO Box 3813, Melfort, S0E 1A
10 km N and 2.5 km W of Gronlid.
2 km lit trail at Melfort campground.

Trail Fee	Total	●	■	◆	Ungroomed	Lodge	Shelters
NA	6	3	3	0	0	T	1
	18.0				1.0 0.0		

30 Carlton Trail Ski Club (Carlton Trail Ski Club), Humboldt

(306) 682-3053; Carlton Trail Ski Club, PO Box 1972, Humboldt, S0K 2A0
6.5 km W of Humboldt on Hwy 5, 6.5 km N on grid rd, follow signs 3 km W.

Trail Fee	Total	●	■	◆	Ungroomed	Lodge	Shelters
NA	3	1	1	1	0	E	1
	20.0				0.0		

Sask

		Groomed Trails										
Trail Fee	Total	●	■	◆	Skating	Ungroomed	Lodge	Wax Room	Rentals	Food	Lessons	Shelters

31 Greenwater Provincial Park, Porcupine Plain

(306) 278-2972; PO Box 430, Porcupine Plain, S0E 1H0
30 km SW of Porcupine Plain or 45 km N of Kelvington on Hwy 38.

Fee	Total	●	■	◆	Skating	Ungroomed	Lodge	Wax Room	Rentals	Food	Lessons	Shelters
NC	6	0	6	0		0	√		√	√		2
	25.0		25.0			0.0						

32 Hudson Bay Ski Trails

(306) 865-2263; Recreation Dept., 302 Main St., Hudson Bay, S0E 0Y0
3 km S of town of Hudson Bay

Fee	Total	●	■	◆	Skating	Ungroomed	Lodge	Wax Room	Rentals	Food	Lessons	Shelters
NC	-	-	-	-		0						0
	12.0					0.0						

33 Nipawin Regional Park, Nipawin

(306) 862-3237; PO Box 1499, Nipawin, S0E 1E0
1.5 km N of Nipawin

Fee	Total	●	■	◆	Skating	Ungroomed	Lodge	Wax Room	Rentals	Food	Lessons	Shelters
NC	2	-	-	-		0						0
	10.0					0.0						

34 Nipawin Ski Trails

(306) 862-9866; Town Office, 2nd Ave. E., Nipawin, S0E 1E0
2 km NW of Nipawin.

Fee	Total	●	■	◆	Skating	Ungroomed	Lodge	Wax Room	Rentals	Food	Lessons	Shelters
NA	4	-	-	-		0						1
	17.0					0.0						

35 Narrow Hills Provincial Park, Smeaton

(306) 426-2082; PO Box 130, Smeaton, S0J 2J0
110 km N of town of Prince Albert on Hwy 120. (formerly Nipawin P.P.)
Novice and intermediate trails. 2 commercial lodges

Fee	Total	●	■	◆	Skating	Ungroomed	Lodge	Wax Room	Rentals	Food	Lessons	Shelters
NC	-	-	-	-		0				C		1
	21.0					0.0						

36 Candle Lake Provincial Park, Meath Park

(306) 929-4656; PO Box 246, Meath Park, S0J 1T0
Approx 60 km NE of town on Prince Albert via Hwys 55 and 120.

Fee	Total	●	■	◆	Skating	Ungroomed	Lodge	Wax Room	Rentals	Food	Lessons	Shelters
NC	3	1	2	0		0						1
	14.0	4.5	9.6			0.0						

37 Lac La Ronge Provincial Park, La Ronge

(306) 425-4234, 1-800-667-7538; PO Box 5000, La Ronge, S0J 1L0
At Nut Point Campground and Don Allen trails near English Bay. 5 km lit trail.

Fee	Total	●	■	◆	Skating	Ungroomed	Lodge	Wax Room	Rentals	Food	Lessons	Shelters
NC	11	6	2	3		2		√				3
	61.0	20.5	32.5	22.5		10.0						

16 Manitoba

Manitoba's long, cold winters will give you plenty of opportunities to take advantage of the province's cross-country skiing facilities.

As in Saskatchewan, the province's largest concentration of trails are operated by the National Parks. Riding Mountain National Park grooms more than 200 km of its trails for cross-country skiing. Many of the provincial parks also offer groomed trails.

Travel Information

Airport: Winnipeg is serviced by Air Canada, Canadian Airlines and NWT Air with connections to several regional airlines.

Buslines: Greyhound, 1-800-661-8747 and Grey Goose Bus Lines, (204) 784-4500 (Winnipeg)

Railway: VIA Rail offers transcontinental service.
104 - 123 Main St., Winnipeg, MB R3C 1A3
1-800-561-8630 (Western Canada)

Road Conditions: (204) 945-3704 (Winnipeg)

Tourist Information Bureau
Travel Manitoba, 700 - 155 Carlton St., Winnipeg, MB R3C 3H8;
(204) 945-3777, 1-800-665-0040 (Canada and USA)

Cross Country Skiing Organizations

Cross Country Manitoba and **CANSI Manitoba**
200 Main Street, Winnipeg, MB R3C 4M2
(204) 925-5639; fax: (204) 925-5624

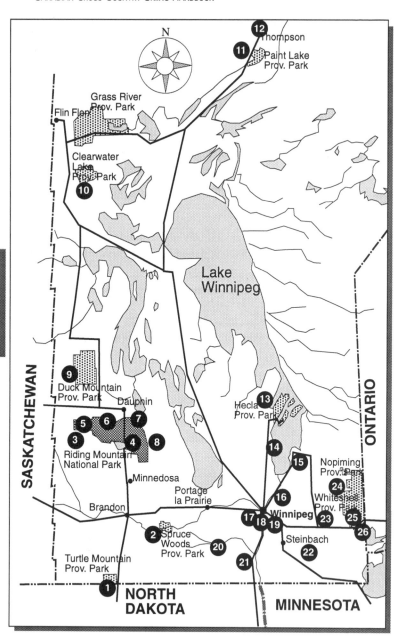

Manitoba

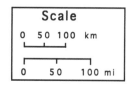

Scale

0   50 100 km

0   50   100 mi

Cross Country Ski Areas

Assiniboine Park	18	Pinawa	23
Beaudry Provincial Park	17	Riding Mountain Nat'l Park	4-8
Birch Ski Area	20	Saint Malo Provincial	
Birds Hill Provincial Park	16	Recreation Park	21
Camp Morton Provincial		Sandilands Prov. Forest	22
Recreation Park	14	Spruce Woods Provincial	
Clearwater Lake Prov. Park	10	Heritage Park	2
Duck Mountain Prov. Park	9	Thompson Ski Club	12
Grand Beach Prov. Park	15	Turtle Mountain Prov. Park	1
Hecla Provincial Park	13	Whitemouth River	
Mystery Mountain		Cross-Country Ski Trails	24
Winter Park	12	Whiteshell Prov. Park	25-26
Paint Lake Provincial Park	11	Windsor Park	19
		Woodland Hills	3

Manitoba

Winter Climate

Manitoba's cross-country ski season generally begins in mid-December and lasts to about late March.

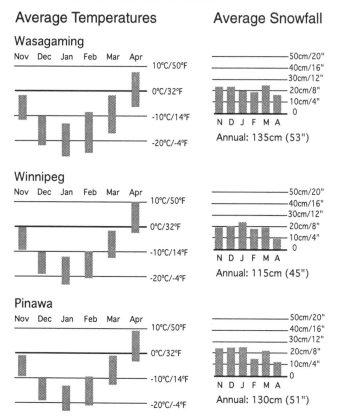

Average Temperatures

Average Snowfall

Wasagaming

Annual: 135cm (53")

Winnipeg

Annual: 115cm (45")

Pinawa

Annual: 130cm (51")

Manitoba Loppet Series

Date	Event	Location
early Dec	Whiteshell Open	Pinawa
early Jan	Grand Beach Classic	Grand Beach
late Jan	Pumpkin Creek Mystery Tour	Roseisle
late Jan	*Manitoba Loppet	Pinawa
early Mar	Riding Mountain Loppet	Riding Mountain

*Canadian Ski Odyssey event

Groomed Trails

Trail Fee	Total	●	■	◆	Skating	Ungroomed	Lodge	Wax Room	Rentals	Food	Lessons	Shelters

1 Turtle Mountain Provincial Park, Boissevain

(204) 534-7204 Turtle Mountain Provincial Park,Dept of Natural Resources, Boissevain, MB R0K 1E0
15 km S of Boissevain on Hwy 10.
Stacked loops around lakes and marshes. BC cabin for overnight use.

Trail Fee	Total	●	■	◆	Skating	Ungroomed	Lodge	Wax Room	Rentals	Food	Lessons	Shelters
NC	4	0	4	0		0	√					3
	41.0	41.0				0.0						

2 Spruce Woods Provincial Heritage Park, Carberry

(204) 834-3223 Spruce Woods Provincial Heritage Park, P.O. Box 900,Carberry, R0K 0H0
8 km S of Carberry. Three trailheads - Seton, Epinette & Yellow Quill.
Seton trails are groomed infrequently. Backcountry cabin for overnight use.

Trail Fee	Total	●	■	◆	Skating	Ungroomed	Lodge	Wax Room	Rentals	Food	Lessons	Shelters
NC	7	5	1	1		3	√					5
	51.0	18.5	8.2	24.4		11.7						

3 Woodland Hills Ranch B&B/Woodland Hills Ski Club, Rossburn

(204) 859-2663; PO Box 520, Rossburn, R0J 1V0
Go 5km N from Vista, then 1.5k E to Farm Vacation sign, then 1.5k N and 0.5k E.
Rolling hills and tree-lined interconnected trails. Possible to go over or around hills.

Trail Fee	Total	●	■	◆	Skating	Ungroomed	Lodge	Wax Room	Rentals	Food	Lessons	Shelters
3⁰⁰	-	-	-	-		0	√					2
	12.0											

4 Riding Mountain National Park Wasagaming area, Wasagaming

(204) 848-2811 Riding Mountain National Park ,Wasagaming, R0J 2H0
Near Wasagaming and 4 trailheads along Hwys 10 and 19.
Grey Owl's cabin is a 8 km ski. Crossing ice is hazardous near beaver dam

Trail Fee	Total	●	■	◆	Skating	Ungroomed	Lodge	Wax Room	Rentals	Food	Lessons	Shelters
Entry	10	6	3	1		1						1
Fee	66.4	20.0	26.7	3.4		4.2						

5 Riding Mountain National Park western sector

(204) 848-2811
2 areas - Moose Lake 40k NW of Rossburn and Sugar loaf 24k S of Grandview.
Stands of aspen & spruce. Potential of viewing wildlife.

Trail Fee	Total	●	■	◆	Skating	Ungroomed	Lodge	Wax Room	Rentals	Food	Lessons	Shelters
Entry	2	0	2	0		0						1
Fee	25.6	25.6				0.0						

Manitoba

Groomed Trails

Trail Fee	Total	●	■	◆	Skating	Ungroomed	Lodge	Wax Room	Rentals	Food	Lesons	Shelters

Manitoba

6 Riding Mountain National Park north central

(204) 848-2811
2 areas–Ranch Creek and Strathclair on Rte 274 S of Gilbert Plains.
Trails meander through hardwood forest.

	Total	●	■	◆	Ungroomed			Shelters
Entry	2	1	1	0	0			0
Fee	20.0	10.0	10.0		0.0			

7 Riding Mountain National Park north east sector

(204) 848-2811
Track-set trails are at N boundary of park on Hwy 10.
Log cabin for overnight stay (by reservation) is 13k along ungroomed trail

	Total	●	■	◆	Ungroomed			Shelters
Entry	5	1	3	1	3			2
Fee	54.8	3.5	25.7	25.6	38.1			

8 Riding Mountain National Park east sector

(204) 848-2811
Groomed trails are W of McCreary near alpine centre.
Ungroomed trails are W of Norgate.

	Total	●	■	◆	Ungroomed			Shelters
Entry	2	1	0	1	2			0
Fee	9.6	3.2		3.2	36.0			

9 Duck Mountain Provincial Park, Swan River

(204) 734-3429 Duck Mountain Provincial Park, P.O. Box 640, Swan River, R0L 1Z0
Three trailheads - Glad Lake (3 km), Wellman Lake (3 k), Childs Lake (8 k).
Trails skirt lakes. Resorts at Wellman and Childs Lakes.

	Total	●	■	◆	Ungroomed			Shelters
NC	3	0	3	0	0			1
	14.0		14.0		0.0			

10 Clearwater Lake Provincial Park, The Pas

(204) 627-8254
N of The Pas on Hwy 10, approx 10 km to Hwy 287, on Hwy 287.
Two sets of stacked loops near Clearwater Lake. Commercial lodges are nearby.

	Total	●	■	◆	Ungroomed	Lodge	Wax Room	Shelters
NC	3	-	-	-	·0	√	√	1
	13.0				0.0			

Trail Fee · Total · **Groomed Trails** (● ■ ◆) · Skating · Ungroomed · Lodge · Wax Room · Rentals · Food · Lessons · Shelters

11 Paint Lake Provincial Park, Thompson

(204) 677-6640 Paint Lake Provincial Park,P.O. Box 28,Elizabeth Rd.,Thompson,R8N 1X4
30 km S of Thompson on Hwy 6. Three trailheads. Paint Lake Resort nearby.

Trail Fee	Total	●	■	◆	Skating	Ungroomed	Lodge	Wax Room	Rentals	Food	Lessons	Shelters
NC	3	2	1	0		0	√			√		1
	12.0	7.0	5.0			0.0						

12 Mystery Mountain Winter Park/Thompson X-C Ski Club, Thompson

(204) 778-8624;
At alpine ski centre 22km N of Thompson.

Trail Fee	Total	●	■	◆	Skating	Ungroomed	Lodge	Wax Room	Rentals	Food	Lessons	Shelters
3⁰⁰	-	-	-	-		0	√		√	√		2
	23.0											

13 Hecla Provincial Park, Riverton

(204) 378-2945 Hecla Provincial Park, P.O. Box 70, Riverton,R0C 2R0
40 km N of Riverton on Hwy 8.
Novice trail on golf course. Int trails along lakeshore Gull Harbour Resort nearby.

Trail Fee	Total	●	■	◆	Skating	Ungroomed	Lodge	Wax Room	Rentals	Food	Lessons	Shelters
NC	3	1	2	0		0	√	√		√		1
	18.0	5.6	12.4			0.0						

14 Camp Morton Provincial Recreation Park, Gimli

(204) 642-8113 Camp Morton Provincial Recreation Park,P.O. Box 6000,Gimli,R0C 1B0
5 km N of Gimli on Hwy 222.
Views of Lake Winnipeg, spruce and hardwoods. Run by Gimli XC Club.

Trail Fee	Total	●	■	◆	Skating	Ungroomed	Lodge	Wax Room	Rentals	Food	Lessons	Shelters
NC	4	4	0	0		0	√					0
	7.7	7.7				0.0						

15 Grand Beach Provincial Park, Grand Beach

(204) 754-2112 Grand Beach Provincial Park, P.O. Box 220, Grand Beach, R0E 0T0
100 km N of Winnipeg on Hwy 59.
Stacked loops through pine forest, on ridge and beaver pond.

Trail Fee	Total	●	■	◆	Skating	Ungroomed	Lodge	Wax Room	Rentals	Food	Lessons	Shelters
NC	5	2	2	1		0	√					4
	19.0	5.8	19.4	2.6		0.0						

Manitoba

16 Birds Hill Provincial Park, Dugald

(204) 222-9151
25 km N of Winnipeg on Hwy 59. 3 trailheads - N & S Drives & Nimowin Rd.
A 4 km skating loop. Two lookouts on intermediate trail.

		●	■	◆						
NC	7	6	1	0	0		√	√		4
	40.9	27.9	13.0		0.0					

17 Beaudry Provincial Park, Winnipeg

(204) 945-6784
10 km W of Winnipeg on Hwy 241. Trails follow Assiniboine River.

		●	■	◆						
NC	4	4	0	0	0					3
	14.0	14.0			0.0					

18 Assiniboine Park, Winnipeg

(204) 257-1264 Assiniboine Park, Winnipeg,1539 Waverly St.,Winnipeg,R3T 4V6
At Croyden Ave and Shaftesbury Blvd in Winnipeg.

		●	■	◆						
NC	-	-	-	-	0	√		√		0
	5.2				0.0					

19 Windsor Park, Winnipeg

(204) 257-1264 10 De Meurons St.,Winnipeg
On De Meurons St. in Winnipeg. Lit trail for night skiing.

		●	■	◆						
NC	-	-	-	-	0	√		√	√	0
	7.5				0.0					

20 Birch Ski Area, Roseisle

(204) 828-3586 Pumpkin Creek X.C. Ski Club, P.O. Box 20, Roseisle, MB R0G 1V0
2k E then 2k S of Roseisle in the Pembina Hills.
Trails are tree-lined and vary from easy to intermediate.

		●	■	◆						
3⁰⁰	6	-	-	-		√				1
5⁰⁰ F	20.0									

21 Saint Malo Provincial Recreation Park, Morris

(204) 746-2556 Saint Malo Provincial Recreation Park,Morris,MB R0G 1K0
2 km E of St. Malo. Trails over campground and on shore of reservoir.

		●	■	◆						
NC	3	3	0	0	0					0
	8.0	8.0			0.0					

Groomed Trails

Trail Fee	Total	●	■	◆	Skating	Ungroomed	Lodge	Wax Room	Rentals	Food	Lessons	Shelters

22 Sandilands Provincial Forest/Sandilands Ski Club, Steinbach

Sandilands Ski Club, P.O. Box 3016, Steinbach, MB R0A 2A0
E of Steinbach on Hwy 210 at junction of Hwy 404. Five parking areas.
Stacked loops plus one linear trail. Maintained by Sandilands Ski Club.

Trail Fee	Total	●	■	◆	Skating	Ungroomed	Lodge	Wax Room	Rentals	Food	Lessons	Shelters
NC	6	-	-	-		0						1
	48.0					0.0						

23 Pinawa Cross Country Ski Trails, Pinawa

Whiteshell Cross Country Ski Club, PO Box 525, Pinawa, MB R0E 1L0
On N side of town. One trail on golf course, rest are mainly in wooded areas.

Trail Fee	Total	●	■	◆	Skating	Ungroomed	Lodge	Wax Room	Rentals	Food	Lessons	Shelters
DA	8	3	2	3	3	2	√					2
	37.0	10.0	8.0	19.0	12.0	11.5						

24 Whitemouth River Cross-Country Ski Trails, Hadashville

(204) 945-6784; Dept. of Natural Resources, 1495 St. James St., Winnipeg, R3H 0W9
N of Hadashville at junction of Hwys 1 & 11.
Stacked loops through jack pine, poplar lowland and black spruce forest.

Trail Fee	Total	●	■	◆	Skating	Ungroomed	Lodge	Wax Room	Rentals	Food	Lessons	Shelters
NC	3	3	0	0		0						1
	10.0	10.0				0.0						

25 Whiteshell Provincial Park, Rennie area, Rennie

(204) 369-5232 Whiteshell Provincial Park, Falcon Lake,R0E 1R0
Five trailheads - one at Rennie, others along Hwy 307 N of Rennie.
Inverness Falls (8 k of trails), Jessica Lk (8 k), Pine Pt (6.5 k) and Otter Falls (10k).
Accommodation available at resorts near trails.

Trail Fee	Total	●	■	◆	Skating	Ungroomed	Lodge	Wax Room	Rentals	Food	Lessons	Shelters
NC	8	-	-	-		0						4
	39.5					0.0						

26 Whiteshell Provincial Park, Falcon Lake, Falcon Lake

(204) 349-2201
At Falcon Lake on TCH. 3 trail heads–at ski hill, golf course and junction of Hwy 44.
Ski hill chalet open weekends. Biathalon range at ski hill.

Trail Fee	Total	●	■	◆	Skating	Ungroomed	Lodge	Wax Room	Rentals	Food	Lessons	Shelters
NC	5	2	3	0		0	E					1
	26.5	8.0	18.5			0.0						

Manitoba

17 Ontario

Ontario, Canada's largest province, offers the widest variety of cross-country ski centres. Ski clubs, resorts, provincial parks and conservation areas all make important contributions to the Ontario ski scene.

Over 70 ski clubs have sprung up around the province, many of which have developed their own trail systems. They are also responsible for the long slate of loppets held each year.

Many vacation resorts offer up a side order of skiing with their vacation packages. For a unique experience, try Chadwick's Kwagama Lake Lodge or Windy Lake Lodge, both accessible by train only.

Haliburton operates one of the largest trail systems in the province. Several resorts along the trails offer lodge-to-lodge ski packages.

Many provincial parks and conservation areas groom their trails for cross-country skiing. Most charge a flat per-car rate. A season pass to all provincial parks costs about $24.

Travel Information

Road report: (416) 235-1110 (Toronto), 1-800-268-1376

Tourist Information Bureau
Ontario Travel publishes a winter guide and offers an accommodation reservation service and a ski report.
Ministry of Culture, Tourism and Recreation
(416) 314-0944 (Toronto); 1-800-ONTARIO (Canada and USA)

Cross Country Skiing Organizations

Cross Country Ontario - Ontario division of Cross Country Canada. In addition to regular CCC functions it also publishes an annual guide to clubs and events.
1185 Eglinton Avenue East, North York, ON M3C 3C6
(416) 426-7262; fax: (416) 426-7346

Ontario Ski Council is an umbrella organization for eleven organizations including Biathlon Ontario, Cross Country Ontario, Nordic Combined Ontario, Ontario Association for Skiers with Disabilities, Canadian Association of Nordic Ski Instructors and Canadian Ski Patrol System.
1185 Eglinton Avenue East, Don Mills, ON M3C 3C6
(416) 426-7262; fax: (416) 426-7346

Winter Climate

In northern Ontario the cross-country ski season lasts from approximately early December to late March. For those regions south of Barrie the season is slightly shorter, more so at areas close to the Great Lakes.

Average Temperatures   ## Average Snowfall

Thunder Bay

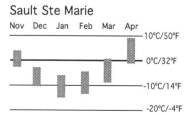

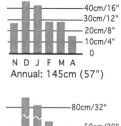

Annual: 145cm (57")

Sault Ste Marie

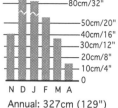

Annual: 327cm (129")

Ontario

170

Huntsville

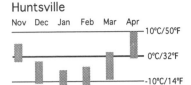

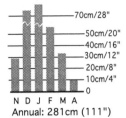

Annual: 281cm (111")

Toronto

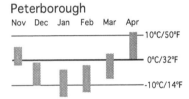

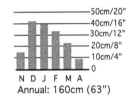

Annual: 135cm (53")

Peterborough

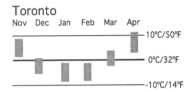

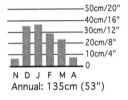

Annual: 160cm (63")

Ontario Loppet Series

Date	Event	Location
early Dec	Porcupine Ski Runners	Timmins
late Jan	Nakkerloppet	Ottawa
mid Jan	Hiawatha Ski Festival	Sault Ste Marie
early Feb	Wildwood Loppet	St. Mary's
early Feb	Algonquin Loppet	Whitney
early Feb	Silver Spoon	Deep River
early Feb	Haliburton Fun Loppet	Haliburton
early Feb	Voyageur Loppet	Alzida
mid Feb	North Bay Classic	North Bay
mid Feb	Temiskaming Nordic	New Liskeard
late Feb	Georgian Bay Loppet	Hepworth
late Feb	South River Classic	South River
early Mar	*Tour of Hardwood	Hardwood Hills
early Mar	Highlands Nordic Classic	Duntroon
late Mar	Wabos Loppet	Sault Ste Marie

* Canadian Ski Odyssey event

Ontario

171

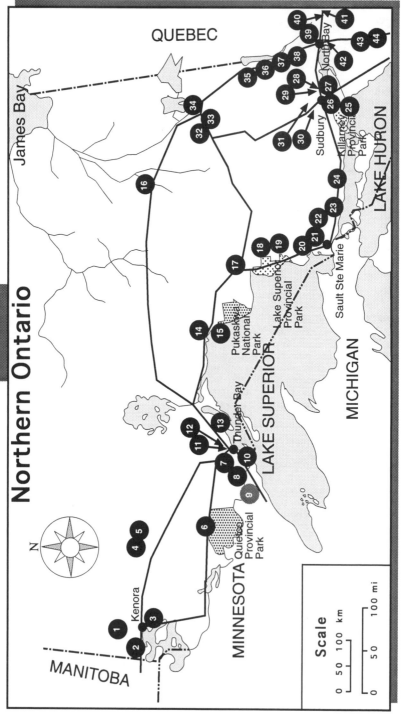

QUEBEC

James Bay

Ontario

Northern Ontario

MANITOBA

Kenora

MINNESOTA

Quetico
Provincial
Park

LAKE SUPERIOR

Thunder Bay

Pukaskwa
National
Park

Lake Superior
Provincial
Park

Sault Ste Marie

MICHIGAN

Sudbury

Killarney
Provincial
Park

North Bay

LAKE HURON

Scale
0	50	100 km
0	50	100 mi

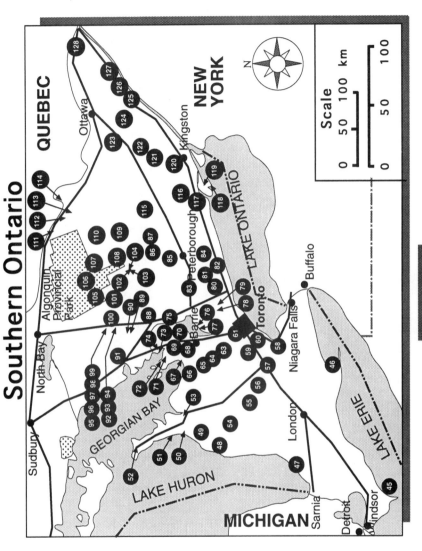

Cross Country Ski Areas

Ontario

Ontario

		Groomed Trails			Skating	Ungroomed	Lodge	Wax Room	Rentals	Food	Lesons	Shelters
Trail Fee	Total	●	■	◆								

1 Club Minaki, Minaki
(807) 543-3952; PO Box 35, Minaki, ON P0X 1J0
1 km S of Minaki on Hwy 596. There are 3 accesses to trails.
3 yurts for overnight rentals. Gun Lake Lodge is at one trailhead.

Trail Fee	Total	●	■	◆	Skating	Ungroomed	Lodge	Wax Room	Rentals	Food	Lesons	Shelters
2⁰⁰	6	-	-	-		0	√	√				3
	25.0	7.5	7.5	10.0	5.0	0.0						

2 Mt. Evergreen, Kenora
(807) 548-5100
E side of Kenora on airport road.

Trail Fee	Total	●	■	◆	Skating	Ungroomed	Lodge	Wax Room	Rentals	Food	Lesons	Shelters
NA	3	1	1	1		0	√			√		0
	8.0					0.0						

3 Rushing River Provincial Park, Kenora
(807) 468-2671; PO Box 5160, 810 Robertson St., Kenora, P9N 3X9
6 km S of Kenora on Hwy 17.
Winding trails through mature stands of Jackpine and along lakeshore.

Trail Fee	Total	●	■	◆	Skating	Ungroomed	Lodge	Wax Room	Rentals	Food	Lesons	Shelters
NC	7	1	4	2		0						0
	21.0	1.0	10.0	10.0		0.0						

4 Nordic Nomad Ski Club, Sioux Lookout
(807) 737-4467; PO Box 1416, Sioux Lookout, P8T 1B9
At curling rink on Seventh Ave N.

Trail Fee	Total	●	■	◆	Skating	Ungroomed	Lodge	Wax Room	Rentals	Food	Lesons	Shelters
Yes	11	-	-	-		0	√	√		√		0
	50.0					5.0	0.0					

5 Northern Comfort Wilderness Adventures, Sioux Lookout
(807) 737-2773 1-800-465-1661 (North America); PO Box 127, Sioux Lookout, P8T 1A1
1.6 km SE on Sturgeon River Rd. Family rate $25.00
Boreal forest, excellent variety of terrain. Backcountry chalet

Trail Fee	Total	●	■	◆	Skating	Ungroomed	Lodge	Wax Room	Rentals	Food	Lesons	Shelters
15⁰⁰	8	6	1	1		1						1
5⁰⁰ C	40.0	30.0	10.0	12.0	5.0	15.0						

6 Brown's Clearwater West Lodge, Atikokan
(807) 597-2884 1-800-900-4240; PO Box 1766, Atikokan, P0T 1C0
Daycare, 12 cottages. Trails for Guests Only.

Trail Fee	Total	●	■	◆	Skating	Ungroomed	Lodge	Wax Room	Rentals	Food	Lesons	Shelters
GO	5	2	3	0		0	√	√		√		0
	35.0	15.0	20.0			0.0						

Ontario

Groomed Trails — Trail Fee | Total | ● | ■ | ◆ | Skating | Ungroomed | Lodge | Wax Room | Rentals | Food | Lesons | Shelters

7 **Kakabeka Falls Provincial Park,** Thunder Bay

(807) 473-9231, Snow phone: (807) 625-5075; PO Box 252, Kakabeka Falls, P0T 1W0
32 km W of Thunder Bay on Hwy 11. 2 km S on Hwy 590 Kakabeka Falls Village.
Stacked loop trails over meadow and terraced terrain.

Trail Fee	Total	●	■	◆	Skating	Ungroomed	Lodge	Wax Room	Rentals	Food	Lesons	Shelters
6^{00}	3	1	2	0		0						0
car	13.4	4.0	9.4			0.0						

8 **Kamview Nordic Centre (Thunder Bay Nordic Trails),** Thunder Bay

(807) 475-7081, Snow phone: (807) 625-5075; RR 3, Site 2, PO Box 9, Thunder Bay, P7C 4V2
5 km SW of Thunder Bay Airport on Hwy 61 then 2 km N on 20th Side Road.
Sheltered trails with views of Nor'Westers. 4 km lighted trails.

Trail Fee	Total	●	■	◆	Skating	Ungroomed	Lodge	Wax Room	Rentals	Food	Lesons	Shelters
8^{25}	11	5	3	3	0	√			√	√	√	0
4^{00} C	30.0	11.0	9.5	9.5	30.0	0.0						

9 **Gunflint Trail,** Grand Marais, Minnesota

1-800-338-6932
From Grand Marais take Gunflint Trail (County Rd 50) N for 45 miles.
50% of trails are single track, rest are double. Lodge-to-lodge skiing. Bar, 4 lodges

Trail Fee	Total	●	■	◆	Skating	Ungroomed	Lodge	Wax Room	Rentals	Food	Lesons	Shelters
5^{50}	12	-	-	-	0	√	√		√	√	√	0
	100.0				25.0	0.0						

10 **Big Thunder Sports Park,** Thunder Bay

(807) 475-4402, (807) 475-7457 (tape), 1-800-667-8386; 11 Little Norway Road, Thunder Bay, P7C 4V2
15 min S on Hwy 61. Turn left on Little Norway Rd.
Varied terrain through maple and pine forest. 5km lighted trail, bar, ski jumping.

Trail Fee	Total	●	■	◆	Skating	Ungroomed	Lodge	Wax Room	Rentals	Food	Lesons	Shelters
7^{50}	8	3	2	3	0	√	√		√	√	√	0
5^{00} C	60.0	10.0	25.0	25.0	60.0	0.0						

11 **Lappe Nordic Ski Center,** Thunder Bay; RR 16, Thunder Bay, P7B 6B3
Hwy 102 N to Dog Lake R then E to Concession 4 Rd, then 3 km W .
Stacked loops. 5 km trail lit for night skiing, Finnish pancake brunch, sauna.

Trail Fee	Total	●	■	◆	Skating	Ungroomed	Lodge	Wax Room	Rentals	Food	Lesons	Shelters
7^{50}	-	-	-	-	0	√	√			√		0
	11.5	5.0	3.0	3.5		0.0						

12 **Wishart Conservation Area,** Thunder Bay
(807) 344-5857; c/o Lakehead Cons. Authority, PO Box 3476, Thunder Bay, P7B 5J9
At N end of city go N on Balsam, W on Wardope, then 13 km N on Onion Lake Rd.

Trail Fee	Total	●	■	◆	Skating	Ungroomed	Lodge	Wax Room	Rentals	Food	Lesons	Shelters
NC	4	2	2	0		0						0
	8.0					0.0						

Groomed Trails — Trail Fee | Total | ● ■ ◆ | Skating | Ungroomed | Lodge | Wax Room | Rentals | Food | Lessons | Shelters

13 Sleeping Giant (Sibley) Provincial Park, Pass Lake

(807) 977-2526, Snow phone: (807) 625-5075; RR 1, Pass Lake, P0T 2M0
6 km S of Hwy 11/17 on Hwy 587 to Pass Lake or 20km to Rita Lake.
Operated by Kamview Nordic. Long loop trails.

Trail Fee	Total	●	■	◆	Skating	Ungroomed	Lodge	Wax Room	Rentals	Food	Lessons	Shelters
6⁰⁰	4	1	2	1		0	E					0
car	60.0	2.0	25.0	33.0		0.0						

14 Marathon International Ski, Marathon

(807) 229-1538 1-800-229-1538; PO Box 1587, Marathon, P0T 2E0
Hwy 17 to Hwy 626,4 4 km on Hwy 626.
Scenic trails overlooking Lake Superior. Mix of easy & challenging trails Bar

Trail Fee	Total	●	■	◆	Skating	Ungroomed	Lodge	Wax Room	Rentals	Food	Lessons	Shelters
Yes	-	-	-	-		0	√	√	√	√	√	0
	15.0	7.0	3.0	5.0		15.0	0.0					

15 Pukaskwa National Park, Hattie Cove

(807) 229-0801; Pukaskwa National Park, Hwy 627, Hattie Cove, P0T 1R0

Trail Fee	Total	●	■	◆	Skating	Ungroomed	Lodge	Wax Room	Rentals	Food	Lessons	Shelters
Entry	0					1						0
Fee	0.0					5.0						

16 Hearst Cross-Country Ski Club, Hearst

5 km N on Hwy 583, turn left at golf course. PO Box 2687, Hearst, P0L 1N0
Two-way trails, rolling forested hills. Two long linear trails and loops.

Trail Fee	Total	●	■	◆	Skating	Ungroomed	Lodge	Wax Room	Rentals	Food	Lessons	Shelters
7⁰⁰	17	15	2	0		0	√	√		√		2
10⁰⁰F	35.0	31.5	3.5			35.0	0.0					

17 Wawa Cross-Country Ski Club, Wawa

Ch. of Com.: (705) 856-1080, 1-800-367-WAWA (Canada, USA)
At Magpie High Falls Rd or Carl M. Beck Windston Rd. PO Box 864, Wawa, P0S 1K0
Access from school yard. Linked loop trails.

Trail Fee	Total	●	■	◆	Skating	Ungroomed	Lodge	Wax Room	Rentals	Food	Lessons	Shelters
DA	3	1	1	1		0						0
	15.0	5.0	6.0	4.0		0.0						

18 Windy Lake Lodge, Sault Ste Marie

(705) 942-0525; Mile 122 1/2, A.C.R., Sault Ste Marie, P6A 5N9
Board the Algoma Central Railway at Sault Ste Marie, disembark at Mile 122.5.
Remote location/rail-only access. Mixed forest, hills and small lakes. 5 cabins (20 beds)

Trail Fee	Total	●	■	◆	Skating	Ungroomed	Lodge	Wax Room	Rentals	Food	Lessons	Shelters
GO	12	2	8	2		2	√	√		√		1
	50.0	7.0	31.0	12.0		15.0	5.0					

Ontario

178

Groomed Trails

Legend: Trail Fee · Total · Groomed Trails (● ■ ◆) · Skating · Ungroomed · Lodge · Wax Room · Rentals · Food · Lessons · Shelters

19 Chadwick's Kwagama Lake Lodge, Hawk Junction

(705) 856-1104; Algoma Central Railway, Mile 118 1/2, Hawk Junction, P0S 1G0
Accessible only by Algoma Central Railway. Disembark at Mile 118 1/2.
Wilderness lodge in rugged setting with trails for all levels. Mountain lookouts.

Trail Fee	Total	●	■	◆	Skating	Ungroomed	Lodge	Wax Room	Rentals	Food	Lessons	Shelters
GO		-	-	-	0		√			√		0
	75.0	75.0			0.0							

20 Stokely Creek Ski Touring Center, Goulais River

(705) 649-3421; RR 1, Goulais River, P0S 1E0
30 k N of Sault Ste Marie on Hwy 17 to Mahler Rd,rt 1 blk to Pickard Rd,go 3k
Double-tracked trails thru hardwood forests and past creeks & waterfalls. 24 rooms

Trail Fee	Total	●	■	◆	Skating	Ungroomed	Lodge	Wax Room	Rentals	Food	Lessons	Shelters
10⁰⁰	25	5	9	12	-		√	√		√	√	0
7⁰⁰	120.0				35.0	8.0						

21 Hiawatha Highlands, Sault Ste Marie

(705) 759-5310, 1-800-361-1522; PO Box 580, 99 Foster Dr., Sault Ste Marie, P6A 5N1
9 km N of Sault Ste Marie on Hwy 17 to 5th Line then 2 km E to lodge.
Typical Canadian Shield, hardwood highlands and cedar lowlands. Bar

Trail Fee	Total	●	■	◆	Skating	Ungroomed	Lodge	Wax Room	Rentals	Food	Lessons	Shelters
16⁰⁰	11	6	3	3	0		√	√	√	√	√	0
	42.0	15.0	15.0	12.0	0.0	19.0						

22 Searchmont Resort, Sault Ste. Marie

(705) 781-2340,1-800-663-ALGO (S Ontario, Mich); PO Box 1029, Sault Ste. Marie, P6A 5N5
Hwy 17 N to Heyden then 27 km E on Hwy 556 to Searchmount.
Trails of all levels groomed for classic and skating. Daycare, 15 chalets.

Trail Fee	Total	●	■	◆	Skating	Ungroomed	Lodge	Wax Room	Rentals	Food	Lessons	Shelters
8⁰⁰	9	-	-	-	0		√	√	√	√	√	0
4⁰⁰ C	50.0				0.0							

23 Wakomata Shores Resort, Thessalon

(705) 841-1067; Hwy 129, RR 3, Thessalon, P0R 1L0
32 km N of Thessalon on Hwy 129, then 3 km on access road.
Bar, 8 rooms with kitchenettes. Guests Only.

Trail Fee	Total	●	■	◆	Skating	Ungroomed	Lodge	Wax Room	Rentals	Food	Lessons	Shelters
GO	3	-	-	-	0					√		0
	15.0				0.0							

24 Blind River Ski Club, Blind River

In town of Blind River. PO Box 1030, Blind River, P0R 1B0

Trail Fee	Total	●	■	◆	Skating	Ungroomed	Lodge	Wax Room	Rentals	Food	Lessons	Shelters
DA	3	3	0	0	0							0
	15.0	15.0			0.0							

Ontario

Groomed Trails

Trail Fee	Total	●	■	◆	Skating	Ungroomed	Lodge	Wax Room	Rentals	Food	Lessons	Shelters

25 Killarney Provincial Park, Killarney
(705) 287-2800; Killarney Provincial Park, Killarney, P0M 2A0

Trail Fee	Total	●	■	◆	Skating	Ungroomed	Lodge	Wax Room	Rentals	Food	Lessons	Shelters
6⁰⁰	0	-	-	-	-							0
car	0.0				Yes							

26 Laurentian University X-C Ski Trails, Sudbury
(705) 675-1151; Laurentian University X-C Ski Trails, Ramsey Lake Rd., Sudbury, P3E 2C6
3 linked trail systems–Laurentain University, Larentian Lake and Idylwylde golf course.

Trail Fee	Total	●	■	◆	Skating	Ungroomed	Lodge	Wax Room	Rentals	Food	Lessons	Shelters
Yes	-	-	-	-	0	√	√	√	√			0
	35.0				0.0							

27 Lake Laurentian Conservation Area, Sudbury
(705) 674-5249; c/o Nickel District Conservation Authority, 200 Brady St., Sudbury, P3E 5K3

Trail Fee	Total	●	■	◆	Skating	Ungroomed	Lodge	Wax Room	Rentals	Food	Lessons	Shelters
NA	6	-	-	-	0							0
	20.0				0.0							

28 Kukagami Lodge, Wahnapitae
(705) 853-4929; PO Box 19, RR 1, Wahnapitae, P0M 3C0
18 km E of Wahnapitae on Hwy 17 to Kukagami Rd, then 19 km N, ski 7 km to lodge.
Parking lot is 7 km from lodge. Luggage is transported by snowmobile.

Trail Fee	Total	●	■	◆	Skating	Ungroomed	Lodge	Wax Room	Rentals	Food	Lessons	Shelters
GO	8	2	5	1	0	√		√				0
	28.0	2.0	20.0	6.0	0.0							

29 Loney's Sportsman Lodge, Garson
(705) 853-4434 ; PO Box 520, Garson, P3L 1S8
27 km E on Hwy 17, 27 km on Kukagami Rd. Bar, 23 rooms

Trail Fee	Total	●	■	◆	Skating	Ungroomed	Lodge	Wax Room	Rentals	Food	Lessons	Shelters
10⁰⁰	8	2	2	3	0	√	√	√	√			0
	35.5				20.0	0.0						

30 Onaping Falls Nordic Ski Club, Chelmsford
At Windy Lake Prov Park N of Sudbury. Onaping Falls Nordic Ski Club, Chelmsford, P0M 1L0

Trail Fee	Total	●	■	◆	Skating	Ungroomed	Lodge	Wax Room	Rentals	Food	Lessons	Shelters
NA	3	0	3	0	0	√			E			0
	30.0		30.0		0.0							

31 Capreol Cross-Country Ski Club, Capreol

Trail Fee	Total	●	■	◆	Skating	Ungroomed	Lodge	Wax Room	Rentals	Food	Lessons	Shelters
NA	6	-	-	-	0			√	√	√		0
	21.0				0.0							

Ontario

Groomed Trails — column headers: Trail Fee | Total | ● | ■ | ◆ | Skating | Ungroomed | Lodge | Wax Room | Rentals | Food | Lesons | Shelters

32 Porcupine Ski Runners, Schumacher; PO Box 250, Schumacher, P0N 1G0
0.8 km E of Schumacher on Hwy 101 or 3.5 km E of Timmins on Hwy 101
Mixed vegetation, spruce, cedar, poplar and birch. Mixed terrain.

Trail Fee	Total	●	■	◆	Skating	Ungroomed	Lodge	Wax Room	Rentals	Food	Lesons	Shelters
7^{00}	9	-	-	-		0	√	√		E	√	0
3^{00}C	30.0	7.0	15.0	8.0	30.0	0.0						

33 Kettle Lakes Provincial Park, Timmins
(705) 363-3511; Mailing Address: 896 Riverside Dr., Timmins, P4N 3W2
E of Timmins. Stacked trail loops.

Trail Fee	Total	●	■	◆	Skating	Ungroomed	Lodge	Wax Room	Rentals	Food	Lesons	Shelters
6^{00}	3	0	3	0		0						1
car	12.0		12.0			0.0						

34 Iroquois Falls Cross-Country Ski Club, Iroquois Falls
2 km E of Hwy 11 on Cemetry Rd. Family Rate $12; PO Box 84, Iroquois Falls, P0K 1E0
Loop trails with cross-overs skirting several lakes, variable terrain.

Trail Fee	Total	●	■	◆	Skating	Ungroomed	Lodge	Wax Room	Rentals	Food	Lesons	Shelters
5^{00}	4	2	1	1		1	√	√		√		2
2^{00}C	25.0	9.0	6.0	10.0	25.0	10.0						

35 Temiskaming Nordic Ski Club, New Liskeard; PO Box 2109, New Liskeard, P0J 1P0
2 km N of Cobalt on Hwy 11, 2 km W on Portage Bay Rd.

Trail Fee	Total	●	■	◆	Skating	Ungroomed	Lodge	Wax Room	Rentals	Food	Lesons	Shelters
Yes	-	-	-	-		0	√	√			√	0
	19.0				14.0	0.0						

36 Smoothwater Outfitters, Temagami
(705) 569-3539; PO Box 40, Temagami, P0H 2H0
10 min. N of Temagami on Hwy 11. (1 hr N of North Bay) Family Rate $25.00
White & red pine, rocky cliffs, lakes, moose ponds, troll caves. 5 rooms & bunkhouse

Trail Fee	Total	●	■	◆	Skating	Ungroomed	Lodge	Wax Room	Rentals	Food	Lesons	Shelters
10^{00}	10	4	4	2		2	√			√		0
5^{00}C	40.0	15.0	15.0	10.0		10.0						

37 Temagami Wilderness Centre, Temagami
(705) 569-3733 (905) 319-0203 (Toronto); RR 1, Temagami, P0H 2H0
Trails for use of guests only. 6 rooms

Trail Fee	Total	●	■	◆	Skating	Ungroomed	Lodge	Wax Room	Rentals	Food	Lesons	Shelters
GO	-	-	-	-		0				√		0
	40.0					0.0						

38 Temagami Shores Inn & Resort, Temagami
(705) 569-3200; PO Box 68, Temagami, P0H 2H0
2 km S of Temagami on Hwy 11. Bar, 19 rooms

Trail Fee	Total	●	■	◆	Skating	Ungroomed	Lodge	Wax Room	Rentals	Food	Lesons	Shelters
GO	-	-	-	-		-				√		0
	12.0					15.0						

Ontario

Groomed Trails

Trail Fee · Total · ● ■ ◆ · Skating · Ungroomed · Lodge · Wax Room · Rentals · Food · Lessons · Shelters

39 North Bay Nordic Ski Club, North Bay
(705) 495-0332 (tape); PO Box 6067, RR#3, North Bay, P1B 8G4
E on Hwy 63 to Peninsula Rd, turn right, turn left at Northshore Rd, then go 2 km
Varied terrain: spruce bog, mixed forest, rock cliff, lake.

Trail Fee	Total	●	■	◆	Skating	Ungroomed	Lodge	Wax Room	Rentals	Food	Lessons	Shelters
7⁰⁰	7	2	1	4		0	√	√	√		√	0
5⁰⁰	42.2	3.7	3.5	35.0	18.0	0.0						

40 Samuel de Champlain Provincial Park, Mattawa
(705) 744-2276; PO Box 147, Mattawa, P0H 1V0
E of Mattawa on Hwy 17.
Operated by volunteers. Deer feeders offer viewing opportunities.

Trail Fee	Total	●	■	◆	Skating	Ungroomed	Lodge	Wax Room	Rentals	Food	Lessons	Shelters
DA	3	0	3	0		0						0
	20.0		20.0			0.0						

41 Mattawa Golf & Ski Resort, Mattawa
(705) 744-5818, 1-800-762-2339; PO Box 609, Mattawa, P0H 1V0

Trail Fee	Total	●	■	◆	Skating	Ungroomed	Lodge	Wax Room	Rentals	Food	Lessons	Shelters
Yes	-	-	-	-		0						0
	20.0					0.0						

42 Wasi Cross-Country Ski Club, Callander
N of Callander to Lake Nosbonsing Rd. General Delivery, Callander, P0H 1H0

Trail Fee	Total	●	■	◆	Skating	Ungroomed	Lodge	Wax Room	Rentals	Food	Lessons	Shelters
Yes	-	-	-	-		0	√					0
	35.0					0.0						

43 South River Community Trails, South River; c/o Proect DARE, PO Box 2000, South River, P0A 1X0
22 km E of town of South River on secondary road.
Operated by Project DARE rehabilitation. Hosts a loppet.

Trail Fee	Total	●	■	◆	Skating	Ungroomed	Lodge	Wax Room	Rentals	Food	Lessons	Shelters
NC	1	0	1	0		0						0
	10.0		10.0			0.0						

44 The Caswell Resort Hotel, Sunridge
(705) 384-7600 1-800-461-5262; PO Box 70, 149 Main St., Sunridge, P0A 1Z0
149 Main St. in Sunridge. Indoor pool and sauna. Bar, 42 rooms

Trail Fee	Total	●	■	◆	Skating	Ungroomed	Lodge	Wax Room	Rentals	Food	Lessons	Shelters
Yes	4	-	-	-		0	√	√	√	√		0
	18.0					0.0						

45 Point Pelee National Park, Leamington
(519) 322-2365; Point Pelee National Park, RR 1, Leamington, N8H 3V4
Hwy 401 exit 48, take Hwy 77 S to Leamington,4 continue to park.
Trails are on peninsula in Lake Erie near marsh.

Trail Fee	Total	●	■	◆	Skating	Ungroomed	Lodge	Wax Room	Rentals	Food	Lessons	Shelters
3²⁵	0	-	-	-		2						0
2⁴⁰ S	0.0					5.0						

Ontario

		Groomed Trails										
Trail Fee	Total	●	■	◆	Skating	Ungroomed	Lodge	Wax Room	Rentals	Food	Lesons	Shelters

46 Backus Woods, Port Rowan

(519) 428-4623; Long Point Region Conservation Authority, RR1, Port Rowan, N0E 1M0
2 km E of junction of Hwys 24 & 59.

Trail Fee	Total	●	■	◆	Ungroomed	Shelters
NA	3	-	-	-	0	0
	12.0				0.0	

47 Pinery Provincial Park, Grand Bend

(519) 243-2220; Pinery Provincial Park, RR#2, Grand Bend, N0M 1T0
5 km SW of Grand Bend on Hwy 21.
Oak and pine forest, dune ridge, wildlife viewing.

Trail Fee	Total	●	■	◆	Ungroomed	Food	Lesons	Shelters
6⁰⁰	5	2	2	1	0	√	√	0
car	36.9	13.2	14.3	9.4	0.0			

48 Sutton Park Inn, Kincardine

(519) 396-3444 1-800-265-3045; PO Box 209, 725 King St. E., Kincardine, N2Z 2Y7
On Hwy 21 N of Kincardine Bar, 65 rooms.

Trail Fee	Total	●	■	◆	Ungroomed	Food	Shelters
Yes	-	-	-	-	0	√	0
	30.0				0.0		

49 Stoney Island Conservation Area, Hanover

(519) 364-1255; Saugeen Valley Conservation. Authority, RR1, Hanover, N4N 3B8
5 km N of Kincardine on Lakeshore Rd just S of junction with Concession road 6.
Hardwood highlands and coniferous lowlands.

Trail Fee	Total	●	■	◆	Ungroomed	Shelters
NC	4	-	-	-	0	0
	10.0				0.0	

50 Sauble Beach Cross Country Ski Club, Sauble Beach

Sauble Beach Cross Country Ski,   Club, General Delivery, Sauble Beach, N0H 2G0
30 km W of Owen Sound 5.5 km N of Sauble Beach
Trails through mature forest next to Sauble Falls Provincial Park.

Trail Fee	Total	●	■	◆	Ungroomed	Lodge	Shelters
6⁰⁰	6	0	6	0	0	√	0
9⁰⁰ F	18.0		18.0		0.0		

51 Red Bay Lodge, Mar

(519) 534-1027; Red Bay Lodge, RR 1, Mar, N0H 1X0
2 km N of Red Bay on Shore rd.
On-site trails operated by Bruce Ski Club. Sauna

Trail Fee	Total	●	■	◆	Ungroomed	Food	Lesons	Shelters
Yes	3	1	1	1	0	√	√	0
	40.0				0.0			

Ontario

Groomed Trails

Trail Fee · Total · ● ■ ◆ · Skating · Ungroomed · Lodge · Wax Room · Rentals · Food · Lesons · Shelters

52 Bruce Peninsula National Park, Tobermory
(519) 596-2233; PO Box 189, Tobermory, N0H 2R0
N tip of Bruce Peninsula.
Linear trail from Cyprus Lake to Bruce Trail on cliff overlooking bay.

Entry	0	-	-	-		1					0
Fee	0.0					2.0					

53 Inglis Falls Conservation Area, Owen Sound
(519) 376-3076; Grey Sauble Conservation Authority, RR4, Owen Sound, N4K 5N6
2 km W on County Rd 18.

NC	1	0	1	0		1					0
	8.0		8.0			10.0					

54 Minto Glen Sports Center, Clifford
(519) 338-2782; Minto Glen Sports Center, RR#3, Clifford, N0G 1M0
W on Hwy 89 from Mount Forest, then N on County Rd 2.
One main trail with many side trails ranging from novice to intermediate.

4^{00}	-	-	-	-		0	√		√	√	0
	10.0					0.0					

55 Allan Park Conservation Area, Hanover
(519) 364-1255; Saugeen Valley Conservation Authority, RR#1, Hanover, N4N 3B8
Hwy 4 between Hanover and Durham turn S. 3 km S of hamlet of Allan Park.
400 acres of forested rolling terrain.

NC	11	3	2	6		0					0
	15.0					0.0					

56 Elora Gorge Conservation Area, Elora
(519) 846-9742; Grand River Cons. Authourity, PO Box 356, Elora, N0B1S0
Hwy 6 to Elora Rd. 8 km W on Elora Rd.
Trails skirt rim of spectacular limestone gorge.

4^{50}	3	1	1	1		0					0
	12.0	5.0	5.0	2.0		0.0					

57 Laurel Creek Conservation Area, Waterloo
(519) 884-6620; 290 Beavercreek Road, Waterloo, N2J 3Z4
NW corner of Waterloo off Westmount Rd N.
Trails over camping and picnic grounds.

4^{00}	3	1	1	1		0	√		√		0
2^{25}C	7.8	2.0	4.0	1.8		0.0					

Ontario

Groomed Trails

| | | ● | ■ | ◆ | Skating | Ungroomed | Lodge | Wax Room | Rentals | Food | Lesons | Shelters |

58 Valens Conservation Area, Cambridge

(905) 659-7715 (519) 621-6029; Hamilton Region Cons Authority, RR#6, Cambridge, N1R 5S7
Hwy 6 to Freelton then W on Regional Rd 97.
Forest, wetland, fields, lookout point.

Trail Fee	Total	●	■	◆	Skating	Ungroomed	Lodge	Wax Room	Rentals	Food	Lesons	Shelters
4^{00}	8	8	0	0		0	√	√				0
car	12.0	12.0				0.0						

59 Hilton Falls Conservation Area, Milton

(905) 854-0262; Halton Region Cons. Authourity, 2596 Britannia Rd. W., RR#2, Milton, L9T 2X6
Hwy 401 exit on Hwy 25 at Milton, N on Hwy 25 to Regional Rd 9 then 5 km W.
Waterfall and gorge, 4 rolling wooded escarpment and wetlands, Bruce Trail

Trail Fee	Total	●	■	◆	Skating	Ungroomed	Lodge	Wax Room	Rentals	Food	Lesons	Shelters
6^{00}	3	0	3	0		0	√		√			0
car	15.5		15.5			0.0						

60 Mountsberg Conservation Area, Milton

(905) 336-1158; Halton Region Cons. Authourity, 2596 Britannia Rd.W., RR#2, Milton, L9T 2X6
Hwy 401 to Hwy 1 or Hwy 6 Go S to Campbell Rd. N on Milborough Line.
Gently rolling open and wooded area, wildlife exhibits.

Trail Fee	Total	●	■	◆	Skating	Ungroomed	Lodge	Wax Room	Rentals	Food	Lesons	Shelters
6^{00}	3	1	2	0		0	√		√			0
car	13.7	1.6	12.1			0.0						

61 Seneca College, King City; 13990 Dufferin St. N., King City, L0G 1K0
In King City go N on Dufferin to Seneca College Campus.
Mixture of fields and forest on the old Eaton estate.

Trail Fee	Total	●	■	◆	Skating	Ungroomed	Lodge	Wax Room	Rentals	Food	Lesons	Shelters
8^{00}	4	2	2	0		0	√	√	√	E		0
4^{00}C	14.0	6.4	7.6		2.1	0.0						

62 Albion Hills Conservation Area, Bolton
(905) 880-0227, (416) 661-6600; Toronto Reg. Cons. Authourity, PO Box 78, Palgrave, L0N 1P0
8 km N of of Bolton on Hy 50.
Adjacent to Bruce Trail in the Caledon Hills on the banks of the Humber.

Trail Fee	Total	●	■	◆	Skating	Ungroomed	Lodge	Wax Room	Rentals	Food	Lesons	Shelters
7^{00}	5	2	1	1		0	√	√	√	√		0
3^{00}C	26.5	4.5	6.0	16.5	7.0	0.0						

Ontario

Column legend: Trail Fee | Total | Groomed Trails (● ■ ◆) | Skating | Ungroomed | Lodge | Wax Room | Rentals | Food | Lessons | Shelters

64 Palgrave Forest Wildlife Area, Bolton

(905) 880-0227 ; Palgrave Forest Wildlife Area, Bolton, L0N 1P0
10 km N of Bolton on Hwy 50.

Trail Fee	Total	●	■	◆	Skating	Ungroomed	Lodge	Wax Room	Rentals	Food	Lessons	Shelters
Yes	3	-	-	-		0						0
	16.0					0.0						

65 Mansfield Outdoor Centre, Mansfield

(705) 435-4479; PO Box 95, Mansfield, L0N 1M0
One hour N of Toronto on Airport Rd. 10 km N of Hwy 89.
Mixed forest on rolling terrain with views. School programs, cabins & dorms.

Trail Fee	Total	●	■	◆	Skating	Ungroomed	Lodge	Wax Room	Rentals	Food	Lessons	Shelters
10^{50}	5	3	2	1		0	√	√	√	√	√	0
7^{00} C	34.0	12.0	18.0	4.0	2.0	0.0						

66 Highlands Nordic, Duntroon

(705) 444-5017 1-800-263-5017 (416, 905, 519, 705); PO Box 110, Duntroon, L0M 1H0
At Duntroon go 3 km W to 10th Line, turn S and go 2 km.
Trails wind thru maplebush on rolling hills overlooking Georgian Bay.

Trail Fee	Total	●	■	◆	Skating	Ungroomed	Lodge	Wax Room	Rentals	Food	Lessons	Shelters
10^{00}	5	2	2	1		0	√	√	√	√	√	0
7^{00}	28.5	5.5	11.5	11.5	28.5	0.0						

67 Wasaga Beach Provincial Park, Wasaga Beach

(705) 429-2516; PO Box 183, Wasaga Beach, L0L 2P0
In town of Wasaga Beach turn S on Blueberry Trail.
Trails over dunes and through mixed forest.

Trail Fee	Total	●	■	◆	Skating	Ungroomed	Lodge	Wax Room	Rentals	Food	Lessons	Shelters
6^{00}	6	3	2	2		0	√	√	√			2
car	26.0	7.0	7.2	12.3	3.0	0.0						

68 Horseshoe Resort, Horseshoe Valley, Barrie

(705) 835-2790, (705) 835-3546 (tape), (416) 283-2988 (Toronto)
PO Box 10, Horseshoe Valley, RR #1, Barrie, L4M 4Y8
Hwy 400 exit 117 10 min.N of Barrie turn right onto Horseshoe Valley Rd.
Luxury resort with all facilities. Trails are a series of stacked loops.
Daycare, bar, 102 rooms, 40 condos, 1-800-461-5627 (reservations).

Trail Fee	Total	●	■	◆	Skating	Ungroomed	Lodge	Wax Room	Rentals	Food	Lessons	Shelters
11^{00}	12	2	5	7		0	√	√	√	√	√	0
7^{00} C	35.0				9.0	0.0						

69 Springwater Provincial Park, Midhurst

(705) 728-7393; Springwater Provincial Park, Midhurst, L0L 1X0
10 km NW of Barrie on Hwy 26.
Fairly flat terrain through mixed coniferous forest.

Trail Fee	Total	●	■	◆	Skating	Ungroomed	Lodge	Wax Room	Rentals	Food	Lessons	Shelters
6^{00}	3	3	0	0		0	√					0
car	12.4	12.4				0.0						

Ontario

Groomed Trails

Header symbols: **Trail Fee · Total · ● ■ ◆ · Skating · Ungroomed · Lodge · Wax Room · Rentals · Food · Lessons · Shelters**

70 Hardwood Hills, Oro Station

(705) 487-3775, 1-800-387-3775 (416, 519, 705, 905); RR#1, Oro Station, L0L 2E0
Hwy 400 N of Barrie take exit 111 and go E on Doran Rd for 10 km.
Racing and recreational trails over rolling hills through maple forest. Snowmaking

Trail Fee	Total	●	■	◆	Skating	Ungroomed	Lodge	Wax Room	Rentals	Food	Lessons	Shelters
13⁰⁰	6	0	3	3		1	√	√	√	√	√	0
7⁰⁰ C	32.0		16.0	16.0	32.0	5.0						

71 Lafontaine Ski Trails, Penetanguishene

(705) 533-2961; RR 3, Penetanguishene, L0K 1P0
Take Robert St. W, turn right on Lafontaine Rd, 4 left at Concession 16.
Varied terrain. Hardwood and pine forest, views of bay.

Trail Fee	Total	●	■	◆	Skating	Ungroomed	Lodge	Wax Room	Rentals	Food	Lessons	Shelters
8⁰⁰	7	2	4	1		0	√	√	√	√	√	1
5⁰⁰ C	42.0	4.0	23.0	15.0	7.0	0.0						

72 Awenda Provincial Park, Penetanguishene

(705) 549-2231; PO Box 973, Penetanguishene, L0K 1P0
11 km NW of Penetanguishene.
Shoreline, wetland and bluff trails. Views of Georgian Bay.

Trail Fee	Total	●	■	◆	Skating	Ungroomed	Lodge	Wax Room	Rentals	Food	Lessons	Shelters
6⁰⁰	4	1	3	0		0		√				0
car	29.0	4.0	25.0			0.0						

73 Mountainview Ski Hills, Midland

(705) 526-8149; RR2, Midland, L4R 4K4
Go W on Foster's Rd at police station in Midland.

Trail Fee	Total	●	■	◆	Skating	Ungroomed	Lodge	Wax Room	Rentals	Food	Lessons	Shelters
5⁰⁰	5	1	2	2		0	√	√		√		0
	20.0	1.5	11.5	7.0	20.0	0.0						

74 Wye Marsh Wildlife Centre, Midland

(705) 526-7809; PO Box 100, Midland, L4R 4K6
5 km E of Midland on Hwy 12.
Nature trails thru mixed forest with clearings and lookouts. Snowshoes incl.

Trail Fee	Total	●	■	◆	Skating	Ungroomed	Lodge	Wax Room	Rentals	Food	Lessons	Shelters
6⁰⁰	6	2	4	0		0	√		√		R	0
4⁰⁰ C	16.4	4.7	10.7			0.0						

75 Bayview-Wildwood Resorts, Severn Bridge

(705) 689-2338 1-800-461-0243 (Ont, except 807); RR 1, Severn Bridge, P0E 1N0
10 km N of Orilla on Hwy 11 turn onto S Sparrow Lake Rd, then 9 km to center.
Marshland, lakeshore and forest. Daycare, rooms and cottages, bar.

Trail Fee	Total	●	■	◆	Skating	Ungroomed	Lodge	Wax Room	Rentals	Food	Lessons	Shelters
12⁰⁰	6	1	2	3		0	√		√	√		0
	16.0	1.0	3.0	12.0		0.0						

Groomed Trails — Trail Fee · Total · ● ■ ◆ · Skating · Ungroomed · Lodge · Wax Room · Rentals · Food · Lesons · Shelters

Ontario

76 The Briars Resort, Jacksons Point

(905) 722-3271, 1-800-465-2376; 55 Hedge Road, RR 1, Jacksons Point, L0E 1L0
0.8 km E of Jackson's Point on Hedge Road. Lakeshore resort on 200 acre grounds.
Trails thru woods and over golf course. Bar, 50 rooms.

Trail Fee	Total	●	■	◆	Skating	Ungroomed	Lodge	Wax Room	Rentals	Food	Lesons	Shelters
7.00	3	3	0	0		0	√	√	√	√	√	0
	8.0	8.0				0.0						

77 Sibbald Point Provincial Park, Sutton West

(905) 722-8061; RR2, Sutton West, L0E 1R0
2 km N of Hwy 48 on County Rd 18.

Trail Fee	Total	●	■	◆	Skating	Ungroomed	Lodge	Wax Room	Rentals	Food	Lesons	Shelters
Yes	1	0	1	0		0						0
	8.0		8.0			0.0						

78 Pleasure Valley, Uxbridge

(905) 649-3334; 2499 Brock Road, RR 4, Uxbridge, L9P 1R4
20 km N of Hwy 401 at Pickering on Brock Road.
Rolling hills, some open vistas, wide variety of vegetation.

Trail Fee	Total	●	■	◆	Skating	Ungroomed	Lodge	Wax Room	Rentals	Food	Lesons	Shelters
12.00	3	1	1	1		0	√	√	√	√	√	1
8.00 C	26.0	3.5	8.5	14.0		0.0						

79 Dagmar Resort, Ashburn

(905) 649-2002; RR 1, Ashburn, L0B 1A0
24 km N of Ajax at 1220 Lakeridge Rd. Snowmaking facilities. Bar

Trail Fee	Total	●	■	◆	Skating	Ungroomed	Lodge	Wax Room	Rentals	Food	Lesons	Shelters
10.00	6	-	-	-		0	√	√	√	√	√	0
8.00 S	22.0	9.0	5.0	8.0		0.0						

80 Heber Down Conservation Area, Oshawa

(905) 579-0411; Central Lake Ontario Cons. Authority, 100 Whiting Ave, Oshawa, L1H 3T3
From Hwy 401 take Hwy 12 5 km N to Taunton Rd W then N on country lane.
Trails over campground.

Trail Fee	Total	●	■	◆	Skating	Ungroomed	Lodge	Wax Room	Rentals	Food	Lesons	Shelters
2.00	3	1	1	1		0	T					0
car	9.5	2.0	3.0	4.5		0.0						

81 Long Sault Conservation Area, Oshawa

(905) 579-0411, (905) 263-2041
Central Lake Ontario Cons. Authority, 100 Whiting Ave, Oshawa, L1H 3T3
Hwy 401 to Bowmanville, Regional Rd 57 N to Reg. Rd 20, 3 km E on Woodley
Hilly terrain but trails for all levels of ability.

Trail Fee	Total	●	■	◆	Skating	Ungroomed	Lodge	Wax Room	Rentals	Food	Lesons	Shelters
2.00	4	1	2	1		0	√	√	√	√		0
car	17.0	2.0	8.6	6.4		0.0						

Groomed Trails

Column headers: Trail Fee | Total | ● | ■ | ◆ | Skating | Ungroomed | Lodge | Wax Room | Rentals | Food | Lessons | Shelters

82 Trillium Trails, Raglan
(905) 655-3754; Trillium Trails, 53 Snow Ridge Ct., Brooklin L0B 1C0
From Hwy 401 in Oshawa, take Simcoe St 16 km N to Raglan.

Trail Fee	Total	●	■	◆	Skating	Ungroomed	Lodge	Wax Room	Rentals	Food	Lessons	Shelters
11^{00}	-	-	-	-		0	√	√	√	√		0
7^{00}C	23.5	2.0	8.0	13.5	23.5	0.0						

83 Ken Reid Conservation Area, Lindsay
(705) 328-2271, 1-800-668-5722 (416,705,905)
Kawartha Region Cons. Authority, RR1, Kenerei Park Rd., Lindsay, K9V 4R1
5 km N of Lindsay on Hwy 35 to Kenerei Park Rd. E then follow signs.

Trail Fee	Total	●	■	◆	Skating	Ungroomed	Lodge	Wax Room	Rentals	Food	Lessons	Shelters
NC	2	2	0	0		0						0
	8.0	8.0			2.0	0.0						

84 Ganaraska Forest Centre, Campbellcroft
(905) 797-2721; Ganaraska Region Cons. Auth., RR 1, Campbellcroft, L0A 1B0
Hwy 115 N to Kirby. East on Ganaraska Rd 9 for about 9km, then left at sign.
Stacked loop trails through reforested areas. School programs

Trail Fee	Total	●	■	◆	Skating	Ungroomed	Lodge	Wax Room	Rentals	Food	Lessons	Shelters
6^{00}	6	0	6	0		0	√	√		E		0
	28.0		28.0			0.0						

85 Warsaw Caves Conservation Area, Warsaw
(705) 745-5791; Otonabee Region Cons. Authority, #200, 380 Armour Road, Peterborough, K9H 7L7
1 km N of Warsaw on Caves Rd.

Trail Fee	Total	●	■	◆	Skating	Ungroomed	Lodge	Wax Room	Rentals	Food	Lessons	Shelters
Yes	2	-	-	-		0						0
	13.0					0.0						

86 Kawartha Nordic Ski Club Trail, Woodview
(705) 749-5605 (tape); PO Box 1371, Peterborough, K9J 7H6
40 km N of Peterborough on Hwy 28 at Haultain Rd just N of Woodview.
Wilderness trails on Peterborough Game Reserve. Looped trails. B&B

Trail Fee	Total	●	■	◆	Skating	Ungroomed	Lodge	Wax Room	Rentals	Food	Lessons	Shelters
7^{00}	10	-	-	-		0	√					3
15^{00}F	45.0	15.0	15.0	15.0	15.0	0.0						

87 Viamede Resort & Conference Centre, Woodview
(705) 652-1166, 1-800-461-1946 (Ontario); Woodview Post Office, Woodview, K0L 3G0
5 km E of Burleigh Falls,4 3 km S on Viamede Rd.
Trails thru game preserve, bar on-site.

Trail Fee	Total	●	■	◆	Skating	Ungroomed	Lodge	Wax Room	Rentals	Food	Lessons	Shelters
5^{00}	20	0	20	0		0	√	√		√	√	0
	25.0		25.0			0.0						

Groomed Trails — columns: Trail Fee | Total | ● | ■ | ◆ | Skating | Ungroomed | Lodge | Wax Room | Rentals | Food | Lessons | Shelters

88 Gravenhurst KOA Nordic Trails, Gravenhurst

(705) 687-2333; RR#3, Gravenhurst, P1P 1R3
Hwy 11 6 km N of Gravenhurst, about 1 km E on Reay Rd.
Flats and short hills, mixed forest, peat marsh. 3 unheated cabins, RV facilities

Trail Fee	Total	●	■	◆	Skating	Ungroomed	Lodge	Wax Room	Rentals	Food	Lessons	Shelters
7⁰⁰	8	5	2	1		0	√	√	√	√		1
3⁰⁰ C	16.5	7.9	5.4	3.2	13.3	0.0						

89 Sherwood Inn, Port Carling

(705) 765-3131, 1-800-461-4233 (Ontario); PO Box 400, Sherwood Road, Port Carling, P0B 1J0
2 km N of Hwy 118 on Hwy 169 to Lake Joseph.
Luxurious 40 room resort-type inn with health club, bar. Trails for Guests Only.

Trail Fee	Total	●	■	◆	Skating	Ungroomed	Lodge	Wax Room	Rentals	Food	Lessons	Shelters
GO	3	1	1	1		0	√		√	√	√	0
	16.0	2.0	4.0	10.0		0.0						

90 Shamrock Lodge, Port Carling

(705) 765-3177 (tape), 1-800-668-8885 (North America); PO Box 160, Port Carling, P0B 1J0
From Port Carling take Muskoka Rd 27 for 4.5 km to Shamrock Rd.
Hardwood forests, gentle slopes, lookout tower, bar, 13 rooms, sauna.

Trail Fee	Total	●	■	◆	Skating	Ungroomed	Lodge	Wax Room	Rentals	Food	Lessons	Shelters
2⁰⁰	4	-	-	-		0	√	√	√	√	√	0
1⁰⁰	13.0					0.0						

91 Georgian Bay Ski & Canoe Club, Parry Sound

10 km on Hwy 124 at Nine Mile Lake. PO Box 42, Parry Sound, P2A 2X2

Trail Fee	Total	●	■	◆	Skating	Ungroomed	Lodge	Wax Room	Rentals	Food	Lessons	Shelters
8⁰⁰	6	4	2	0		0	√	√			√	0
2⁰⁰ C	35.0				10.0	0.0						

92 Divine Lake Resort, Sydney

(705) 385-1212, 1-800-263-6600; PO Box XD3, RR 1, Port Sydney, P0B 1L0

Trail Fee	Total	●	■	◆	Skating	Ungroomed	Lodge	Wax Room	Rentals	Food	Lessons	Shelters
Yes	-	-	-	-		0						0
	12.0					0.0						

93 Hill & Gully Riders Snowmobile Club, Port Sydney

(705) 385-2271; PO Box 1001, Port Sydney, P0B 1L0
Rolling wooded terrain.

Trail Fee	Total	●	■	◆	Skating	Ungroomed	Lodge	Wax Room	Rentals	Food	Lessons	Shelters
NA	-	-	-	-		0				√		0
	20.0		20.0			0.0						

Ontario

Groomed Trails — Trail Fee | Total | ● | ■ | ◆ | Skating | Ungroomed | Lodge | Wax Room | Rentals | Food | Lesons | Shelters

94 Pine Lodge Country Inn, Port Sydney

(705) 385-2271, 1-800-461-7463; RR 1, Port Sydney, P0B 1L0
2 km E of Hwy 11 on Muskoka Rd 10. 19 rooms, sauna

Trail Fee	Total	●	■	◆	Skating	Ungroomed	Lodge	Wax Room	Rentals	Food	Lesons	Shelters
Guests	5	-	-	-		0			√			0
Only	25.0					0.0						

95 Cedar Grove Lodge, Huntsville

(705) 789-4036, 1-800-461-4269 (Canada, USA); PO Box 996, Huntsville, P0A 1K0
10 km east of Huntsville on Hwy 60. Turn onto Grassmere Resort Road.
6 km loop on lakeshore, shorter trails around peninsula. Daycare, 19 cottages, 8 rooms.

Trail Fee	Total	●	■	◆	Skating	Ungroomed	Lodge	Wax Room	Rentals	Food	Lesons	Shelters
NC	-	-	-	-		0	√					0
	12.0					0.0						

96 Blue Water Acres, Huntsville

(705) 635-2880, (705) 635-1483, 1-800-461-4279 (Ont except 807) ;
3 km S of Huntsville on Muskoka Rd 9. Year-round lakeside resort.
Rolling hills, meadows , scenic lookouts, bar, 40 chalets.

Trail Fee	Total	●	■	◆	Skating	Ungroomed	Lodge	Wax Room	Rentals	Food	Lesons	Shelters
pkg	3	1	1	1		0	√		√	√		0
	20.0					0.0						

97 Arrowhead Provincial Park, Huntsville

(705) 789-5105; RR#3, Huntsville, P0A 1K0
8 km N of Huntsville on Hwy 11.
All are loop trails except one to lookout and water fall.

Trail Fee	Total	●	■	◆	Skating	Ungroomed	Lodge	Wax Room	Rentals	Food	Lesons	Shelters
6^{00}	7	2	4	1		0	√	√	√			0
car	23.0	7.0	13.3	2.7	3.0	0.0						

98 Deerhurst Resort Trail System, Huntsville

(705) 789-6411, 1-800-268-9411; RR #4, Huntsville, P0A 1K0
8 km E of Huntsville on Muskoka Rd 23.
Bar. Trails for Guests Only.

Trail Fee	Total	●	■	◆	Skating	Ungroomed	Lodge	Wax Room	Rentals	Food	Lesons	Shelters
Guests	-	-	-	-		0			√	√		0
Only	15.0					0.0						

99 Grandview Inn, Huntsville

(705) 789-4417, 1-800-461-4454 (Canada); RR #4, Huntsville, P0A 1K0
8 km E of Huntsville on Hwy 60.
Luxury resort nestled in evergreen forest, open field and marsh, bar, 156 condos

Trail Fee	Total	●	■	◆	Skating	Ungroomed	Lodge	Wax Room	Rentals	Food	Lesons	Shelters
5^{00}	6	1	3	2		0	√	√	√	√		0
	15.0	1.0	7.5	6.5		0.0						

Trail Fee	Total	Groomed Trails ●	■	◆	Skating	Ungroomed	Lodge	Wax Room	Rentals	Food	Lessons	Shelters

Ontario

100 Bondi Village, Dwight

(705) 635-2261; RR#1, Dwight, P0A 1H0
Hwy 35 to Muskoka Rd. 2 km SW on Muskoka Rd.
Mixed hardwood and spruce open field and lakeshore. 10 cottages

Trail Fee	Total	●	■	◆	Skating	Ungroomed	Lodge	Wax Room	Rentals	Food	Lessons	Shelters
3⁰⁰	-	-	-	-		0	√		N			1
NCC	16.0	8.0	4.0	4.0		0.0						

101 Nordic Inn, Dorset

(705) 766-2343; PO Box 155, Dorset, P0A 1E0
2 km N of Dorset on Hwy 35.
Forest, woodlands and a variety of wildlife. Bar, rooms

Trail Fee	Total	●	■	◆	Skating	Ungroomed	Lodge	Wax Room	Rentals	Food	Lessons	Shelters
8⁰⁰	4	1	2	1		0	√	√		√		0
	23.0	2.0	7.0	14.0		0.0						

102 Haliburton Nordic Trails, Haliburton

(705) 457-1640 (tape), 1-800-461-7677; PO Box 670, Haliburton, K0M 1S0
Hwy 35, 118 or 121 to any of the various resorts along the trails.
Deciduous forests, scenic views, some hills, night skiing. Bar, inns, lodges, B&B

Trail Fee	Total	●	■	◆	Skating	Ungroomed	Lodge	Wax Room	Rentals	Food	Lessons	Shelters
9⁰⁰	34	9	17	8		0	√	√	√	√	√	6
4⁵⁰ C	190.0	33.0	78.0	73.0	23.0	0.0						

103 Haliburton Forest & Wildlife Reserve, Haliburton

(705) 754-2198, 1-800-267-4482 (S. Ontario); RR 1, Haliburton, K0M 1S0
On Kennisis Lake Rd.

Trail Fee	Total	●	■	◆	Skating	Ungroomed	Lodge	Wax Room	Rentals	Food	Lessons	Shelters
NA	-	-	-	-		0						0
	15.0					0.0						

104 Domain of Killien, Haliburton

(705) 457-1100; PO Box 810, Haliburton, K0M 1S0
Hwy 121 to Haliburton,4 left on Hwy 118, then rt on Harburn Rd for 12 km.
Rooms with jacuzzi, wilderness cabin, interlinking trails, bar, 5 rooms, 8 cottages.

Trail Fee	Total	●	■	◆	Skating	Ungroomed	Lodge	Wax Room	Rentals	Food	Lessons	Shelters
GO	-	-	-	-		0	√	√	√	√		0
	28.0	14.0	7.0	7.0		0.0						

Groomed Trails

Trail Fee	Total	●	■	◆	Skating	Ungroomed	Lodge	Wax Room	Rentals	Food	Lessons	Shelters

105 **Algonquin Provincial Park,** Fen Lake Ski Trail
P.O. Box 219, Whitney K0J 2M0
(705) 633-5572
West Gate of Park on Hwy 60.
Deciduous trees. Tracks of moose, deer, wolves can often be seen.

Trail Fee	Total	●	■	◆	Skating	Ungroomed	Lodge	Wax Room	Rentals	Food	Lessons	Shelters
6⁰⁰	3	2	0	1	0	√						2
car	15.5	6.3		9.2		0.0						

106 **Algonquin Provincial Park,** Minnesing Ski Trail
(705) 633-5572
22 km E of West Gate on Hwy 60. Three Stacked loops.

Trail Fee	Total	●	■	◆	Skating	Ungroomed	Lodge	Wax Room	Rentals	Food	Lessons	Shelters
6⁰⁰	4	2	2	0	0	T						2
car	27.8	18.4	9.4			0.0						

107 **Algonquin Provincial Park,** Leaf Lake Ski Trail **A**
(705) 633-5572
East Gate of park 5 km N of Whitney on Hwy 60.
Varied terrain with beautiful vistas. Accomodation nearby in Whitney.

Trail Fee	Total	●	■	◆	Skating	Ungroomed	Lodge	Wax Room	Rentals	Food	Lessons	Shelters
6⁰⁰	7	3	1	2	0	√						2
car	46.2	15.9	5.0	25.3		0.0						

108 **Algonquin Nordic Wilderness Lodge,** Harcourt
(705) 745-9497
S.E. corner of Algonquin Park. 20 km N of Harcourt.
Secluded lodge located on lake in Algonquin Park.

Trail Fee	Total	●	■	◆	Skating	Ungroomed	Lodge	Wax Room	Rentals	Food	Lessons	Shelters
pkg	10	4	3	3	0	√	√		√	√		1
	80.0	25.0	25.0	30.0		0.0						

109 **Silent Lake Provincial Park,** Bancroft **A**
(613) 332-3940; PO Box 500, Bancroft, K0L 1C0
24 km S of Bancroft off Hwy 28.
Long loop around lake. Hardwood groves and cedar swamps.

Trail Fee	Total	●	■	◆	Skating	Ungroomed	Lodge	Wax Room	Rentals	Food	Lessons	Shelters
6⁰⁰	4	3	1	1	0	√	√	√				2
car	45.0	13.5	13.0	19.0	5.0	0.0						

110 **Mount Madawaska,** Barry's Bay
(613) 756-2931, 1-800-668-8249; PO Box 632, Barry's Bay, K0J 1B0
5 km S of Barry's Bay on Hwy 62. Open Wed to Sun. Bar

Trail Fee	Total	●	■	◆	Skating	Ungroomed	Lodge	Wax Room	Rentals	Food	Lessons	Shelters
Yes	7	-	-	-	0				√	√		0
	30.0					0.0						

Ontario

		Groomed Trails										
Trail Fee	Total	●	■	◆	Skating	Ungroomed	Lodge	Wax Room	Rentals	Food	Lesons	Shelters

111 Deep River Cross Country, Deep River; PO Box 1222, Deep River, K0J 1P0
Groomed trails in town. Wilderness trails in Algonquin park.

Trail Fee	Total	●	■	◆	Skating	Ungroomed	Lodge	Wax Room	Rentals	Food	Lesons	Shelters
NC	-	-	-			-	√					0
	25.0					100.0						

112 Forest Lea X-C Ski Trail, Pembrooke
(613) 732-3661; PO Box 220, Pembrooke, K8A 6X4
13 km W on Forest Lea Rd (Alice Township Rd 14).

Trail Fee	Total	●	■	◆	Skating	Ungroomed	Lodge	Wax Room	Rentals	Food	Lesons	Shelters
NA	5	-	-			0						0
	12.0					0.0						

113 Nangor Resort, Westmeath
(613) 587-4456 ; PO Box 3, Westmeath, K0J 2L0. Bar

Trail Fee	Total	●	■	◆	Skating	Ungroomed	Lodge	Wax Room	Rentals	Food	Lesons	Shelters
Yes	4	-	-			√	√	√	√			0
	30.0					0.0						

114 Petawawa Ski Club, Petawawa

Hwy 17 to Larentian Dr. Pembrooke.

Trail Fee	Total	●	■	◆	Skating	Ungroomed	Lodge	Wax Room	Rentals	Food	Lesons	Shelters
Yes	2	-	-			0	√	√		√		0
	7.0					0.0						

115 Bon Echo Provincial Park, Cloyne
(613) 336-2228; RR 1, Cloyne, K0H 1K0
10 km N of Cloyne on Hwy 41.

Trail Fee	Total	●	■	◆	Skating	Ungroomed	Lodge	Wax Room	Rentals	Food	Lesons	Shelters
6⁰⁰	2	0	2	0		0						0
car	10.0		10.0			0.0						

116 Vanderwater Conservation Area, Belleville
(613) 968-3434; Moira River Cons. Authourity, PO Box 698, Belleville, K8N 5B3
Hwy 37 to Thomasburg,4 Turn E, follow signs. (1/2 hr N of Belleville)
One extended loop along Moira River. Two cutoffs make shorter loops.

Trail Fee	Total	●	■	◆	Skating	Ungroomed	Lodge	Wax Room	Rentals	Food	Lesons	Shelters
2⁰⁰	3	1	2	0		0						0
1⁰⁰ C	15.0	1.8	12.7			0.0						

117 Quinte Conservation Area, Belleville
(613) 968-3434; Moira River Cons. Authourity, PO Box 698, Belleville, K8N 5B3
2 min. W of Belleville on Hwy 2. Corner Wallbridge- Loyalist Rd & Hwy 2.
Flat terrain through old apple orchard, red cedar mixed forest & pasture.

Trail Fee	Total	●	■	◆	Skating	Ungroomed	Lodge	Wax Room	Rentals	Food	Lesons	Shelters
2⁰⁰	3	3	0	0		0						0
1⁰⁰ C	5.0	5.0				0.0						

Ontario

Groomed Trails

Trail Fee / Total	●	■	◆	Skating	Ungroomed	Lodge	Wax Room	Rentals	Food	Lessons	Shelters

118 Sandbanks Provincial Park, Picton

(613) 393-3319; RR 1, Picton, K0K 2T0
18 km SW of Picton on County Rd 12.
Closely linked network of trails near shores of Lake Ontario.

Trail Fee	Total	●	■	◆	Skating	Ungroomed	Lodge	Wax Room	Rentals	Food	Lessons	Shelters
DA	9	9	0	0		0	√					0
	12.0	12.0				0.0						

119 Macauly Mountain Conservation Area, Picton

(613) 476-7408; Prince Edward Region Cons. Authority, PO Box 310, Union St., Picton, K0K 2T0
2 km E of Picton on Waupoos Rd. (County Rd 8).

Trail Fee	Total	●	■	◆	Skating	Ungroomed	Lodge	Wax Room	Rentals	Food	Lessons	Shelters
NC	1	0	1	0		0						0
	11.0		11.0			0.0						

120 Little Cataraqui Creek Conservation Area, Glenburnie

(613) 546-4228; Little Cataraqui Cons. Authority, Box 160, Glenburnie, K0H 1S0
Hwy 401 exit 617 Kingston 2 km N on Hwy 10.
Marshes, fields and forests.

Trail Fee	Total	●	■	◆	Skating	Ungroomed	Lodge	Wax Room	Rentals	Food	Lessons	Shelters
6⁰⁰	4	2	1	1		0	√	√	√	√		0
car	13.0	3.1	6.7	3.1		0.0						

121 Frontenac Provincial Park, Sydenham

(613) 376-3489; PO Box 11, Sydenham, K0H 2T0
12 km N of Sydenham on city Rd 19.
Diverse environment of lakes, cliffs, swamps and upland forests.

Trail Fee	Total	●	■	◆	Skating	Ungroomed	Lodge	Wax Room	Rentals	Food	Lessons	Shelters
6⁰⁰	0	-	-	-		-	√					0
car	0.0					160.0						

122 Foley Mountain Conservation Area, Westport

(613) 273-3255; Rideau Valley Cons. Authority, PO Box 244, Westport, K0G 1X0
1 km N of Westport on County Rd 10.

Trail Fee	Total	●	■	◆	Skating	Ungroomed	Lodge	Wax Room	Rentals	Food	Lessons	Shelters
6⁰⁰	2	0	1	1		1						0
car	4.0		2.0	2.0		1.5						

123 Mount Pakenham, Pakenham

(613) 624-5290, (613) 624-5672 (tape), 1-800-665-7105 (Ottawa area)
PO Box 190, Pakenham, K0A 2X0
30 minutes W of Ottawa on Hwy 417 Bar

Trail Fee	Total	●	■	◆	Skating	Ungroomed	Lodge	Wax Room	Rentals	Food	Lessons	Shelters
6⁰⁰	8	4	4	0		5	√	√	√	√	√	2
	16.0	8.0	8.0			15.0						

195

Trail Fee	Total	Groomed Trails ● ■ ◆			Skating	Ungroomed	Lodge	Wax Room	Rentals	Food	Lessons	Shelters

124 Murphy's Point Provincial Park, Perth

(613) 267-5060; RR #5, Perth, K7H 3C7
14 km E of Perth on Lanark County Rd 1 then 14 km S on County Rd 21.
Mainly linked loops..

Trail Fee	Total	●	■	◆	Ungroomed	Lodge	Wax Room	Food	Shelters
5⁰⁰	4	0	4	0	0	√	√		0
car	25.0		25.0		0.0				

125 Triangle Cross-Country Ski Club, Brockville

Triangle Cross-Country Ski Club of Brockville, PO Box 1277, Brockville, K6V 5W2
Hwy 401 exit 675, N on County Rd #5 to McIntosh Mill, follow sign.
Frontenac Axis: granite rock valleys, hardwood trees, ponds, deer yards.

Trail Fee	Total	●	■	◆	Ungroomed	Lodge	Wax Room	Food	Shelters
5⁰⁰	-	-	-	-	8	√	√	√	2
	24.0	8.0	8.0	8.0	2.0 18.0				

126 Gordon MacCormack Maitland Trails, Maitland

(613) 348-3993; PO Box 189, Maitland, K0E 1P0
At Maitland Recreation Centre. 8 km perimeter trail with secondary trails.

Trail Fee	Total	●	■	◆	Ungroomed	Shelters
NC	4	-	-	-	0	0
	15.0				0.0	

127 Upper Canada Bird Sanctuary Parks of the St. Lawrence, Morrisburg

(613) 543-3704; Parks of the St. Lawrence, RR 1, Morrisburg, K0C 1X0
14 km E of Morrisburg on Hwy 2 or 4 km E of Ingleside.

Trail Fee	Total	●	■	◆	Ungroomed	Shelters
NC	3	3	0	0	0	0
	10.0	10.0			0.0	

128 Carillon Provincial Park, Chute-a-Blondeau

(613) 674-2825; PO Box 130, Chute-a-Blondeau, K0B 1B0

Trail Fee	Total	●	■	◆	Ungroomed	Shelters
NA	3	-	-	-	0	0
	12.0				0.0	

Ontario

18 Quebec

Quebec is doubly blessed, with both excellent ski terrain and bountiful snow. Some of the biggest and best cross-country ski areas in the country are found in Quebec, from the Gatineau Park, north of Hull to Mont-Sainte-Anne. Should you ever tire of what Quebec has to offer, there are plenty more ski areas within an hour's drive south of the border.

Backcountry enthusiasts are also well-provided for with a plethora of trails. Thanks to the tireless efforts of Jackrabbit Johannsen, who pioneered the first trails, there are dozens of trails linking towns and ski centres in the Laurentians north of Montreal. Many provincial parks and reserves rent huts for overnight sojourns. Backcountry skiers from all over the east are enticed to the Chic-Choc mountains in the Gaspé.

The *joie de vivre* of the francophone population adds an extra flavour to ski trips in this province. Tourists should have no communication problems in the southwest where most people are bilingual. In other regions, most people speak French only.

One caveat is that most of Quebec's privately-operated ski areas include a lot of overlap in the calculation of the total length of their trails. The totals given by some operators are more than double that obtained without overlap.

Travel Information

Road report: (514) 873-4121.

Tourist Information Bureau
Tourisme Quebec publishes separate four-season guides in both official languages for each of the 19 tourism regions of the province. PO Box 979, Montreal, Quebec H3C 2W3;
(514) 873-2015 (Montreal); 1-800-363-7777 (Canada and USA)

Ski report: Friday edition of *The Gazette*

Weather Report: Environment Canada (514) 283-4006.

Cross Country Skiing Organizations

Ski de Fond Quebec, Quebec division of Cross Country Canada, and **Biathlon Quebec** and **CANSI Quebec** are all located in the Big Owe at 4545 ave. Pierre de Coubertin, C.P. 1000, Succ. M, Montreal, QC H1V 3R2; (514) 252-3089; fax: (514) 254-1499

Winter Climate

In southern Quebec the ski season generally starts in mid-December and lasts until about late March. Parc de la Gaspésie and nothern regions have a longer season.

Average Temperatures   Average Snowfall

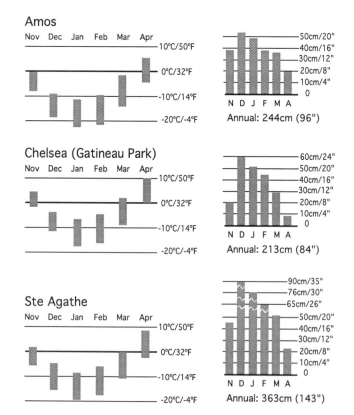

Amos
Annual: 244cm (96")

Chelsea (Gatineau Park)
Annual: 213cm (84")

Ste Agathe
Annual: 363cm (143")

Quebec

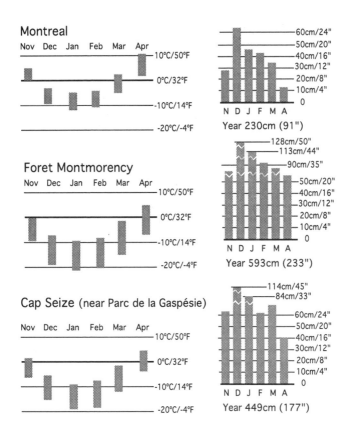

Montreal

Year 230cm (91")

Foret Montmorency

Year 593cm (233")

Cap Seize (near Parc de la Gaspésie)

Year 449cm (177")

Loppets

Date	Event	Location
late Jan	Grand fond (42k)	Rimouski
late Jan	Defi Yves Carbonneau	Mont Orford
late Jan	Peter Austin Classic (20k)	St-Jovite
early Feb	Loppet Mont Orford (30k)	Mont Orford
early Feb	Marathon de la vallée (40k)	Gaspésie
early Feb	Canadian Ski Marathon (160k)	Lachute/Gatineau
mid Feb	30-km Mouski	Val-Neigette
mid Feb	Keskinada World Loppet (50k)	Gatineau Park
late Feb	Viking Loppet (50k)	Viking Club
late Feb	Bec-Scie	La Baie
early Mar	*La Loppet Mont-Ste-Anne (65k)	Mont-Ste-Anne
mid Mar	Tour de Mont-Valin (55k)	Mont-Valin

*Canadian Ski Odyssey

Quebec

Quebec

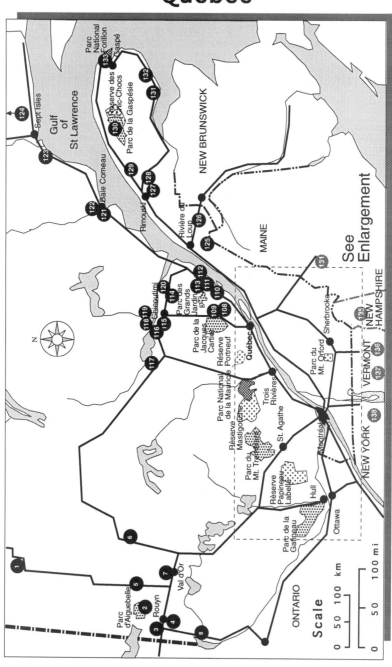

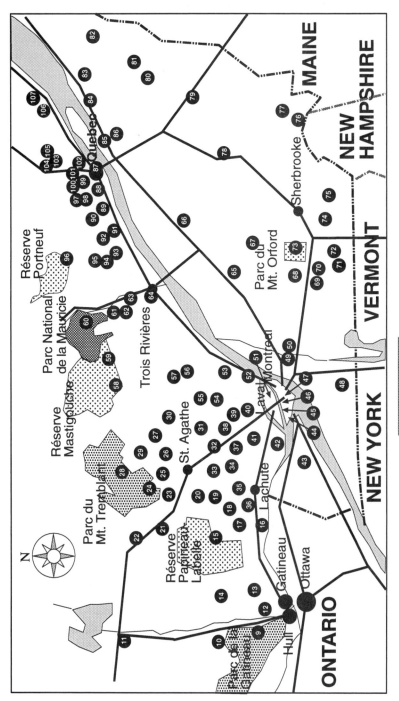

Cross Country Ski Areas

Quebec

Quebec

Groomed Trails

Column headers (left to right): Trail Fee | Total | ● | ■ | ◆ | Skating | Ungroomed | Lodge | Wax Room | Rentals | Food | Lessons | Shelters

1 Club de ski de fond Nordic, Matagami
(819) 739-2030

Trail Fee	Total	●	■	◆	Skating	Ungroomed	Lodge	Wax Room	Rentals	Food	Lessons	Shelters
5⁰⁰	6	0	6	0		0	√	√				0
	20.0	20.0				0.0						

2 Parc d'Aiguebelle, Rouyn-Noranda
(819) 762-8154; Bureau 104, 180 boul. Rideau, Rouyn-Noranda, J9X 1N9
Approx 10 km N of Saint-Norbert-de-Mont-Brun in park. Open Fri-Sun 10am-4:30
Interesting rock formations (kettles, eskers, etc.) over 2 billion yrs old.

Trail Fee	Total	●	■	◆	Skating	Ungroomed	Lodge	Wax Room	Rentals	Food	Lessons	Shelters
3⁰⁰	8	8	0	0		0						7
	32.0	32.0				0.0						

3 Club de ski de fond d'Evian, Evian
(819) 768-2591; 450 rue de l'eglise, Evian, J0Z 1Y0
450 rue de l'eglise, Evian. Open Wednesday to Sunday.

Trail Fee	Total	●	■	◆	Skating	Ungroomed	Lodge	Wax Room	Rentals	Food	Lessons	Shelters
7⁰⁰	18	7	4	7		0	√	√		√		0
	40.0					0.0						

4 Club de ski de fond de Granada, Granada
(819) 762-1037
40 Rang 2-3 Est South of Rouyn.
Open 1-4:30pm Mon to Tues, 10am-4:30pm Wed to Sun.

Trail Fee	Total	●	■	◆	Skating	Ungroomed	Lodge	Wax Room	Rentals	Food	Lessons	Shelters
3⁰⁰	5	3	1	1		0	√	√	√	√		2
	18.0					0.0						

5 Les Pieds Fartés, Amos
(819) 732-8435
Approx 6 km W of Amos on Hwy 395.

Trail Fee	Total	●	■	◆	Skating	Ungroomed	Lodge	Wax Room	Rentals	Food	Lessons	Shelters
5⁰⁰	11	2	6	3		0	√	√		√		3
	54.0				7	0.0						

6 Club 2 Temps, Lebel-sur-Quevillon
(819) 755-4157
Boulevard Quevillon Open 1 to 5 pm weekdays, 10am to 5pm weekends.

Trail Fee	Total	●	■	◆	Skating	Ungroomed	Lodge	Wax Room	Rentals	Food	Lessons	Shelters
5⁰⁰	7	4	2	1		0	√	√	√	√		0
	25.0					0.0						

Quebec

Groomed Trails

Trail Fee | Total | ● | ■ | ◆ | Skating | Ungroomed | Lodge | Wax Room | Rentals | Food | Lessons | Shelters

7 Club de ski de fond de Val d'Or, Val d'Or
(819) 825-4398
Chemin de l'areoport in Val-d'Or.
4 km lit trail for night skiing. Open 12 to 9pm weekdays, 10am to 9 pm weekends.

Trail Fee	Total	●	■	◆	Skating	Ungroomed	Lodge	Wax Room	Rentals	Food	Lessons	Shelters
6⁰⁰	10	4	4	2		0	√	√	√	√		0
	50.0					0.0						

8 Domaine de la Baie Gillies, Fugereville
(819) 747-2548
Four-season outdoor recreation center with rooms & dormitory for rent.

Trail Fee	Total	●	■	◆	Skating	Ungroomed	Lodge	Wax Room	Rentals	Food	Lessons	Shelters
6⁰⁰	8	1	4	3		0	√		√	√		1
	20.0					0.0						

9 Parc de la Gatineau, Old Chelsea

(819) 827-2020, 1-800-465-1867 (Ont, Que); c/o National Capital Commision, Old Chelsea, J0X 1N0
N of Hull on Chemin de la Mine (4 accesses) OR near Old Chelsea (9 accesses).
Excellent variety of trails; some views; huts for rent. Host of Keskinada Worldloppet.

Trail Fee	Total	●	■	◆	Skating	Ungroomed	Lodge	Wax Room	Rentals	Food	Lessons	Shelters
7⁰⁰	40	15	11	14		0	√		√	√	√	11
	185.0					0.0						

10 Edielweiss Ski Center, Wakefield

(819) 459-2328

Trail Fee	Total	●	■	◆	Skating	Ungroomed	Lodge	Wax Room	Rentals	Food	Lessons	Shelters
NC	1	1	0	0		0	√	√	√	√		0
	25.0					0.0						

11 Club de ski de fond Ferme-Neuve, Ferme-Neuve
(819) 587-3101

Trail Fee	Total	●	■	◆	Skating	Ungroomed	Lodge	Wax Room	Rentals	Food	Lessons	Shelters
3⁰⁰	8	3	3	2		0	√	√		√		0
	70.0					0.0						

12 Nakkertok Ski Club, Cantley
(613) 824-0591
Hwy 50 N of Gatineau exit at Laverendrye in Cantley. Go to end of ave Gatineau.
Trails are for MEMBERS ONLY. Trailside cabins can be rented for overnight.

Trail Fee	Total	●	■	◆	Skating	Ungroomed	Lodge	Wax Room	Rentals	Food	Lessons	Shelters
MO	7	-	-	-		0	√	√				4
	50.0	15.0	15.0	20.0		0.0						

Groomed Trails

Column headers: Trail Fee | Total | ● | ■ | ◆ | Skating | Ungroomed | Lodge | Wax Room | Rentals | Food | Lesons | Shelters

13 Base de Plein-Air des Outaouais, Poltimore

(819) 423-6692; chemin des Voyageurs, Poltimore, J0X 2S0
On rue des Voyageurs in Poltimore.
An 80-bed outdoor recreation center for year-round activities. Bar

Trail Fee	Total	●	■	◆	Skating	Ungroomed	Lodge	Wax Room	Rentals	Food	Lesons	Shelters
6^{50}	6	2	2	2		0					√	1
	43.0					0.0						

14 Centre de ski Mont Sainte-Marie, Mont Sainte-Marie

(819) 467-5200, 1-800-567-1256; rue du Lac Sainte-Marie, Mont Sainte-Marie, J0X 1X0
Approx 10 km E of Lac-Sainte-Marie at alpine ski center.

Trail Fee	Total	●	■	◆	Skating	Ungroomed	Lodge	Wax Room	Rentals	Food	Lesons	Shelters
Yes	-	-	-	-		0						0
	25.0					0.0						

15 Reserve faunique de Papineau-Labelle, Duhamel

(819) 454-2013; Reserve faunique de Papineau-Labelle, Accueil Gagnon, Duhamel, J0X 3C0
15 km N of Duhamel on Hwy 321.
Trails are intermediate to advanced. Backcountry huts can be rented.

Trail Fee	Total	●	■	◆	Skating	Ungroomed	Lodge	Wax Room	Rentals	Food	Lesons	Shelters
5^{00}	0					1						11
	0.0					94.0						

16 Chateau Montebello, Montebello

(819) 423-6341, 1-800-441-1414; 392 rue Notre-Dame, Montebello, J0V 1L0
Hwy 148 on W side of Montebello.
World's largest log structure and host of the Canadian Ski Marathon.
Linked with municipal trails. Daycare, bar, 210-room luxury hotel.

Trail Fee	Total	●	■	◆	Skating	Ungroomed	Lodge	Wax Room	Rentals	Food	Lesons	Shelters
6^{00}	8	3	3	2		0	√	√	√	√		0
	27.0	7.9	9.8	9.4		0.0						

17 Auberge Suisse Montevilla/Montebello municipal trails

(819) 423-6692, 1-800-363-0061; 970 Montevilla, Montebello, J0V 1L0
At north end of town of Montebello. 1 km lighted trail. 5 chalets

Trail Fee	Total	●	■	◆	Skating	Ungroomed	Lodge	Wax Room	Rentals	Food	Lesons	Shelters
6^{00}	7	2	3	2		0				√		0
	41.0	8.0	17.0	16.0		0.0						

18 Centre Touristique de la Petite-Rouge, St-Emile-de-Suffolk

(819) 426-2191; 65 rue des Pruniers, St-Emile-de-Suffolk, J0V 1Y0
Hwy 323 to Saint-Emile-de-Suffolk.
Center specializes in hosting groups. Bar, chalets (124 beds)

Trail Fee	Total	●	■	◆	Skating	Ungroomed	Lodge	Wax Room	Rentals	Food	Lesons	Shelters
5^{00}	5	1	2	2		0	√	√	√	√		2
10^{00}F	30.0					0.0						

Quebec

Trail Fee	Total	Groomed Trails ●	■	◆	Skating	Ungroomed	Lodge	Wax Room	Rentals	Food	Lessons	Shelters

19 Hotel mon Chez-Nous, Lac des Plages
(819) 426-2186
Hwy 323 at Lac des Plages. Hotel has 38 rooms

Trail Fee	Total	●	■	◆	Skating	Ungroomed	Lodge	Wax Room	Rentals	Food	Lessons	Shelters
3^{00}	5	2	3	0		0	√	√		√		2
	30.0					0.0						

20 Huberdeau
Auberge du Lac à la Loutre: (819) 687-8888; 122 chemin Trudel, Huberdeau, J0T 1G0
At N end of town of Huberdeau. Single track loop trails, some challenging hills.

Trail Fee	Total	●	■	◆	Skating	Ungroomed	Lodge	Wax Room	Rentals	Food	Lessons	Shelters
3^{00}	10	2	3	5		0	√			√		1
	30.0	6.0	15.0	10.0		0.0						

21 Club de ski de fond Labelle, Labelle
(819) 686-2431; rue Belle-Pente, Labelle, J0T 1H0
A few km W of Labelle on S shore of Lac Labelle.

Trail Fee	Total	●	■	◆	Skating	Ungroomed	Lodge	Wax Room	Rentals	Food	Lessons	Shelters
3^{50}	5	1	3	1		0	√	√	√	√		0
	40.0					0.0						

22 Club de Six Cantons, l'Annociation
(819) 275-1303; CP 802, L'Annociation, QC J0T 1T0
4.5 km E of l'Annociation on Route de la Macaza

Trail Fee	Total	●	■	◆	Skating	Ungroomed	Lodge	Wax Room	Rentals	Food	Lessons	Shelters
5^{00}	6	2	4	0		0						3
	50.0					0.0						

23 Centre de ski de fond Mont Tremblant/Saint-Jovite, St-Jovite
(819) 425-5588; C.P. 203, Mont-Tremblant, J0T 1Z0
Just N of St. Jovite and at base of Mont Tremblant alpine ski center.
Trails are around the townsite so they cross a lot of streets. Near all services.

Trail Fee	Total	●	■	◆	Skating	Ungroomed	Lodge	Wax Room	Rentals	Food	Lessons	Shelters
6^{00}	35	5	20	11		0	√	√	√	√		0
	100.0				10.0	0.0						

24 Parc du Mont Tremblant western sector (Lac-Monroe), Lac-Superieur ▲
(819) 688-2281/6176; C.P. H5 Chemin Lac Superieur, Lac-Superieur, J0T 1P0
Approx 10 km N of Lac Superieur. Good early-season snow.
50-km & 33-km loops (see backcountry section). Bar

Trail Fee	Total	●	■	◆	Skating	Ungroomed	Lodge	Wax Room	Rentals	Food	Lessons	Shelters
5^{25}	8	4	1	3	2		√	√	√	√	√	7
	56.0	20.5	8.2	19.4	10	77.0						

25 Base de plein air Le Petit Bonheur, Lac Superieur
(819) 326-4281, (514) 875-5555, 1-800-567-6788 (Quebec)
1400 chemin du Lac-Quenouille, Lac Superieur, J0T 1P0
Approx 5 km N of Lac Carre towards Lac Superieur turn E at sign.
A 4-season family and group outdoor center with 450 beds.

Trail Fee	Total	●	■	◆	Skating	Ungroomed	Lodge	Wax Room	Rentals	Food	Lessons	Shelters
7^{00}	8	2	3	3		0	√	√	√	√		0
	45.0	10.8	11.0	18.0		0.0						

Quebec

Column headers: Trail Fee | Total | ● ■ ◆ (Groomed Trails) | Skating | Ungroomed | Lodge | Wax Room | Rentals | Food | Lessons | Shelters

26 Parc des campeurs, Sainte-Agathe
(819) 324-0482
Exit 83 off Hwy 15, go W to Hwy 329 at Lac des Sables.

Trail Fee	Total	●	■	◆	Skating	Ungroomed	Lodge	Wax Room	Rentals	Food	Lessons	Shelters
3^{00}	4	1	1	3	0		√	√	√	√		0
	27.0	3.0	5.0	19.0	0.0							

27 Centre de ski de fond l'Estérel, Ville d'Estérel

Hotel: (514) 228-2571; 1-800-363-3623; 39 boul. Fridolin-Simard, Ville de l'Esterel, J0T 1E0
Exit 69 off Hwy 15, then about 15 km N on Hwy 370 to l'Estérel.
A full-service resort with indoor pool, saunas, gym, bar, 135-rooms.

Trail Fee	Total	●	■	◆	Skating	Ungroomed	Lodge	Wax Room	Rentals	Food	Lessons	Shelters
5^{00}	13	4	5	4		1	√	√	√	√	√	0
	55.0	9.0	13.6	25.6	18.0	11.0						

28 Parc du Mont-Tremblant, east sector (La Pimbina), Saint-Donat
(819) 424-2954 /2833; Route 125 nord, Saint-Donat, J0T 2C0
10 km N of St. Donat on Hwy 125.
Backcountry trails connecting with Lac Monroe for multi-day trips are difficult.

Trail Fee	Total	●	■	◆	Skating	Ungroomed	Lodge	Wax Room	Rentals	Food	Lessons	Shelters
6^{00}	7	4	2	1		2	√	√				3
	32.0	12.1	13.0	6.3		20.0						

29 Club de ski de fond de Saint-Donat, Saint-Donat
(819) 424-7012; C.P. 129, Saint-Donat, J0T 2C0
Three areas: La Donatienne, Vue des Cimes and Montagne Noir.

Trail Fee	Total	●	■	◆	Skating	Ungroomed	Lodge	Wax Room	Rentals	Food	Lessons	Shelters
NC	4	2	1	1	0							0
	32.0				0.0							

30 Base de plein air l'Interval, Sainte-Lucie-des-Larentides
(819) 326-4069; 3565, 91e Avenue, Sainte-Lucie-des-Laurentides, J0T 2J0
Approx 5 km N of Sainte-Lucie-des-Larentides on S shore of Lake Legault.
Beautiful views from the top of Mt. Legault. 88-bed outdoor centre.

Trail Fee	Total	●	■	◆	Skating	Ungroomed	Lodge	Wax Room	Rentals	Food	Lessons	Shelters
3^{50}	0					10	√	√		√		0
	0.0					45.0						

31 Station touristique Val-David/Val-Morin (Far Hills), Val David
Far Hills Inn: (819) 322-2014, (514) 866-2219 (Montreal), 1-800-567-6636
Far Hills Inn, 2510 rue de l'eglise #2, Val David, J0T 2N0
Exit 76 off Hwy 15, follow signs to Far Hills, Val-Morin or Val-David.
Includes Far Hills ski centre, linked to the Petit Train linear park. Bar, inns

Trail Fee	Total	●	■	◆	Skating	Ungroomed	Lodge	Wax Room	Rentals	Food	Lessons	Shelters
8^{00}	21	10	7	4		4	√	√	√	√	√	0
	130.0				18.0	10.0						

Quebec

		Groomed Trails										
Trail Fee	Total	●	■	◆	Skating	Ungroomed	Lodge	Wax Room	Rentals	Food	Lessons	Shelters

32 Centre de plein air Sainte-Adèle, Sainte-Adèle

(514) 229-2921, ext 207 (tourist bureau); (514) 229-3555 (Chantercler)
Network of trails around Ste-Adèle, Chanteler alpine ski center and golf course.
Pick up trail maps at tourist bureau or Chantecler.

Trail Fee	Total	●	■	◆	Skating	Ungroomed	Lodge	Wax Room	Rentals	Food	Lessons	Shelters
NC	25	8	12	5		0						0
	60.0					0.0						

33 Miramont-sur-la-lac, St-Adolphe-d'Howard

(819) 327-3330, (514) 875-9042, 1-800-567-6707 (Que, Ont)
Approx 4 km N of Saint-Adolphe-d'Howard on Hwy 329. 3199 chemin du Village, St-Adolphe,J0T 2B0
Full-service resort with indoor pool, bar, condos, chalets.

Trail Fee	Total	●	■	◆	Skating	Ungroomed	Lodge	Wax Room	Rentals	Food	Lessons	Shelters
NC	3	0	2	1		0			√	√		0
	30.0					0.0						

34 Centre de ski de fond de Morin-Heights/Viking Ski Club Trails, Morin-Heights

(514) 226-2417; Centre de ski, 612, rue du Village, Morin-Heights, J0R 1H0
Hwy 364 to Morin Heights, at E side of town turn N at sign for ski centre.
Trails are single-tracked except 10 km aerobic corridor link with Viking trails.
Non-members are permitted on Viking trails but not in chalet or parking lot.

Trail Fee	Total	●	■	◆	Skating	Ungroomed	Lodge	Wax Room	Rentals	Food	Lessons	Shelters
6⁰⁰	14	6	6	2		-	√	√		√	√	0
	75.0	24.0	23.0	9.0	10.0	75.0						

35 Centre de ski de fond La Randonnée, Brownsburg

(514) 533-6687; 300, rue Hotel-de-ville, Brownsburg, J0V 1A0
Rue Principale in Brownsburg.

Trail Fee	Total	●	■	◆	Skating	Ungroomed	Lodge	Wax Room	Rentals	Food	Lessons	Shelters
5⁰⁰	9	1	7	1		0	√					0
	24.0		13.0			0.0						

36 Club de Montagne d'Argenteuil (Rivière Rouge), Calumet

(819) 242-2168; C.P. 612, Calumet, J0V 1J0
Approx 1 km W of Grenville on Hwy 148, turn N on Kilmar Road, go about 2 km.
Chalet is base for white-water rafting in summer. Views of the Rivière Rouge. Bar

Trail Fee	Total	●	■	◆	Skating	Ungroomed	Lodge	Wax Room	Rentals	Food	Lessons	Shelters
7⁰⁰	12	6	3	3		0	√	√	√	√	√	0
1⁰⁰ C	53.0	16.8	12.3	24.0	17	0.0						

37 Centre de ski de fond Gai-Luron, Bellefeuille

(819) 224-5302; 1435, montée Sainte-Therese, Bellefeuille, J0R 1A0
Exit 45 off Hwy 15 at St. Jérome, W across overpass, N on country road. Bar

Trail Fee	Total	●	■	◆	Skating	Ungroomed	Lodge	Wax Room	Rentals	Food	Lessons	Shelters
6⁰⁰	6	2	3	1		0	√	√	√	√		0
	28.0					0.0						

Groomed Trails

| Trail Fee | Total | ● | ■ | ◆ | Skating | Ungroomed | Lodge | Wax Room | Rentals | Food | Lesons | Shelters |

Quebec

38 Club de ski de fond Mt Rolland, Mont-Rolland

Hotel des monts: (514) 229-4980; 1340 rue Saint-Joseph, Mont-Rolland, J0R 1G0
Exit 67 off Hwy 15 to Mont-Rolland. Maps available at Hotel des Monts.
Connected to linear park and BC long-distance trails such as the Johannsen.

Trail Fee	Total	●	■	◆	Skating	Ungroomed	Lodge	Wax Room	Rentals	Food	Lesons	Shelters
NC	9	2	6	1		-				√		0
	50.0	12.0	32.5	2.3		Yes						

39 Parc lineaire le Petit Train du Nord, Saint-Jérome to Val-David

Tourist Bureau: (514) 436-4051 (St-Jerome), (514) 990-5625 (Montreal)
300, rue Longpre, #110, Saint-Jerome, J7T 3B9
Linear park linking St.-Jérome, Prévost, Mont-Rolland and Val-David.
Trail is a converted railway bed so is straight and flat. Services available at several towns.

Trail Fee	Total	●	■	◆	Skating	Ungroomed	Lodge	Wax Room	Rentals	Food	Lesons	Shelters
3⁰⁰	1	1	0	0		0	√		√	√		2
	45.0	45.0				45.0	0.0					

40 Parc regional de la Riviere-du-Nord, Saint-Jérome

(514) 431-1676; 1051 boul. International, RR#2, Saint-Jerome, J7Z 5T5
Exit 45 off Hwy 15 at St. Jérome then N to park.
Winter hiking, nature interpretation centre, waterfalls. Located on linear park.

Trail Fee	Total	●	■	◆	Skating	Ungroomed	Lodge	Wax Room	Rentals	Food	Lesons	Shelters
3⁰⁰	12	9	3	0		0	√	√		√		0
car	28.0					9.0	0.0					

41 Parc du Domaine Vert, Mirabel

(514) 435-6510; 10423, montee Sainte-Marianne, Mirabel, J7E 4H5
Exit 23 off Hwy 15 then W for approx 1 km, then N to the park.
Regional park with lots of easy trails, chalet, trailside cabins and horseback riding.

Trail Fee	Total	●	■	◆	Skating	Ungroomed	Lodge	Wax Room	Rentals	Food	Lesons	Shelters
6²⁵	9	7	1	1		0	√	√	√	√		1
	50.0					10.0	0.0					

42 Parc d'Oka, Oka

(514) 479-8337; 2020 chemin d'Oka, C.P. 1200, Oka, J0N 1E0
1 km E of Oka on Hwy 344.
Easy lakeside trails and some more challenging hillside trails.

Trail Fee	Total	●	■	◆	Skating	Ungroomed	Lodge	Wax Room	Rentals	Food	Lesons	Shelters
6⁷⁵	7	3	2	2		0	√	√	√	√	√	4
	53.0	37.0	3.0	13.0		26.0	0.0					

43 Centre de plein air Les Forestiers, Saint-Clet

(514) 452-4736; Centre de plein air Les Forestiers, Les Cedres, J0P 1L0
Hwy 340 W of Vaudreuil at 1677 chemin St-Dominique.

Trail Fee	Total	●	■	◆	Skating	Ungroomed	Lodge	Wax Room	Rentals	Food	Lesons	Shelters
7⁰⁰	9	1	8	0		0	√	√	√	R	R	1
	48.0					0.5	0.0					

Groomed Trails — Trail Fee | Total | ● | ■ | ◆ | Skating | Ungroomed | Lodge | Wax Room | Rentals | Food | Lessons | Shelters

44 Parc du Cap St Jacques, Montréal
(514) 280-6871
20099 Gouin Blvd West in Pierrefonds in the NW corner of Montreal.
Some nature trails are plowed for winter walking.

Trail Fee	Total	●	■	◆	Skating	Ungroomed	Lodge	Wax Room	Rentals	Food	Lessons	Shelters
NC	4	4	0	0		0	√	√		√			0
	27.0	27.0				0.0							

45 Parc régional du Bois-d'Ile-Bizard, Montréal
(514) 280-6784
At 2115 chemin Bord-du-Lac on Ile-Bizard.

Trail Fee	Total	●	■	◆	Skating	Ungroomed	Lodge	Wax Room	Rentals	Food	Lessons	Shelters
NC	3	-	-	-		0	E						0
	17.5				2.0	0.0							

46 Parc régional du Bois-de-Liesse, Montréal
(514) 280-6729
9432 Gouin Blvd West near Hwy 13.
Nature trails are cleared for walking in winter.

Trail Fee	Total	●	■	◆	Skating	Ungroomed	Lodge	Wax Room	Rentals	Food	Lessons	Shelters
NC	4	4	0	0		0	√						0
	22.0	22.0				0.0							

47 Parc du Mont-Royal, Montreal
(514) 872-2644; Lessons (City of Montreal): (514) 722-8149
Corner of Aves Parc and Mount Royal or at Beaver Lake (meter parking)
Ski trails up and around Mt. Royal are within a kilometre of downtown.

Trail Fee	Total	●	■	◆	Skating	Ungroomed	Lodge	Wax Room	Rentals	Food	Lessons	Shelters
NC	3	2	1	0		0	√			√	√		0
	12.0	7.0	5.0			0.0							

48 Parc régional écologique et recreatif de Saint-Bernard, St-Bernard-de-Lacolle
(514) 246-3348; 219 rang Saint-Andre, St-Bernard-de-Lacolle, J0J 1V0
2 km S of Hwy 202 on Hwy 217.

Trail Fee	Total	●	■	◆	Skating	Ungroomed	Lodge	Wax Room	Rentals	Food	Lessons	Shelters
NC	5	3	1	1		0	√						0
	12.0	9.2	1.5	1.3		0.0							

49 Parc du Mont Saint-Bruno, Saint-Bruno-de-Montarville
(514) 653-7544; 330, rang des Vingt-Cinq Est, Saint-Bruno-de-Montarville, J3V 4P6
Exit 102 off Hwy 20, then S on chemin des 25 to park. Parking costs $3.25.
Views of Montreal and the St. Lawrence valley. Old mill and lakes.

Trail Fee	Total	●	■	◆	Skating	Ungroomed	Lodge	Wax Room	Rentals	Food	Lessons	Shelters
6²⁵	9	4	4	1		0	√	√		√	√		1
+prkg	27.0	7.0	16.0	2.0	Yes	0.0							

Groomed Trails

Trail Fee	Total	●	■	◆	Skating	Ungroomed	Lodge	Wax Room	Rentals	Food	Lesons	Shelters

50 Centre de conservation de la nature Mont-Saint-Hilaire

(514) 467-1755 ; 422, chemin des Moulins, Mont-Saint-Hilaire, J3G 4S6
Exit 113 off Hwy 20, then S to Mt. St. Hilaire, follow signs to centre.
Views of Montreal and the St. Lawrence valley. Ungroomed trails are quite steep.

Trail Fee	Total	●	■	◆	Skating	Ungroomed	Lodge	Wax Room	Rentals	Food	Lesons	Shelters
4^{00}	3	1	1	1		2	√	√		√		0
2^{00} C	8.0					7.0						

51 Bois Duvernay, Laval
(514) 662-4906
2830 blvd Saint-Elzéar in Laval.

Trail Fee	Total	●	■	◆	Skating	Ungroomed	Lodge	Wax Room	Rentals	Food	Lesons	Shelters
NC	-	-	-	-		0	√					0
	20.0					0.0						

52 Les sentiers de la Presqu'ile, Le Gardeur
(514) 585-8015 / 0121; 2001 rue Jean-Pierre, Le Gardeur, J6A 1N4
2001, rue Jean-Pierre in Le Gardeur.

Trail Fee	Total	●	■	◆	Skating	Ungroomed	Lodge	Wax Room	Rentals	Food	Lesons	Shelters
7^{00}	9	6	2	1		0	√	√	√	√	√	1
	45.0					0.0						

53 Chez Ti-Jean ski de fond, L'Epiphanie
(514) 588-5980; 825, rang Petit-Saint-Esprit, L'Epiphanie, J0K 1J0
At 825, rang Petit-St-Esprit in L'Epiphanie.

Trail Fee	Total	●	■	◆	Skating	Ungroomed	Lodge	Wax Room	Rentals	Food	Lesons	Shelters
6^{50}	8	3	3	1		0	√	√	√	√	√	1
	37.0				6.0	0.0						

54 Les Sentiers de la Cabane, Sainte-Anne-des-Plaines
(514) 478-2090; 270, 1re Avenue, Sainte-Anne-des-Plaines, J0N 1H0
Hwy 335 to Sainte-Anne-des-Plaines.

Trail Fee	Total	●	■	◆	Skating	Ungroomed	Lodge	Wax Room	Rentals	Food	Lesons	Shelters
6^{00}	5	4	1	0		0	√	√	√	√		1
	31.0					0.0						

55 Centre de plein air chez Martine, Laurentides
(514) 439-7687; 1135 rang Double, Laurentides, J0R 1C0
Approx 2 km N of town of Laurentides on Hwy 337, then about 4 km W.

Trail Fee	Total	●	■	◆	Skating	Ungroomed	Lodge	Wax Room	Rentals	Food	Lesons	Shelters
6^{00}	12	4	6	1		0	√	√	√	√	√	0
	60.0				Yes	0.0						

Quebec

56 Station Touristique Montagne Coupée, Saint-Jean-de-Matha
(514) 886-3891, 1-800-363-8614; 1000 rue de la Montagne-Coupée, Saint-Jean-de-Matha, J0K 2S0
About 2 km S of St.-Jean- de-Matha on Hwy 131.
Panoramic view from hill. Mix of fields and forest. Daycare, bar, inn

Trail Fee	Total	●	■	◆	Skating	Ungroomed	Lodge	Wax Room	Rentals	Food	Lessons	Shelters
8⁵⁰	15	5	11	3		1	√	√	√	√	√	0
	55.0	5.0	30.0	10.0		25.0	10.0					

57 Centre de plein air Saint-Jean-de-Matha, Saint-Jean-de-Matha
(514) 886-9321; 945 route 131, Saint-Jean-de-Matha, J0K 2S0
Approx 5 km N of St.-Jean -de-Matha on Hwy 131.
Based at golf club. Daycare, bar, auberge

Trail Fee	Total	●	■	◆	Skating	Ungroomed	Lodge	Wax Room	Rentals	Food	Lessons	Shelters
7⁵⁰	10	3	2	3		0	√	√	√	√	√	0
	66.0					6.0	0.0					

58 Réserve faunique de Mastigouche, Secteur Catherine, St.-Charles-de-Mandeville
(819) 265-2098 C.P. 450, St-Alexis-des-Monts, J0K 1V0
18 km N of St.-Charles-de-Mandeville.
Easy trails for day skiers, intermediate for over night trips to several BC huts.

Trail Fee	Total	●	■	◆	Skating	Ungroomed	Lodge	Wax Room	Rentals	Food	Lessons	Shelters
3⁰⁰	4	2	2	0		0	√	√				2
	43.3	12.8	30.5				0.0					

59 Réserve faunique de Mastigouche, Secteur Pins Rouge, St-Alexis-des-Monts
(819) 265-2098, (819) 265-3807; C.P. 450, St-Alexis-des-Monts, J0K 1V0
24 km N of St.-Alexis-des-Monts.
Intermediate trails are for long randonnées to huts, easy trails are for day skiers.

Trail Fee	Total	●	■	◆	Skating	Ungroomed	Lodge	Wax Room	Rentals	Food	Lessons	Shelters
3⁰⁰	4	2	2	0		0	√	√				12
	51.0	13.6	37.3				0.0					

60 Parc national de la Mauricie, Saint-Jean-des-Piles
(819) 536-2638; PO Box 758, Shawinigan, G9N 6V9
5 km N of St.-Jean-de-Piles or 8 km N of St-Gérard.
Lots of gently rolling trails. Overnight lodges on trail.

Trail Fee	Total	●	■	◆	Skating	Ungroomed	Lodge	Wax Room	Rentals	Food	Lessons	Shelters
4⁰⁰	12	5	5	2		0	√	√				7
	80.0	45.0	21.5	13.5		27.0	0.0					

61 Club de golf de Grand-Mère, Grand-Mère
(819) 538-8651, (819) 533-4776; , 10, 6e Avenue, Grand-Mere, G9T 2H8
On N side of Grand-Mère at 10 - 6th Ave.

Trail Fee	Total	●	■	◆	Skating	Ungroomed	Lodge	Wax Room	Rentals	Food	Lessons	Shelters
3⁰⁰	5	4	1	0		0	√	√		√		0
	19.0						0.0					

Quebec

Groomed Trails

Trail Fee Total	●	■	◆	Skating	Ungroomed	Lodge	Wax Room	Rentals	Food	Lesons	Shelters

62 Station de ski Vallée du Parc, Grand-Mère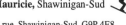

(819) 538-1639, 1-800-363-1639; 10000, boul. Vallee-du-Parc, Grand-Mere, G9T 5L1
N of Shawinigan at 10000 Boul. Vallée du Parc.
Many trails are lit for night skiing. Daycare

Trail Fee	Total	●	■	◆	Skating	Ungroomed	Lodge	Wax Room	Rentals	Food	Lesons	Shelters
3⁰⁰	10	2	6	2		0	√	√	√	√	√	0
	65.0				Yes	0.0						

63 Station de ski Val-Mauricie, Shawinigan-Sud

(819) 537-8732; 109e rue, Shawinigan-Sud, G9P 4E8
109th Street in Shawinigan-Sud.

Trail Fee	Total	●	■	◆	Skating	Ungroomed	Lodge	Wax Room	Rentals	Food	Lesons	Shelters
NC	4	2	2	0		0	√	√		√		0
	15.0					0.0						

64 Club de golf Ki-8-Eb, Trois-Rivières

(819) 375-8918; 8200, boul. des Forges, Trois-Rivieres, G9A 5H5
8200 Boul. des Forges on N side of Trois Rivières.

Trail Fee	Total	●	■	◆	Skating	Ungroomed	Lodge	Wax Room	Rentals	Food	Lesons	Shelters
3⁰⁰	8	2	5	1		0	√	√		√		1
	30.0					0.0						

65 Cité des Loisirs, Drummondville

(819) 478-5475; 950, chemin Hemming, Drummondville, J2B 6W6
From center of Drummondville cross bridge, turn right on chemin Hemming

Trail Fee	Total	●	■	◆	Skating	Ungroomed	Lodge	Wax Room	Rentals	Food	Lesons	Shelters
5⁰⁰	11	8	3	0		0	√	√	√	√		1
	30.0					0.0						

66 Domaine de Lac Louise, Saint-Louis-de-Blanford

(819) 364-7002
Exit 235 off H;w Route 263 Nord, Saint-Louis-de-Blandford, G0Z 1B0y 20, S on Hwy 162.

Trail Fee	Total	●	■	◆	Skating	Ungroomed	Lodge	Wax Room	Rentals	Food	Lesons	Shelters
4⁵⁰	4	2	1	1		0	√	√		√		1
	28.0					0.0						

67 Club de ski de fond Bellevue, Melbourne

(819) 826-3869; 70, chemin Lay, Melbourne, J0B 2B0
Exit 88 off Hwy 55 at Melbourne, then W on Hwy 116 to chemin Lay. Bar

Trail Fee	Total	●	■	◆	Skating	Ungroomed	Lodge	Wax Room	Rentals	Food	Lesons	Shelters
8⁰⁰	15	5	5	5		0	√	√	√	√		2
	77.0	10.0	10.0	13.0		0.0						

Quebec

Groomed Trails

Columns: Trail Fee · Total · ● · ■ · ◆ · Skating · Ungroomed · Lodge · Wax Room · Rentals · Food · Lessons · Shelters

68 Parc de la Yamaska, Granby

(514) 776-7182; 950, 8e Rang Ouest, Granby, J0E 2G0
About 8 km NE of Granby. Enter S side of park on 8th Rang East.
Stacked loop trails go partially around lake and to old sugar shack.

Trail Fee	Total	●	■	◆	Skating	Ungroomed	Lodge	Wax Room	Rentals	Food	Lessons	Shelters
NC	3	1	2	0		0	√	√		√		3
	26.0					0.0						

69 Centre de plein air Davignon, Bromont

(514) 534-2277, 1-800-363-8952; 319, rue Gale, Bromont, J0E 1L0
approx 3 km S of Bromont. 230-bed outdoor recreation center.

Trail Fee	Total	●	■	◆	Skating	Ungroomed	Lodge	Wax Room	Rentals	Food	Lessons	Shelters
7^{00}	5	2	2	1		0	√	√	√	E		1
	22.0					0.0						

70 Station de ski Bromont, Bromont

(514) 534-2200, (514) 866-4270 (Montreal); 150, rue Champlain, Bromont, J0E 1L0
150 Champlain St. in Bromont. Daycare on weekends

Trail Fee	Total	●	■	◆	Skating	Ungroomed	Lodge	Wax Room	Rentals	Food	Lessons	Shelters
8^{50}	9	4	2	3		0	√	√	√	√		1
	67.0				15	0.0						

71 Sutton en Haut, Sutton

(514) 538-2271, Hotel: (514)538-3212; 297, rue Maple, Sutton, J0E 2K0
1 km E of Sutton on Maple Rd, 1 km from alpine ski center.

Trail Fee	Total	●	■	◆	Skating	Ungroomed	Lodge	Wax Room	Rentals	Food	Lessons	Shelters
7^{00}	15	6	5	4		0	√	√	√	√		1
	58.0	14.0	14.0	7.0	7.0	0.0						

72 Ski de fond Repos du Fermier (Farmer's Rest), Lac Brome

(514) 243-6843; 2651, chemin Mont-Echo, Lac Brome, J0E 1V0
Approx 10 km S of Lac-Brome (Knowlton) at 2651 chemin Mt-Echo.

Trail Fee	Total	●	■	◆	Skating	Ungroomed	Lodge	Wax Room	Rentals	Food	Lessons	Shelters
10^{00}	11	4	3	4		0	√	√	√	√	√	2
	53.0	14.8	12.0	20.6	3.0	0.0						

73 Parc du Mont-Orford, Magog

(819) 843-9855; C.P. 200, Magog, J1X 3W8
Exit 118 off Hwy 10 then about 5 km N on Hwy 141.
Guided wildlife observation ski tours, ice slide.

Trail Fee	Total	●	■	◆	Skating	Ungroomed	Lodge	Wax Room	Rentals	Food	Lessons	Shelters
8^{50}	12	4	2	6		0	√	√	√	√	√	5
4^{25} C	56.0	13.0	6.3	24.1	20.0	0.0						

Groomed Trails

Table columns: Trail Fee | Total | ● | ■ | ◆ | Skating | Ungroomed | Lodge | Wax Room | Rentals | Food | Lessons | Shelters

74 Skiwippi, North Hatley/Ayer's Cliff

Auberge Hatley: (819) 842-2451; 325 chemin Virgin, North Hatley, J0B 2C0
Trail along Lake Massawippi connects 3 inns up to 20 km apart. Inn-to-inn tours with gourmet meals and baggage and car transfer from $450 pp/do for 3 nights.

Trail Fee	Total	●	■	◆	Skating	Ungroomed	Lodge	Wax Room	Rentals	Food	Lessons	Shelters
NC	3			3						√		
	50.0											

75 Parc de la Gorge de Coaticook, Coaticook

(819) 849-2331; 135 rue Michaud, Coaticook, J1A 1A9
400 St-Marc in Coaticook.
A 50 metre deep gorge with suspension bridge and observation towers.

Trail Fee	Total	●	■	◆	Skating	Ungroomed	Lodge	Wax Room	Rentals	Food	Lessons	Shelters
5⁰⁰	10	4	4	2		0				√		4
	50.0											

76 Parc du Mont-Mégantic, Notre-Dame-des-Bois

(819) 888-2800; 119, route du Parc, Notre-Dame-des-Bois, J0B 2E0
Approx 3 km N of Notre-Dame-des-Bois then about 5 km W on access road.
High elev. gives it one of the longest ski seasons in southern Quebec. Bar

Trail Fee	Total	●	■	◆	Skating	Ungroomed	Lodge	Wax Room	Rentals	Food	Lessons	Shelters
5⁰⁰	8	2	4	2		0	√	√		√		4
	50.0					0.0						

77 Club Méganski, Lac Mégantic

(819) 583-3965; Club-Vacances Baie-des-Sables, Lac Mégantic, G6B 2S5
Near NW corner of Lac-Mégantic lake, approx 5 km W of town of Lac-Mégantic.

Trail Fee	Total	●	■	◆	Skating	Ungroomed	Lodge	Wax Room	Rentals	Food	Lessons	Shelters
5⁰⁰	6	2	3	1		0	√			√		2
	40.0					0.0						

78 Club de golf et curling, Thetford Mines

(418) 335-2931; 675, rue Notre-Dame, Thetford Mines, G6G 5T1
675, rue Notre Dame N in Thetford Mines.

Trail Fee	Total	●	■	◆	Skating	Ungroomed	Lodge	Wax Room	Rentals	Food	Lessons	Shelters
4⁰⁰	7	6	1	0		0	√					1
	65.0					0.0						

79 Club motoneige Beauceville, Beauceville

(418) 774-9727; Rang Saint-Charles, Beauceville, G0S 1A0
Rang St.-Charles in Beauceville

Trail Fee	Total	●	■	◆	Skating	Ungroomed	Lodge	Wax Room	Rentals	Food	Lessons	Shelters
3⁰⁰	10	8	2	0		0	√	√	√	√		1
	93.0					0.0						

Quebec

		Groomed Trails			Skating	Ungroomed	Lodge	Wax Room	Rentals	Food	Lessons	Shelters
Trail Fee	Total	●	■	◆								

80 Station de ski du Mont-Orignal, Lac-Etchemin

(418) 625-1551; 160, rang Grande-Riviere, Lac-Etchemin, G0R 1S0
160 Rang Grande-Riviere at Lac-Etchemin.

Trail Fee	Total	●	■	◆	Skating	Ungroomed	Lodge	Wax Room	Rentals	Food	Lessons	Shelters
6⁰⁰	5	3	1	1		0	√	√		√		2
5⁰⁰ Y	41.1					0.0						

81 Station touristique du Massif du sud, Saint-Philemon

(418) 469-3676; 1989, route du Massif, C.P. 70, Saint-Philemon, G0R 4A0
About 2 km W of Saint-Philemon on Hwy 216.
Panoramic views from the top of Mt. du Midi. Daycare

Trail Fee	Total	●	■	◆	Skating	Ungroomed	Lodge	Wax Room	Rentals	Food	Lessons	Shelters
5⁰⁰	9	4	1	1		0	√	√	√	√		1
3⁰⁰ Y	15.0	10.0	2.0	3.0		0.0						

82 Centre de plein air de Sainte-Perpetue, Sainte-Perpetue

(418) 359-3363; Rang Tache Est, Sainte-Perpetue, G0R 3Z0
Rang Tache East in Sainte-Perpetue.

Trail Fee	Total	●	■	◆	Skating	Ungroomed	Lodge	Wax Room	Rentals	Food	Lessons	Shelters
4⁰⁰	8	3	2	3		0	√	√		√		0
	44.0					0.0						

83 Club sportif des Appalaches, Saint-Eugene

(418) 247-3271; 25, chemin des Appalaches Est, Saint-Eugene, G0R 1X0
Exit 400 off Hwy 20 then S on Hwy 285 to St-Eugene
Beautiful views of the St. Lawrence valley. Huts for rent for overnighting.

Trail Fee	Total	●	■	◆	Skating	Ungroomed	Lodge	Wax Room	Rentals	Food	Lessons	Shelters
6⁵⁰	15	3	6	5		0	√	√	√	√		6
3⁰⁰ C	75.0	10.0	13.0	47.0		0.0						

84 Centre de plein air de Montmagny, Montmagny

(418) 248-6721; C.P. 461, Montmagny, G5V 3S9
Exit 378 off Hwy 20 then 18 km S on Hwy 283.

Trail Fee	Total	●	■	◆	Skating	Ungroomed	Lodge	Wax Room	Rentals	Food	Lessons	Shelters
7⁵⁰	13	6	5	2		0	√	√		√		4
3⁰⁰ Y	60.0	30.0	20.0	10.0	10.0	0.0						

85 Club de ski de fond La Balade, St-Jean-Chrysostome

(418) 839-1551
At rue des Erables and du Moulin in St-Jean-Chrysostome. NC for children < 12.

Trail Fee	Total	●	■	◆	Skating	Ungroomed	Lodge	Wax Room	Rentals	Food	Lessons	Shelters
4⁰⁰	-	-	-	-		0	√	√	√	√		1
2⁵⁰ Y	55.0	2.0	20.0	33.0	5.0	0.0						

Quebec

Groomed Trails ● ■ ◆

Trail Fee · Total · Skating · Ungroomed · Lodge · Wax Room · Rentals · Food · Lesons · Shelters

---

86 Ski de fond des Grandes-Prairies, Saint-Romuald
(418) 839-1919
At 4th Ave and 5th St in St-Romuald. NC for under 16 years old.

Trail Fee	Total	●	■	◆	Skating	Ungroomed	Lodge	Wax Room	Rentals	Food	Lessons	Shelters
3^{00}	-	-	-	-		0	√	√		E		0
	25.0	10.0	10.0	5.0	7.0	0.0						

87 Champs de Bataille, Quebec
(418) 849-9054
On the Plains of Abraham in the center of the city.

Trail Fee	Total	●	■	◆	Skating	Ungroomed	Lodge	Wax Room	Rentals	Food	Lessons	Shelters
NC	4	3	1	0		0	√				√	1
	11.0	7.0	4.0		2.5	0.0						

88 Centre de ski de fond Cap-Rouge, Cap Rouge
(418) 650-7722, (418) 650-1433 (tape); 4600, rue Saint-Felix, Cap Rouge, G1Y 3B3
Exit 302 off Hwy 40 5 km W of Hwy 73 then S on Jean-Gauvin.
Trails on golf course and municipal park.

Trail Fee	Total	●	■	◆	Skating	Ungroomed	Lodge	Wax Room	Rentals	Food	Lessons	Shelters
NC	12	11	1	0		0	E	√				1
	43.0	37.6	6.4			0.0						

89 Centre de plein air Dansereau, Pont-Rouge
(418) 873-4150; 30 rue Dansereau, Pont-Rouge, QC G0A 2X0
30 rue Dansereau in Pont-Rouge in front of church.

Trail Fee	Total	●	■	◆	Skating	Ungroomed	Lodge	Wax Room	Rentals	Food	Lessons	Shelters
3^{00}	6	4	1	1		0	√	√	√	√		2
8^{00} F	32.0					0.0						

90 Le Grand Portneuf, Pont-Rouge
(418) 329-2238; Route 365, Pont-Rouge, G0A 2X0
About 8 km N of Pont-Rouge on Hwy 365.

Trail Fee	Total	●	■	◆	Skating	Ungroomed	Lodge	Wax Room	Rentals	Food	Lessons	Shelters
5^{00}	6	1	4	1		0	√	√	√	√		1
	55.0					0.0						

91 Centre Ski-neuf, Portneuf Station
(418) 286-6966 (weekends)
Exit 261 off Hwy 40 then N to 451 Bvld Gauthier in Pontneuf.

Trail Fee	Total	●	■	◆	Skating	Ungroomed	Lodge	Wax Room	Rentals	Food	Lessons	Shelters
NC	6	3	3	0		0	√	√		√		2
	30.0	20.0	10.0			0.0						

92 Les Portes de l'Enfer, St-Alban
(418) 268-3801 Chalets for rent.

Trail Fee	Total	●	■	◆	Skating	Ungroomed	Lodge	Wax Room	Rentals	Food	Lessons	Shelters
4^{00}	-	-	-	-		0	√			√		1
NCC	63.0	16.0	17.0	30.0		0.0						

Quebec

Groomed Trails

| Trail Fee | Total | ● | ■ | ◆ | Skating | Ungroomed | Lodge | Wax Room | Rentals | Food | Lessons | Shelters |

93 Centre Nature Sainte-Basile, Sainte-Basile

(418) 329-3177; 1, avenue Centre-Nature, Sainte-Basile, G0A 3G0
1 ave. Centre Nature in St-Basile-Sud. 2 km trail lit for night skiing.

Trail Fee	Total	●	■	◆	Skating	Ungroomed	Lodge	Wax Room	Rentals	Food	Lessons	Shelters
4⁰⁰	7	3	4	0		0	√	√	√	√		1
NCC	70.0	14.0	56.0			0.0						

94 Gite de l'Ecureuil, Saint-Casimir

(418) 339-3102 / 2543
N of St-Casimir on Hwy 363.

Trail Fee	Total	●	■	◆	Skating	Ungroomed	Lodge	Wax Room	Rentals	Food	Lessons	Shelters
3⁵⁰	7	2	4	1		0	√	√	√	√		1
1⁵⁰ C	55.6	14.1	18.0	23.5		0.0						

95 Les Sapins Verts, Saint-Ubalde

(418) 277-2415
About 10 km N of Saint-Ubalde on chemin du Lac Blanc.

Trail Fee	Total	●	■	◆	Skating	Ungroomed	Lodge	Wax Room	Rentals	Food	Lessons	Shelters
3⁰⁰	6	2	2	0		0						1
	52.0					0.0						

96 Réserve faunique de Portneuf, Rivière-a-Pierre

(418) 323-2021
Approx 7 km N of Rivière-a-Pierre to Talbot sector, then 20 km N to Travers.
Talbot sector has 22 km of mainly linear trails. Travers has 31 km of loops.

Trail Fee	Total	●	■	◆	Skating	Ungroomed	Lodge	Wax Room	Rentals	Food	Lessons	Shelters
NC	7	2	5	0		0						10
	53.0					0.0						

97 Domaine Notre-Dame, Sainte-Catherine-de la Jacques Cartier

(819) 875-2583
Turn W off Hwy 367 on Hwy 358 towards Pont-Neuf.

Trail Fee	Total	●	■	◆	Skating	Ungroomed	Lodge	Wax Room	Rentals	Food	Lessons	Shelters
3⁰⁰	10	-	-			0	√	√	√	√		0
	30.0	5.0	25.0			0.0						

98 Centre de ski Duchesnay, Sainte-Catherine-de-la-Jacques-Cartier

(418) 875-2147, (418) 875-4222; Route 367 Nord, Sainte-Catherine-de-la-Jacques-Cartier, G0A 3M0
Approx 3 km N of Ste-Catherine on SW shore of Lac-St-Joseph.
Good views from top of mountain.

Trail Fee	Total	●	■	◆	Skating	Ungroomed	Lodge	Wax Room	Rentals	Food	Lessons	Shelters
3⁵⁰	10	4	4	2		0	√	√	√	√		5
	125.0	22.0	40.0	63.0		0.0						

Quebec

Groomed Trails

Column symbols: Trail Fee | Total | ● ■ ◆ | Skating | Ungroomed | Lodge | Wax Room | Rentals | Food | Lessons | Shelters

99 Village des Sports, Valcartier

(418) 844-3725; 1860, boulevard Valcartier, Saint-Gabriel-de-Valcartier, QC
About 2 km N of Saint-Gabriel on Hwy 371 at 1860 Blvd Valcartier.

Trail Fee	Total	●	■	◆	Skating	Ungroomed	Lodge	Wax Room	Rentals	Food	Lessons	Shelters
5^{00}	10	6	4	0		0	√	√	√	√		1
	40.0					0.0						

100 Base Militaire de Valcartier, Valcartier

(418) 844-3272
Operated by Club de ski de fond Castor on Valcartier military base.

Trail Fee	Total	●	■	◆	Skating	Ungroomed	Lodge	Wax Room	Rentals	Food	Lessons	Shelters
6^{00}	-	-	-	-		0	√	√	√	√		1
	66.0	3.9	19.5	43.0	66.0	0.0						

101 Centre de ski de fond de Val-Bélair, Val-Bélair

(418) 842-7769; 1560, av. de la Montagne Ouest, Val-Belair, G3K 1X5
Exit 5 off Hwy 573N, then SW on Ste-Genevieve, NW on De l'Eglise.
Nice view from the summit of Mt. Bélair.

Trail Fee	Total	●	■	◆	Skating	Ungroomed	Lodge	Wax Room	Rentals	Food	Lessons	Shelters
3^{00}	8	3	2	3		0	√	√	√	√	√	1
2^{00} S	51.7	7.5	10.4	33.8		0.0						

102 Centre de ski de fond Charlesbourg, Charlesbourg

(418) 849-9054; 375, St-Alexandre, Charlesbourg, G2M 1C3
Exit 155 off Hwy 155 then E on Geoges Muir, N on Notre-Dame, 375 St-Alexandre

Trail Fee	Total	●	■	◆	Skating	Ungroomed	Lodge	Wax Room	Rentals	Food	Lessons	Shelters
8^{00}	22	12	4	6		0	√	√	√	√	√	2
	119.0	37.0	36.0	41.0	5.0	0.0						

103 Les Sentiers du Moulin, Lac-Beauport

(418) 849-9652; 99, chemin du Moulin, Lac-Beauport, G0A 2C0
On N shore of Lac-Beauport at 99 chemin du Moulin. Children < 13: $3.00

Trail Fee	Total	●	■	◆	Skating	Ungroomed	Lodge	Wax Room	Rentals	Food	Lessons	Shelters
9^{00}	16	8	6	2		0	√	√	√	√	√	5
7^{00} Y	148.0	12.0	20.0	15.0	11.0	0.0						

104 Le Refuge, St-Adolphe-de-Stoneham

(418) 848-6155 Trails link with those of Les Sentiers du Moulin.

Trail Fee	Total	●	■	◆	Skating	Ungroomed	Lodge	Wax Room	Rentals	Food	Lessons	Shelters
5^{00}	14	8	3	3		0	√	√	√	√		0
15^{00}F	112.5	32.7	33.6	48.0		0.0						

105 Club "Mont-Torbillon", Lac-Beauport

(418) 849-4418; 55, montée du Golf, Lac-Beauport,
On N shore of Lac-Beauport at 55 montée du Golf.

Trail Fee	Total	●	■	◆	Skating	Ungroomed	Lodge	Wax Room	Rentals	Food	Lessons	Shelters
6^{00}	5	1	3	1		0	√	√	√	√		0
	40.0					0.0						

Groomed Trails

| Trail Fee | Total | ● | ■ | ◆ | Skating | Ungroomed | Lodge | Wax Room | Rentals | Food | Lesons | Shelters |

106 Parc du Mont-Sainte-Anne, St-Ferréol-les-neiges

(418) 827-4561, (418) 827-5727, (514) 861-6670 (Montreal)
Accommodation reservation: 1-800-463-1568; Rang Saint-Julien, St-Ferreol-les-Neiges, G0A 3R0
About 50 km W of Quebec City at St-Ferréol-les-neiges. NC < 13 years, family $26.00.
Best combined X-C/alpine ski centre in Canada. Wide variety of trails, bar, hotel, condos

Trail Fee	Total	●	■	◆	Skating	Ungroomed	Lodge	Wax Room	Rentals	Food	Lesons	Shelters
11⁰⁰	22	8	9	5		1	√	√	√	√	√	8
9⁰⁰ S	135.0	30.0	34.0	40.0	70.0	50.0						

107 Sentiers des Caps de Charlevoix, Saint-Tite-des-Caps

(418) 435-4163
Approx 15 km E of St-Tite on Hwy 138.

Trail Fee	Total	●	■	◆	Skating	Ungroomed	Lodge	Wax Room	Rentals	Food	Lesons	Shelters
5⁰⁰	-	-	-	-		0	√	√	√	√		0
3⁰⁰ C	25.0	15.0	5.0	5.0		0.0						

108 Camp Mercier, Parc de la Jacques Cartier

(418) 848-2422, (418) 848-1037, 1-800-463-1000; 3000, rue Alexandra, bur. 101, Beauport, G1E 7C8
Approx 50 km N of Quebec City on Hwy 175. No charge < 13 years.
Connected to Mt Ste-Anne and Foret Montmorency. Long snow season. chalets & dorm

Trail Fee	Total	●	■	◆	Skating	Ungroomed	Lodge	Wax Room	Rentals	Food	Lesons	Shelters
8⁰⁰	15	5	6	2		2	√	√	√	√	√	6
6⁰⁰ S	192.0	20.0	33.0	4.0	12.0	102.0						

109 Foret Montmorency

(418) 846-2046
Approx 60 km N of Quebec City on Hwy 175, then 3 km E on Route 33.
Connected to Camp Mercier. Operated by University of Laval.

Trail Fee	Total	●	■	◆	Skating	Ungroomed	Lodge	Wax Room	Rentals	Food	Lesons	Shelters
5⁰⁰	8	3	3	2		0	√	√		√		3
	38.0	8.0	15.0	15.8	12.0	0.0						

110 Le Genévrier, Baie-Saint-Paul

(418) 435-6520; 1175, boul. Mgr.-De Laval, Baie-Saint-Paul, G0A 1B0
2 km N of Baie St-Paul on Hwy 138. 16 chalets for rent

Trail Fee	Total	●	■	◆	Skating	Ungroomed	Lodge	Wax Room	Rentals	Food	Lesons	Shelters
4⁵⁰	6	4	1	1		0	√	√	√	√		1
2⁵⁰ C	60.0	28.0	17.0	15.0		0.0						

111 Mont Grand-Fonds, La Malbaie

(418) 665-4405; C.P. 244, La Malbaie, G5A 1T8
About 15 km N of town of Riviere-Malbaie on chemin des Loisirs. Chalets, daycare

Trail Fee	Total	●	■	◆	Skating	Ungroomed	Lodge	Wax Room	Rentals	Food	Lesons	Shelters
7⁵⁰	14	3	5	6		0	√	√	√	√		4
5⁵⁰ S	132.0	6.9	56.0	69.0	4.0	0.0						

Quebec

Groomed Trails

Trail Fee | Total | ● ■ ◆ | Skating | Ungroomed | Lodge | Wax Room | Rentals | Food | Lessons | Shelters

112 Centre Plein Air Les Sources Joyeuses de la Malbaie, La Malbaie

(418) 665-4858; C.P. 235, La Malbaie, G5A 1T7
141, rang Ste-Madeleine W of La Malbaie.

Trail Fee	Total	●	■	◆	Skating	Ungroomed	Lodge	Wax Room	Rentals	Food	Lessons	Shelters
4⁰⁰	7	-	-	-		0	√			√		0
1⁵⁰ C	48.0	4.0	31.0	13.0		6.0	0.0					

113 Parc des Grands-Jardins, Saint-Urbain

(418) 435-3101
About 25 km N of St-Urbain on Hwy 381 at NE side of park.
Mountainous terrain with taiga and tundra vegetation.

Trail Fee	Total	●	■	◆	Skating	Ungroomed	Lodge	Wax Room	Rentals	Food	Lessons	Shelters
3⁰⁰	4	3	1	0		-	√	√				1
	35.0					Yes						

114 Centre de plein air Bec-Scie, La Baie

(418) 544-5433; C.P. 305, La Baie, G7B 3R4
1000 chemin des Chutes in La Baie.

Trail Fee	Total	●	■	◆	Skating	Ungroomed	Lodge	Wax Room	Rentals	Food	Lessons	Shelters
6⁰⁰	10	4	4	2		0	√					0
	90.0					27.0	0.0					

115 Club de ski de fond Le Norvégien, Jonquière

(418) 542-5822; 4885 chemin Saint-Benoit, Jonquiere, G7X 7W4
4885 chemin Saint-Benoit in Jonquière. 4 km long trail is illuminated.

Trail Fee	Total	●	■	◆	Skating	Ungroomed	Lodge	Wax Room	Rentals	Food	Lessons	Shelters
5⁰⁰	11	3	2	2		0	√	√	√	√	√	1
	60.0					12.0	0.0					

116 Club de ski de fond d'Alma, Alma

(418) 662-5835; 3795, route du Lac E, C.P.565, Alma, G8B 5V2
3795 route du Lac Est. Well-designed trails overlook the Saguenay in places.

Trail Fee	Total	●	■	◆	Skating	Ungroomed	Lodge	Wax Room	Rentals	Food	Lessons	Shelters
6⁰⁰	10	4	3	3		0	√	√				1
	90.0						0.0					

117 Club Tobo-Ski, Saint-Félicien

(418) 679-1158/5243

About 10 km S of St-Félicien at alpine ski centre.

Trail Fee	Total	●	■	◆	Skating	Ungroomed	Lodge	Wax Room	Rentals	Food	Lessons	Shelters
4⁰⁰	7	3	2	2		0	√	√		√		1
	36.0						0.0					

Quebec

Groomed Trails

Trail Fee | Total | ● | ■ | ◆ | Skating | Ungroomed | Lodge | Wax Room | Rentals | Food | Lesons | Shelters

118 Centre de plein air St-Nazaire, St-Nazaire

(418) 662-4154/ 668-2523; Rte 172E, St-Nazaire, QC J0H 1V0
E of St-Nazaire then N on secondary road.

Trail Fee	Total	●	■	◆	Skating	Ungroomed	Lodge	Wax Room	Rentals	Food	Lesons	Shelters
4⁰⁰	5	4	1	0		0						0
	28.0					0.0						

119 Club de ski de fond de Mt Valin, St-David-de-Falardeau

(418) 690-4248, Le Valinouet alpine centre: (418) 673-3455; C.P. 67, Saint-David G0V 1C0
E of St-David-de-Falardeau near Valinouet alpine ski centre.
Longest ski season in Quebec. Hosts Tour de Mt-Valin. condos and chalets

Trail Fee	Total	●	■	◆	Skating	Ungroomed	Lodge	Wax Room	Rentals	Food	Lesons	Shelters
5⁰⁰	5	-	-	-		0	√	√		√		4
	38.0	10.0	18.0	10.0	15.0	0.0						

120 Parc du Saguenay, Rivière d'Eternité

(418) 272-3008; 24 Notre-Dame, Rivière d'Eternité, QC G0V 1P0
Challenging backcountry trails for experts. See

Trail Fee	Total	●	■	◆	Skating	Ungroomed	Lodge	Wax Room	Rentals	Food	Lesons	Shelters
NC	0	0	0	0		1						2
						31.0						

121 Sentier de la rivière Amedée, Baie Comeau

(418) 589-7991
N end of Blvd Blanche in Baie-Comeau Ouest.
Moonlight skiing offered by club.

Trail Fee	Total	●	■	◆	Skating	Ungroomed	Lodge	Wax Room	Rentals	Food	Lesons	Shelters
4⁰⁰	10	3	5	2		0	√	√			√	2
2⁰⁰ C	25.0				10.0	0.0						

122 Sentier Nor-Fond, Baie-Comeau

(418) 296-2484; Club de ski Norfond, Baie Comeau, QC
4 km trail lit for night skiing. Club runs moonlight ski tours and waxing clinics

Trail Fee	Total	●	■	◆	Skating	Ungroomed	Lodge	Wax Room	Rentals	Food	Lesons	Shelters
5⁰⁰	11	2	1	8		0	√	√				5
2⁰⁰ C	34.0					0.0						

123 Base de plein air Les Goélands, Port-Cartier

(418) 766-8706; C.P. 33, Port-Cartier, G5B 2G7 12-rooms for rent on-site

Trail Fee	Total	●	■	◆	Skating	Ungroomed	Lodge	Wax Room	Rentals	Food	Lesons	Shelters
6⁰⁰	12	7	3	1		0	√	√		√		1
4⁰⁰ C	50.0					0.0						

124 Club de ski de fond Anik, Fermont

(418) 287-5374; C.P. 338, Fermont, G0G 1J0

Trail Fee	Total	●	■	◆	Skating	Ungroomed	Lodge	Wax Room	Rentals	Food	Lesons	Shelters
7⁰⁰	4	1	2	1		0	√	√	E			2
	22.0					0.0						

Groomed Trails

Trail Fee	Total	●	■	◆	Skating	Ungroomed	Lodge	Wax Room	Rentals	Food	Lessons	Shelters

125 Pohénégamook Sante Plein Air, Pohénégamook

(418) 859-2405, 1-800-463-1364; 1723 chemin Guerette, Pohenegamook, G0L 1J0
1723 chemin Guérette. A health spa and recreation centre.

Trail Fee	Total	●	■	◆	Skating	Ungroomed	Lodge	Wax Room	Rentals	Food	Lessons	Shelters
4⁵⁰	7	2	3	2		0	√	√		√		1
	45.0					0.0						

126 Parc du Mont-Comi, Saint-Donat-de-Rimouski

(418) 739-4858; RR 2, Saint-Donat-de-Rimouski, G0K 1L0

Trail Fee	Total	●	■	◆	Skating	Ungroomed	Lodge	Wax Room	Rentals	Food	Lessons	Shelters
4⁵⁰	7	3	2	2		0	√	√	√	√		1
	25.0					0.0						

127 Val-Neigette, Sainte-Blandine
(418) 735-2880

Trail Fee	Total	●	■	◆	Skating	Ungroomed	Lodge	Wax Room	Rentals	Food	Lessons	Shelters
4⁰⁰	4	2	1	1		0	√	√		√		1
	32.0					0.0						

128 Centre de plein air de Saint-Damase, Saint-Damase
(418) 776-2828; 302, route 297 sud, Saint-Damase, G0J 2J0
In town of St-Damase at 302 route 329 South. Daycare

Trail Fee	Total	●	■	◆	Skating	Ungroomed	Lodge	Wax Room	Rentals	Food	Lessons	Shelters
2⁰⁰	5	2	2	1		0	√	√		√		2
	35.0					0.0						

129 Station de ski Val d'Irène, Sainte-Irène

(418) 629-3450; 115, route Val d'Irene, Sainte-Irene, G0J 2P0
W of town of Ste-Irène. chalets and rooms

Trail Fee	Total	●	■	◆	Skating	Ungroomed	Lodge	Wax Room	Rentals	Food	Lessons	Shelters
3⁰⁰	4	2	1	1		0	√	√	√	√		1
	25.0					0.0						

130 Parc de la Gaspésie, Sainte-Anne-des-Monts

(418) 763-3301; Auberge du Mt-Albert: (418) 763-2288
Great backcountry skiing in the Chic-Choc mountains. Taiga and tundra vegetation.

Trail Fee	Total	●	■	◆	Skating	Ungroomed	Lodge	Wax Room	Rentals	Food	Lessons	Shelters
NA	1	-	-	-		-	√					16
	10.0					185.0						

131 Centre de plein air de Saint-Siméon, Saint-Siméon
(418) 534-2155; Rang 3, Saint-Siméon, G0C 3A0
Approx 3 km NE of town of St-Siméon.

Trail Fee	Total	●	■	◆	Skating	Ungroomed	Lodge	Wax Room	Rentals	Food	Lessons	Shelters
2⁰⁰	4	2	2	0		0				√		1
	18.0					0.0						

Quebec

132 Base de plein air de Bellefeuille, Pabos-Mills

(418) 689-6727; 70, route Lemarquand, Pabos-Mills, G0C 1R0
In town of Pabos-Mills. 8 cottages for rent.

Trail Fee	Total	●	■	◆	Skating	Ungroomed	Lodge	Wax Room	Rentals	Food	Lessons	Shelters
2⁵⁰	6	5	1	0		0	√	√	√	√		0
	18.0					0.0						

133 Parc National Forillon, Gaspé

(418) 368-5505; 122 boul. Gaspé, C.P. 1220, Gaspé, G0C 1R0
About 15 km N of town of Gaspé on Hwy 132. Family rate $6.00

Trail Fee	Total	●	■	◆	Skating	Ungroomed	Lodge	Wax Room	Rentals	Food	Lessons	Shelters
2⁵⁰	5	3	2	0		0	√	√	√			3
1²⁵ C	40.0				6.0	0.0						

134 Sugarloaf Touring Center, Sugarloaf, Maine

(207) 237-6830 Condos, inn: 1-800-THE-LOAF; Box 518, Carrabassett Valley, ME 04947

Trail Fee	Total	●	■	◆	Skating	Ungroomed	Lodge	Wax Room	Rentals	Food	Lessons	Shelters
10⁰⁰	20	11	8	1		0	√	√	√	√	√	0
	90.0				Yes							

135 Balsams Wilderness, Dixville Notch, New Hampshire

(603) 255-3400, snowphone: 255-3951, Reservations: 1-800-255-0600
An elegant full-service resort.

Trail Fee	Total	●	■	◆	Skating	Ungroomed	Lodge	Wax Room	Rentals	Food	Lessons	Shelters
NA	-	-	-		0	√	√	√	√	√	-	
	75.0					25.0						

136 Craftsbury Nordic Ski Center, Craftsbury Common, Vermont

1-800-729-7751; PO Box 31, Craftsbury, VT 05827 Dormitory and inn.

Trail Fee	Total	●	■	◆	Skating	Ungroomed	Lodge	Wax Room	Rentals	Food	Lessons	Shelters
10⁰⁰	-	-	-		-	√	√	√	√	√	-	
	100.0				100.0	50.0						

137 Stowe Mountain Resort/Trapp Family Lodge, Stowe, Vermont

Trapp Family Lodge: (802) 253-8511, 1-800-826-7000; lodge, condos, inn

Trail Fee	Total	●	■	◆	Skating	Ungroomed	Lodge	Wax Room	Rentals	Food	Lessons	Shelters
10⁰⁰	-	-	-			√	√	√	√	√	√	1
	100.0				88.0	80.0						

138 Mount Van Hoevenberg, Lake Placid, New York

(518) 523-2811
Site of the 1980 Olympic Winter Games. Trails for all levels of abilities.

Trail Fee	Total	●	■	◆	Skating	Ungroomed	Lodge	Wax Room	Rentals	Food	Lessons	Shelters
10⁰⁰	-	-	-	-		-	√	√	√	√	√	0
	50.0	4.6	22.0	15.0	Yes	Yes						

Quebec

Backcountry Huts and Lodges

Huts in most provincial parks and reserves can be booked by by calling SEPAQ at a toll-free number, 1-800-665-6527, from within the province or (418) 890-6527 (Quebec City) from outside the province. Distances from trailhead to the hut are indicated for most huts. Prices are approximate and include taxes. Trail fees are not usually charged for ungroomed trails.

Parc l'Aiguebelle
Reservations: (819) 762-8154
Wood burning stoves
Seven huts with a capacity of 4 persons
Cost: $13 p.p., p.n.

Parc de la Gatineau
Reservations: (from first week of December) (819) 827-2020
Trails are usually groomed.

Leblanc Lake	$35	10 persons
Taylor Lake	$23	6 "
Brown Lake	$23	16 "

Réserve Faunique Papineau-Labelle
Reservations from Oct. 1:
(819) 454-2013
Huts have gas stoves and lanterns.
Cost is $18 per person per night.
Minimum 2 nights on weekends.

La Hote	11km	15 persons
Sourd	24km	6&8 "
Barrage	30km	15 "
Fascinant	16km	6 "
Heron	10km	15 "
Calliergon	9km	4 "
Trille	9km	4 "
Wisik	9km	4 "
Ernest	9km	10 "

Parc du Mont Tremblant
Reservations from early Nov. (only one month in advance)
(819) 688-2281
Trails are ungroomed except for a few kilometres at the start.
Cost is approximately $13 per person per night. Capacity of each hut is 16 to 20 persons.

Secteur de la Diable
Lac Ernie 11km
Le Liteau 11km
La Cache 21km

Secteur de la Pimbina
Lac des Sables 16 km

*Réserve Faunique Mastigouche
Reservations: (from Oct. 1)
(819) 265-3925
Trails are mainly groomed. Huts have gas stoves and lanterns.
Cost is $12-$17 per person per night. Baggage transport service available.

Secteur Pins Rouge

Lac Shawinigan	13k	52/4 huts
Lac Jouet	12k	12 persons
Lac Pimbina	16k	24/2 huts
Dickerman	27k	48/6 huts

Secteur Catherine

Lac Joe	8 k	16 persons
Lac Hollis	14 k	10 "
Petit Lac William	11k	24 "

Parc National de la Mauricie
Reservations from mid-November (Sept. 1 for groups)
Season: Dec 20 to March 30
Info-nature: (819) 537-4555
C.P. 174, Shawinigan, QC G9N 6T9
All trails are groomed. Lodges have heating, electricity and showers. Kitchen facilities for occupants of Andrew are in Wabenaki, 100 metres away. Children: $10.50. On weekends there is a two-night minimum ($45-$47).
Wabenaki Lodge $19 3 km
27 persons in 2 dormitories
Andrew Lodge $21 3 km
16 persons in 4 rooms.

Parc du Mont-Orford

Information: (819) 843-9855
4 chalets on groomed trails.
Capacity: 6, 15, 20, 40
Cost: $10 p.p. + trail fee
Capacity: 10 to 40 persons

*Parc du Mont-Mégantic

Information: (819) 888-2800
119 Rte du Parc, Notre-Dame des
Bois, QC J0B 2E0
Heated chalets on groomed trails.
$27 for 3 persons + $5 per extra
person + trail fee. Capacity: up to 8
with 4 sleeping on the floor

Pléiades	3km
La Grande Ours	3 km
Andromède	6km
Orion	7km

*Réserve faunique de Portneuf

Reservations from Oct. 1
Information: (418) 323-2021
Rivière à Pierre, Comité de
Portneuf, QC G0A 3A0
Most of the 13 chalets scattered
throughout the reserve are
accessible by road and ski trail. Cost
varies from $15 per person for ten
people to $46 pp for two. Capacities
vary from 2 to 10 people per chalet.

*Parc de la Jacques Cartier

Reservations from Oct. 1
(418) 890-6527 (Camp Mercier)
Season: mid-November to end of
April. Approximately $20/person.

Quatre Jumeaux sector (70-km loop)

Lac a la Chute	15 k	8 persons
Lac des Allies	24 k	8 "
Quatre Jumeaux	34 k	8 "
Remillard	48 k	8 "

Vallée de la Jacques Cartier sector
(linear trail, 82 k return)

Sautauriski	20k	12 persons
Camp Trois	41k	12 "

* Reservations can be made through
Société des éstablishments de plein air
du Québec (SEPAQ) by calling:
1-800-665-6527 from within Quebec
or (418) 890-6527 (Quebec City), 8:30
to 4:30 Monday to Friday.

Camp Mercier to Mont-Ste-Anne

Information:
(418) 848-2422 (Camp Mercier)
(418) 827-4561 (Mont-Ste-Anne)
A 63-km traverse connecting Camp
Mercier to Mont Sainte-Anne.
Trail is not normally groomed.
Cost: $20 per person

Rivière Noire	22k	8 persons
Lac l'Esperance	46k	8 "

Mont-Sainte-Anne

Information: (418) 827-4561
Reservation: 1-800-463-1568
Season: mid-December to late
March. Cost is $20 p.p. per night
plus trail fees.
Chalets are on the main network of
groomed trails at Mont-Ste-Anne.

Ruisseau Rouge	4km	6 persons
Chaudron	6km	6 "

*Parc du Saguenay

24 rue Notre-Dame,
Rivière-Eternité, QC G0V 1P0
(418) 272-3008
A demanding 31-km traverse from
Rivière Eternité to Anse-St-Jean.
Baggage transfer service is
available. Cost is $15 p.p. per night.
Capacity: 12 per hut

Refuge Lac à la Chute	13k
Refuge du Marais	21k

La traversée de Charlevoix

Information: Eudore Fortin,
(418) 639-2284
C.P. 171, Saint-Urbain, QC G0A 4K0
A six-day 100-km traverse from
Parc des Grands-Jardin to Mont
Grand Fonds passing by the
spectacular gorges of the Malbaie
River. It is one of the most gruelling
tours in Quebec, so skiers must be
at least strong intermediates. Six log
huts with a capacity of 8 persons (a
minimum of 4 is required) can be
reserved along the trail at a cost of
$85 p.p. Alternatively there are six
spacious chalets with a capacity of
15 persons (min. of 10) at $150 p.p.
A baggage transfer service between
cabins is available, as well as a car-
jockey service.

Quebec

*Parc des Grand-Jardins

Information: (418) 435-3101
Season: mid-December to early April
"Sur la piste du caribou" ("On the trail of the caribou") is a guided ecotour to observe caribou in the wild. Distances to be skied range up to 25 km per day over easy to moderate terrain. Cost for a two-and-a-half day tour is about $200 including meals and guide. Huts are also available on a self-sufficient basis for $16 to $20 per person. Baggage transfer service.

La Galette	0km	12 persons
Lac Pointu	5km	2x6 "
Chateau Bromont	13km	2x6 "
Eudore	0.2km	12 "

*Parc de la Gaspésie

Administered by Club des Grand Yetis (418) 763-7782
85 blvd Sainte-Anne Ouest
Sainte-Anne-des-Monts, QC G0E 2G0
Season: mid-December to late April
About 185 km of backcountry trails plus great telemarking in the Chic-Chocs. One of the most popular backcountry areas in eastern Canada. Baggage transportation is available. Eight unheated backcountry huts each with a capacity of 8 persons are available for long randonnées. Rates are about $15 p.p..

* Reservations can be made through Société des établishments de plein air du Québec (SEPAQ) by calling:
1-800-665-6527 from within Quebec or (418) 890-6527 (Quebec City), 8:30 to 4:30 Monday to Friday..

Quebec

19 New Brunswick

New Brunswick's rolling forested hills combined with a better-than-average snowfall and moderate temperatures make it ideal for cross-country skiing. Ski clubs make up the majority of ski centre operators in the province, although some provincial and national parks have groomed trails.

Travel Information

Airports are located at Saint John, Fredericton, Moncton, Charlo, Chatham, Saint Leonard and Bathurst.

Railway service is provided to Campbellton, Bathurst, Newcastle, Moncton and Sackville by VIA Rail.

Language: New Brunswick is officially bilingual with many Acadian settlements along the coast where French is the primary language.

Tourist Information Bureau
New Brunswick Tourism publishes an annual winter guide.
Department of Economic Development and Tourism
PO Box 12345, Fredericton, NB E3B 5C3;
1-800-561-0123 (Canada and USA);
Internet: nbtourism@gov.nb.ca

Cross Country Skiing Organizations

Cross Country Canada - New Brunswick division: in addition to its regular CCC functions also publishes an annual ski guide.
C.P. 1241, Moncton, NB E1C 8P9;
(506) 387-4077; fax: (506) 856-2946

New Brunswick

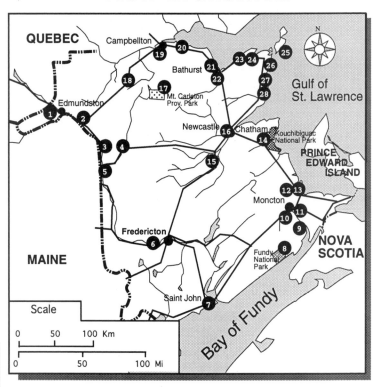

Cross-Country Ski Areas

Les Aventuriers	20	Fundy Outdoor Club	9
Bathurst Snow Bear Club	22	Kahoutek Cross Country	3
Beaver Cross Country Ski Club	13	Kouchibouguac National Park	14
Chignecto Ski Club	8	Les Montagnards	19
Club de Plein Air de Caraquet	24	Mataquac Provincial Park	6
Club de ski de fond Les Mesanges	26	Miramichi Cross Country	16
Club de ski de fond ACA Ski	25	Mount Carleton Prov. Park	17
Club de ski de fond de Dieppe	11	Perth-Andover Cross Country	5
Club de ski de fond Husky	18	Pine Strip Ski Club	15
Club de ski de fond Les Bayeux	23	Riverview	10
Club de ski de fond Skirakdoo	2	Rockwood Park Cross Country	7
Club de ski de fond St-Antoine	12	Rough Waters Cross Country	21
Club de ski Gailurons	28	Sugarloaf Provincial Park	19
Club de sport République	1	Le Sureau Blanc	27
Fundy National Park	8	Tobique Nordic Ski Club	4

Winter Climate

New Brunswick's cross-country ski season usually begins in mid to early December and lasts until about early- to mid-March.

Average Temperatures

Average Snowfall

Fredericton

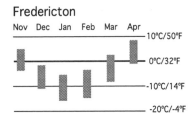

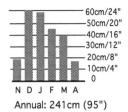

Annual: 241cm (95")

Alma

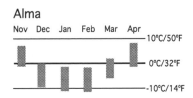

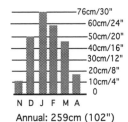

Annual: 259cm (102")

Charlo

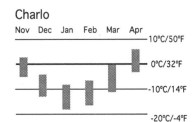

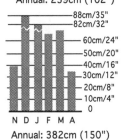

Annual: 382cm (150")

Loppet Schedule

C = classic, F = free technique

Date	Event and Technique	Location
late Jan	Wostawea Loppet (C)	Mactaquac Provincial Park
mid Jan	Rough Waters Loppet (C)	Bathurst
early Feb	Loppet Les Gailurons (C)	Rivière-du-Portage
early Feb	Fundy Loppet (F)	Fundy National Park
mid Feb	Loppet Boules de Neige (F)	Kouchibouguac National Park
early Mar	*Vasaloppet (C)	Charlo

*Canadian Ski Odyssey

Trail Fee	Total	●	■	◆	Skating	Ungroomed	Lodge	Wax Room	Rentals	Food	Lessons	Shelters

Groomed Trails

1 Club Sport République, St. Jacques
570 Rue Principal, St-Jacques E7B 1Y2
2 km from town, go 4 km to the end of Rossignol Rd. Trails are double-track

5⁰⁰	6	2	2	2		0	√	√		√	√	0
	29.0					4.0	0.0					

2 Club de ski de fond Skirakdoo, St. Leonard
(506) 423-7177; PO Box 372, St. Leonard, E0L 1M0
A few km N of town on Trans Canada, then E on Diamond Rd.
Canteen sells drinks and candy. Two-day ski clinics are held a couple times a year.

3⁰⁰	6	3	3	0	1	0	√	√				4
	45.0					5.0	0.0					

3 Kahoutek Cross Country, Grand Falls
PO Box 800, Grand Falls, E3Z 1C3

NA	-	-	-	-		0	√					0
	10.0						0.0					

4 Tobique Nordic Ski Club, Plaster Rock
PO Box 511, Plaster Rock, E0J 1W0

NA	-	-	-	-		0	√					0
	35.0						0.0					

5 Perth-Andover Cross Country Ski Club, Perth-Andover
PO Box 966, Perth-Andover, E0J 1V0

NA	-	-	-	-		0	√					0
	8.0						0.0					

6 Mataquac Provincial Park, Mactaquac
(506) 363-3011; Mataquac Provincial Park, Mactaquac, E0H 1P0
On N side of Mactaquac dam about 24 km W of Fredericton.

NC	3	2	1	0		0	E					1
	13.5	6.0	7.5				0.0					

7 Rockwood Park Cross Country Ski Club, Saint John
Interpretation Centre: (506) 658-2883; PO Box 1971, Saint John, E2L 4L1
At Rockwood Park and golf course near city centre.
Trails are on golf course and through park. Interp. centre or club house may be open.

NC	-	-	-	-		0	√					0
	25.0	10.0	10.0	5.0	1.0	0.0						

N.B.

Groomed Trails

Legend columns: Trail Fee · Total · ● · ■ · ◆ · Skating · Ungroomed · Lodge · Wax Room · Rentals · Food · Lesons · Shelters

8 Fundy National Park/Chignecto Ski Club, Alma

(506) 887-6000; PO Box 40, Alma E0A 1B0/Chignecto Ski Club, PO Box 119, Alma, E0A 1B0
At Alma 80km S of Moncton on Hwy 114.
Loop trails, overnight cabin (4 beds) at end of 8 km trail. Jackrabbit program, Loppet

Trail Fee	Total	●	■	◆	Skating	Ungroomed	Lodge	Wax Room	Rentals	Food	Lesons	Shelters
Entry	7	2	4	1		2	√	√		C	C	3
Fee	40.0	4.5	22.3	12.8	40.0	12.2						

9 Fundy Outdoor Club, Hillsborough

25 km S of Moncton near Hillsborough.

Trail Fee	Total	●	■	◆	Skating	Ungroomed	Lodge	Wax Room	Rentals	Food	Lesons	Shelters
Yes	6	2	2	2		0	√	√			√	0
	25.0	5.0	15.0	5.0		0.0						

10 Riverview Cross Country Ski Club, Riverview

In Bridgedale on Manning Rd 1 mile E of Point Park.
Outer loop is 8.5 km, inner loops are shorter. Family rate $8.00.

Trail Fee	Total	●	■	◆	Skating	Ungroomed	Lodge	Wax Room	Rentals	Food	Lesons	Shelters
3^{00}	4	3	1	0	-	0	√				√	0
1^{00}C	15.0				5.5	0.0						

11 Club de ski de fond de Dieppe, Dieppe

Trail Fee	Total	●	■	◆	Skating	Ungroomed	Lodge	Wax Room	Rentals	Food	Lesons	Shelters
NA	-	-	-	-		0	√					0
	12.0					0.0						

12 Club de ski de fond St-Antoine, St-Antoine

Ave Clement in St. Antoine. PO Box 92, St-Antoine, E0A 2X0
One-way trails except for a 2-km linear trail.

Trail Fee	Total	●	■	◆	Skating	Ungroomed	Lodge	Wax Room	Rentals	Food	Lesons	Shelters
NA	5	5	0	0		0	√	√		√		1
	12.0	12.0				0.0						

13 Beaver Cross Country Ski Club, Cocagne

RR #1, Box 162, Cocagne, E0A 1K0

Trail Fee	Total	●	■	◆	Skating	Ungroomed	Lodge	Wax Room	Rentals	Food	Lesons	Shelters
Yes	-	-	-	-		0	√					0
	20.0					0.0						

Groomed Trails

Trail Fee · Total · ● ■ ◆ · Skating · Ungroomed · Lodge · Wax Room · Rentals · Food · Lesons · Shelters

14 Kouchibouguac National Park, Kouchibouguac

(506) 876-2443; Kouchibouguac National Park, Kouchibouguac, E0A 2A0
Nature interpretation programs on weekends. Loppet Boules de Neige.

Trail Fee	Total	●	■	◆	Skating	Ungroomed	Lodge	Wax Room	Rentals	Food	Lesons	Shelters
Entry	-	-	-	-		0	√	√				2
Fee	25.0				10.0	0.0						

15 Pine Strip Ski Club, Blackville

PO Box 322, Blackville, E0C 1C0

Trail Fee	Total	●	■	◆	Skating	Ungroomed	Lodge	Wax Room	Rentals	Food	Lesons	Shelters
NA	-					0	√					0
	21.0					0.0						

16 Miramichi Cross Country Ski Club, Newcastle

433 King George Highway, Newcastle, E1V 1L7
In town of Newcastle on Route 126 beside firehall.
Interlinked network of trails. Loppet.

Trail Fee	Total	●	■	◆	Skating	Ungroomed	Lodge	Wax Room	Rentals	Food	Lesons	Shelters
7⁰⁰ F	7	3	3	1		0	√	√		√	√	0
	22.0	5.3	11.7	5.0		0.0						

17 Mount Carleton Provincial Park

(506) 235-2025
About 40 km E of St. Quentin on Hwy 180
Mt. Carleton is the highest mountain the Maritimes at 820m (2690 ft)
Trails are single-track plus a narrow skating lane. BC skiing on snowmobile trails.

Trail Fee	Total	●	■	◆	Skating	Ungroomed	Lodge	Wax Room	Rentals	Food	Lesons	Shelters
NC	1	0	1	0		-						1
	7.5			7.5	7.5	Yes						

18 Club de ski de fond Husky, Saint Quentin

Centre de plein du Vieux Moulin: (506) 235-1110; PO Box 161, Saint Quentin, E0K 1J0
At Vieux Moulin outdoor centre. 1 km lighted trail. Jackrabbit progrm, bar, dormitory.

Trail Fee	Total	●	■	◆	Skating	Ungroomed	Lodge	Wax Room	Rentals	Food	Lesons	Shelters
3⁰⁰	5	0	2	3		0	√		√	√		1
	25				Yes	0.0						

Groomed Trails

Trail Fee · Total · ● · ■ · ◆ · Skating · Ungroomed · Lodge · Wax Room · Rentals · Food · Lessons · Shelters

19 Sugarloaf Provincial Park/Les Montagnards Ski Club, Atholville

(506) 789-2366, Alpine ski centre: (506) 789-2392, 1-800-561-0123 (NB)
Sugarloaf Provincial Park, PO Box 629, Atholville, E0K 1A0
Just S of Campbellton. One 4km trail is around base of mountain, others are at top.
Pisten-Bulley grooming. Bar and restaurant are nearby in alpine ski chalet.

Trail Fee	Total	●	■	◆	Skating	Ungroomed	Lodge	Wax Room	Rentals	Food	Lessons	Shelters
NC	-	-	-	-	0		√	√	C	C	√	0
	27.0	7.0	10.0	10.0	27.0	0.0						

20 Les Aventuriers , Charlo

(506) 684-5525; PO Box 149, Charlo E0K 1M0
In Charlo at two access points: Craig Rd and Mountain Brook Rd.
3 km lighted trail. Annual loppet and early-season Masters ski camp.

Trail Fee	Total	●	■	◆	Skating	Ungroomed	Lodge	Wax Room	Rentals	Food	Lessons	Shelters
3.00	4	3	0	1	2	0	√	√	√		√	0
	32.5	25.0		7.5	12.5	0.0						

21 Rough Waters Cross Country Ski Club, Bathurst

(506) 546-9693; RR #4, Site 6, Box 27, Bathurst, E2A 3Y7
On Rough Waters Rd in East Bathurst.
Stacked loop trails (long loop with cut-offs). Home-made food sold on weekends

Trail Fee	Total	●	■	◆	Skating	Ungroomed	Lodge	Wax Room	Rentals	Food	Lessons	Shelters
3.00	1	1	0	0	0		√			E		0
	15.0	15.0				0.0						

22 Bathurst municipal trails/Snow Bear Club, Bathurst

(506) 548-0437, Rec. Dept.: 548-0410; PO Box 1026, Bathurst, E2A 3Z1
On Golf St. in Bathurst.

Trail Fee	Total	●	■	◆	Skating	Ungroomed	Lodge	Wax Room	Rentals	Food	Lessons	Shelters
3.50	5	5	0	0	1	0	√	√		√		3
	26.0	26.0			4.5	0.0						

23 Club de ski de fond Les Bayeux, Grande-Anse

Club de ski de fond Les Bayeux, Grande-Anse, E0B 1R0

Trail Fee	Total	●	■	◆	Skating	Ungroomed	Lodge	Wax Room	Rentals	Food	Lessons	Shelters
NA	-	-	-	-	0		√					0
	15.0					0.0						

N.B.

Groomed Trails

24 Club de Plein Air de Caraquet, Caraquet

PO Box 415, Caraquet, E0B 1K0

Trail Fee	Total	●	■	◆	Skating	Ungroomed	Lodge	Wax Room	Rentals	Food	Lesons	Shelters
NA	-	-	-	-	0	√						0
	20.0				0.0							

25 Club de ski de fond ACA Ski, Lameque

(506) 344-5161; PO Box 727, Lameque, E0B 1V0

On rue de la Tourbe. Double-track trails. Canteen sells juice and chips. Jackrabbits

Trail Fee	Total	●	■	◆	Skating	Ungroomed	Lodge	Wax Room	Rentals	Food	Lesons	Shelters
3⁰⁰	2	2	0	0	0	√	√					3
	20.0				0.0							

26 Club de ski de fond Les Mesanges, Inkerman Ferry

RR #1, Site 11, Box 1, Inkerman Ferry, E0B 2J0

Trail Fee	Total	●	■	◆	Skating	Ungroomed	Lodge	Wax Room	Rentals	Food	Lesons	Shelters
NA	-	-	-	-	0	√						0
	10.0				0.0							

27 Le Sureau Blanc, Sheila

PO Box 547, Sheila, E0C 1Z0

Trail Fee	Total	●	■	◆	Skating	Ungroomed	Lodge	Wax Room	Rentals	Food	Lesons	Shelters
NA	-	-	-	-	0	√						0
	20.0				0.0							

28 Club de ski Gailurons, Riviere-du-Portage

RR #1, Site 1, Bte 4, Riviere-du-Portage, E0C 1Y0

Near Tracadie-Sheila. Loppet.

Trail Fee	Total	●	■	◆	Skating	Ungroomed	Lodge	Wax Room	Rentals	Food	Lesons	Shelters
3⁰⁰	8	-	-	-	0	√					√	0
5⁰⁰ F	25.0	15.0	5.0	5.0	0.0							

N.B.

20 Prince Edward Island

Prince Edward Island may be Canada's smallest province, but it has its fair share of avid skiers. Most ski centres are to be found in the province's parks, except for the Souris Striders Ski Club trails.

Travel Information

Airports: Charlottetown, Summerside

Ferry service from Cape Tormentine, N.B. runs year-round.

Tourist bureau
PEI Visitor Services offers an accomodation reservation service
PO Box 940, Charlottetown, PEI C1A 7M5;
Information: (902) 836-4500, 1-800-463-4734 (North America)
Reservations: 1-800-265-6161

Cross Country Skiing Organizations

Cross Country P.E.I.
PO Box 21131, Charlottetown, PEI C1A 9H6;
(902) 368-4110

P.E.I.

Prince Edward Island

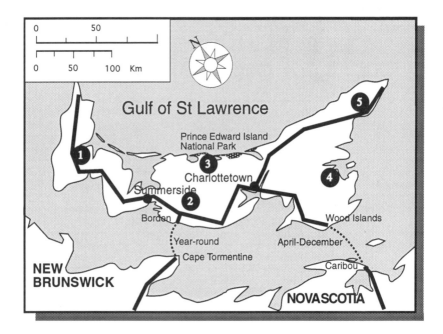

Cross Country Ski Areas

Brookvale Provincial Ski Park   2

Brudenall River Park   4

Mill River Provincial Park   1

Prince Edward Island
  National Park   3

Souris Striders   5

Winter Climate

Due to the milder temperatures that favour the region, the cross-country ski season in this region only lasts from late December to early March.

Average Temperatures Average Snowfall

Charlottetown

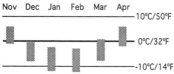

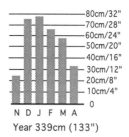

Year 339cm (133")

Summerside

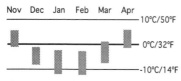

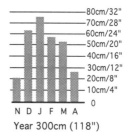

Year 300cm (118")

P.E.I.

Loppets

Date	Event	Location
early Feb	Souris Loppet	Souris
late Feb	Brookvale Loppet	Brookvale

Groomed Trails — Trail Fee, Total, ● ■ ◆, Skating, Ungroomed, Lodge, Wax Room, Rentals, Food, Lesons, Shelters

1 Mill River Provincial Park, Woodstock

(902) 859-2448;
Dept of Economic Development and Tourism, Parks Division West, PO Box 399, O'Leary, C0B 1V0
2 km N of Woodstock on Hwy 2.
8 km trail lit for night skiing. Bar, hotel: 1-800-565-8790

Trail Fee	Total	●	■	◆	Skating	Ungroomed	Lodge	Wax Room	Rentals	Food	Lesons	Shelters
NA	-					0	√		√	√		0
	10.0	10.0				0.0						

2 Brookvale Provincial Ski Park, Brookvale

(902) 658-2925; Brookvale Provincial Ski Park, Crapaud, PEI C0A 1J0
8.5 km of racing trails with several cutoffs.

Trail Fee	Total	●	■	◆	Skating	Ungroomed	Lodge	Wax Room	Rentals	Food	Lesons	Shelters
NA	-	-	0	-		0	√	√			R	0
	18.5	10.0		8.5	Yes	0.0						

3 Prince Edward Island National Park, Dalvay

(902) 672-6350; 2 Palmer's Lane, Charlottetown, C1A 5V6
Three areas—one at Dalvay, W of Dalvay and on golf course.

Trail Fee	Total	●	■	◆	Skating	Ungroomed	Lodge	Wax Room	Rentals	Food	Lesons	Shelters
NC	-	-	0	0		0						0
	10.0	10.0				0.0						

4 Brudenell River Park, Roseneath

(902) 652-2356, Brudenell River Resort: 1-800-565-RODD
Dept of Economic Development and Tourism, Parks Division, PO Box 370, Roseneath, C0A 1R0

Trail Fee	Total	●	■	◆	Skating	Ungroomed	Lodge	Wax Room	Rentals	Food	Lesons	Shelters
NA	-	-	0	0		0	√		√			0
	7.0	7.0				0.0						

5 Souris Trails, Souris

Souris Striders, PO Box 478, Souris, C0A 2B0
Operated by Souris Striders cross-country ski club.

Trail Fee	Total	●	■	◆	Skating	Ungroomed	Lodge	Wax Room	Rentals	Food	Lesons	Shelters
NA	-	-	0	0		0	√					0
	12.0	12.0				0.0						

P.E.I.

21 Nova Scotia

Nova Scotia is graced with a variety of terrain and climate. The south shore is a temperate zone, with mild temperatures and snowfall. Snowfalls increase and temperature ranges fall as you travel towards the north end of Cape Breton.

Both of Nova Scotia's National Parks, Kejimkujik and Cape Breton Highlands, groom trails for cross-country skiers. "Keji" is geared toward novice and intermediate skiers, with its gently rolling hills. CBHNP is the more rugged of the two, with trails for all levels of skiers.

Wentworth Hostel is the unofficial headquarters for skiers who want to use the nearby ungroomed logging roads, where the Nova Scotia ski team sometimes trains.

Travel Information

Ferry Service: operates year-round between St. John and Digby.

Airlines: connections from outside the province are provided by KLM from Amsterdam, Northwest Air from Boston, Air Canada and Canadian Airlines International from the rest of Canada. Within Atlantic Canada scheduled connections are provided by Air Atlantic and Air Nova.

Bus service: Acadian Lines operates throughout Nova Scotia and connects with Greyhound from New York and SMT from New Brunswick.

Rail service: Via Rail connects Halifax with the rest of Canada.

Tourist information and accomodation reservations
Tourism Nova Scotia, PO Box 130, Halifax, NS B3J 2M7; (902) 425-5781 (Halifax), 1-800-565-0000 (Canada and USA); fax: (902) 420-1286; Internet: hlfxwtcc.econ.rboyd@gov.ns.ca

N.S.

Nova Scotia

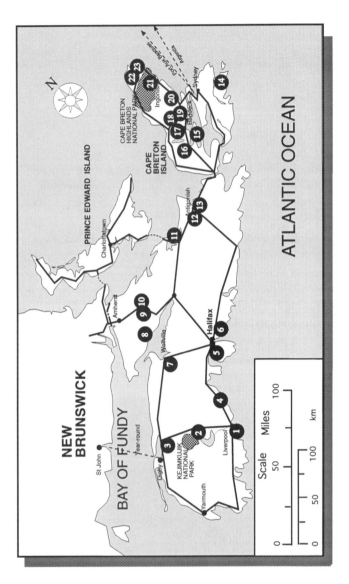

N.S.

Cross Country Ski Areas

Antigonish Golf Club	12	Middle River Ski Club	17
Beaver Mountain Provincial Park	13	North Highland Nordic Ski Trails	22
Big Baddeck	19	Old Orchard Inn	7
Cape Breton Highlands National Park	21	Rails to Trails	1
Dayspring	4	Shubie Park, Dartmouth	5
Five Islands Prov. Park	8	Saint Ann's Gaelic College	20
Fortress Louisbourg National Historic Park	14	Ski Margaree Valley	18
Highland Hill Ski Trail	15	Ski Wentworth	9
Highland Ski Touring	23	Trenton Steeltown Centennial Park	11
Jack Lake Trails	6	Upper Clements Wildlife Park	3
Kejimkujik National Park	2	Wentworth Hostel	10

Cross Country Organizations

Cross Country Canada - Nova Scotia division P.O. Box 3010, Halifax, NS B3J 3G6; (902) 425-5450; fax: (902) 425-5606

Winter Climate

Due to the effects of the Gulf Stream, winters on the south coast of Nova Scotia are moderate. Cape Breton Highlands have a long ski season, lasting from late December to mid-April.

Average Temperatures

Average Snowfall

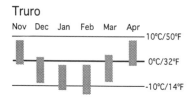

Kejimkujik

Truro

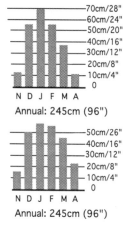

Annual: 245cm (96")

Annual: 245cm (96")

Halifax

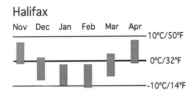

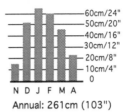

Annual: 261cm (103")

Igonish Beach

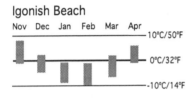

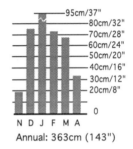

Annual: 363cm (143")

Loppets

Date	Event	Location
early Jan	Black Brook Ski Tour	CBHNP
early Jan	Ceilidh Loppet	Gaelic College, St Ann's
mid Jan	Middle River Loppet	Middle River
late Jan	Honey Pot Selection	Honey Pot
late Jan	Big Farm Classic	Big Baddeck
early Feb	Breton Nordic Loppet	East Bay
mid Feb	Clan Nordic Ski Tour	Highland Hill
late Feb	Ski Margaree	Margaree
early Mar	North Highlands Loppet	
Cape North		

N.S.

Groomed Trails — Trail Fee, Total, ● ■ ◆, Skating, Ungroomed, Lodge, Wax Room, Rentals, Food, Lessons, Shelters

1 Rails to Trails, Liverpool
Tourist Bureau: (902) 354-5741, 1-800-655-5741
T'railway linking Liverpool and Summerville.
Region has short snow season so check with Tourist Bureau.

Trail Fee	Total	●	■	◆	Skating	Ungroomed	Lodge	Wax Room	Rentals	Food	Lessons	Shelters
NC	1	1	0	0		0						0
	8.0	8.0				0.0						

2 Kejimkujik National Park, Maitland Bridge

(902) 682-2772; PO Box 236, Maitland Bridge, B0T 1B0
5 trailheads throughout park.
Overnight cabin at end of 27 km trail can be reserved. Inn, B&B close by.

Trail Fee	Total	●	■	◆	Skating	Ungroomed	Lodge	Wax Room	Rentals	Food	Lessons	Shelters
Entry	4	1	2	1		-				C		4
Fee	50.0	5.5	12.0	8.0		65.0						

3 Upper Clements Wildlife Park, Annapolis Royal
8 km W of Annapolis Royal on Hwy 1. RR 2, Annapolis Royal, B0S 1A0
Trails for all abilities amongst wildlife enclosures.

Trail Fee	Total	●	■	◆	Skating	Ungroomed	Lodge	Wax Room	Rentals	Food	Lessons	Shelters
NC	-	-	-	-		0						0
	10.0					0.0						

4 Dayspring Recreation Complex, Dayspring
(902) 543-1354

Trail Fee	Total	●	■	◆	Skating	Ungroomed	Lodge	Wax Room	Rentals	Food	Lessons	Shelters
NA	-	-	-	-		0						0
	7.0					0.0						

5 Shubie Park, Dartmouth Recreation Dept. Dartmouth
Parks Dept.: (902) 464-2121; Mailing Address: 20 Graham St., Dartmouth, B3A 3H7

Trail Fee	Total	●	■	◆	Skating	Ungroomed	Lodge	Wax Room	Rentals	Food	Lessons	Shelters
NC	3	-	-	-		0						0
	8.5					0.0						

6 Jack Lake Trails, Bedford
Bedford Recreation Dept.: (902) 835-9757
On Hammond Plains Rd in Bedford.

Trail Fee	Total	●	■	◆	Skating	Ungroomed	Lodge	Wax Room	Rentals	Food	Lessons	Shelters
NC	7					0						0
	5.0					0.0						

N.S.

Groomed Trails — legend across top: Trail Fee | Total | ● | ■ | ◆ | Skating | Ungroomed | Lodge | Wax Room | Rentals | Food | Lessons | Shelters

7 Old Orchard Inn, Wolfville

(902) 542-5751; PO Box 1090, Wolfville, B0P 1X0
Exit 11 off Hwy 101 at Greenwich.
Woods and open fields. Guide available. Trails for guests only.

Trail Fee	Total	●	■	◆	Skating	Ungroomed	Lodge	Wax Room	Rentals	Food	Lessons	Shelters
GO	5	5				0	√	√	√		√	0
	15.0	15.0				0.0						

8 Five Islands Provincial Park, Five Islands

(902) 254-2980; Five Islands Provincial Park, Five Islands, B0M 1K0
24 km E of Parrsboro on Hwy 2.
Varied terrain with some steep hills.

Trail Fee	Total	●	■	◆	Skating	Ungroomed	Lodge	Wax Room	Rentals	Food	Lessons	Shelters
NC	2					0						0
	7.5					0.0						

9 Ski Wentworth, Wentworth

(902) 548-2089; Ski Wentworth, Wentworth, B0M 1Z0
At Ski Wentworth alpine center.

Trail Fee	Total	●	■	◆	Skating	Ungroomed	Lodge	Wax Room	Rentals	Food	Lessons	Shelters
Yes	5					0	√				√	0
	15.0					0.0						

10 Wentworth Hostel, Wentworth

(902) 548-2379; Wentworth Hostel, RR 1, Wentworth, B0M 1Z0
W on Wentworth Valley Rd. At 1.5 km turn S, follow signs to hostel.
Old logging roads behind hostel (a quaint 100-yr old farm house). 40-bed hostel

Trail Fee	Total	●	■	◆	Skating	Ungroomed	Lodge	Wax Room	Rentals	Food	Lessons	Shelters
NC	0					16	√	√	√		R	0
	0.0					60.0						

11 Trenton Steeltown Centennial Park, Trenton

(902) 752-1019; P.O. Box 328, Trenton, B0K 1X0
In town of Trenton.

Trail Fee	Total	●	■	◆	Skating	Ungroomed	Lodge	Wax Room	Rentals	Food	Lessons	Shelters
NC	3	1	1	1		0			C	C		0
	6.0	2.0	2.0	2.0		0.0						

12 Antigonish Golf Club, Antigonish

(902) 863-3686; Antigonish Recreation Dept., 24 Main St., Antigonish, B2G
In town of Antigonish. Rentals available from town's Recreation Dept.

Trail Fee	Total	●	■	◆	Skating	Ungroomed	Lodge	Wax Room	Rentals	Food	Lessons	Shelters
NA	3	3	0	0		0						0
	9.0	9.0				0.0						

N.S.

Groomed Trails

Trail Fee	Total	●	■	◆	Skating	Ungroomed	Lodge	Wax Room	Rentals	Food	Lessons	Shelters

13 Beaver Mountain ProvincialPark, Antigonish
(902) 863-3343
Exit 30 off Hwy 104, then go 3 km S to park.

Trail Fee	Total	●	■	◆	Skating	Ungroomed	Lodge	Wax Room	Rentals	Food	Lessons	Shelters
NA	2	-	-	-		0						0
	6.0					0.0						

14 Fortress Louisbourg National Historic Park, Louisbourg
(902) 733-2280
One trail at watertower, other on Kenneth Cove Rd behind fortress.
Beautiful ocean view at Kenneth Cove. Trail thru hardwood and fir.

Trail Fee	Total	●	■	◆	Skating	Ungroomed	Lodge	Wax Room	Rentals	Food	Lessons	Shelters
Entry	2	1	1	0		1						1
fee	9.2	6.0	3.3			16.5						

15 Highland Hill Ski Trail, MacKinnon's Harbor
Barra Glen Rd, then turn on Highland Hill Rd and go to end of road.
Overlooks the Bras d'Or Lakes. Gentle to moderate terrain.

Trail Fee	Total	●	■	◆	Skating	Ungroomed	Lodge	Wax Room	Rentals	Food	Lessons	Shelters
NA	3	-	-	-		0						0
	11.0					0.0						

17 Middle River Ski Club, Baddeck; RR #3, Baddeck, B0E 1B0
Two trailheads - Gold Brook Rd and Garry River.
Gold Brook is thru forest. Garry Rd has panoramic views.

Trail Fee	Total	●	■	◆	Skating	Ungroomed	Lodge	Wax Room	Rentals	Food	Lessons	Shelters
Yes	3	-	-	-		0						0
	21.0					0.0						

18 Ski Margaree Valley, Margaree Valley

Trail Fee	Total	●	■	◆	Skating	Ungroomed	Lodge	Wax Room	Rentals	Food	Lessons	Shelters
NA	1					3						0
	10.0					12.0						

19 Big Baddeck
Big Farm Rd in Big Baddeck.

Trail Fee	Total	●	■	◆	Skating	Ungroomed	Lodge	Wax Room	Rentals	Food	Lessons	Shelters
NC	-					0						0
	5.2					0.0						

20 St. Ann's Gaelic College, St. Ann's
Trailhead behind MacKenzie Hall on the college campus.
Trail passes several heritage sites adjacent to St. Ann's Bay. Beginner and intermediate.

Trail Fee	Total	●	■	◆	Skating	Ungroomed	Lodge	Wax Room	Rentals	Food	Lessons	Shelters
NA	1	-	-	-		0						
	3.5					0.0						

N.S.

Groomed Trails

| Trail Fee | Total | ● | ■ | ◆ | Skating | Ungroomed | Lodge | Wax Room | Rentals | Food | Lessons | Shelters |

21 Cape Breton Highlands National Park, Igonish Beach

(902) 285-2691; Cape Breton Highlands National Park, Igonish Beach, B0C 1L0
Two trailheads—one in Ingonish, the other 10 km N at Black Brook.

Entry	3	2	1	0		0		√		√		0
Fee	35.0	11.0	24.0		35.0	0.0						

22 North Highland Nordic Ski Trails, Cape North
(902) 383-2453
Behind community center in the village of Cape North.
Trails wind thru spruce and hardwood overlooking bay and mountains.

Yes	4	1	1	0		0			0
	12.0	5.0	7.0		12.0	0.0			

23 Highland Ski Touring, Dingwall
(902)383-2952; Highland Ski Touring, RR 1, Dingwall, B0C 1G0
5 km along South Ridge Road near Cape North.
Novice trail winds thru fields and forest. Other trail is on scenic ridge.

4⁰⁰	2	1	1		0	√	√	√	√	0
	12.0	5.0		7.0	0.0					

N.S.

22 Newfoundland and Labrador

Newfoundlanders are famous for their warmth and hospitality. With plentiful snow and its northern location, Newfoundland and Labrador are great destinations for late-season skiing. Gros Morne National Park has fabulous touring and telemark terrain and snow that usually lasts well into April. The Menihek Ski Club in Labrador hosts the final loppet of the Canadian Ski Oyssey on the first weekend in April.

Travel Information

Ferry service from North Sydney, N.S. to Port aux Basques operates year-round. Ferry to Argentia does not operate in winter. Schedule information: (902) 794-5700

Airports: Direct links to London, Montreal and Toronto are available through Air Canada and Canadian Airlines International. Air Nova and Air Atlantic offer service within Newfoundland and Labrador.

Tourist Information Bureau
Department of Tourism, Culture and Recreation
PO Box 8730, St. John's, NF A1B 4K2;
(709) 729-2830, 1-800-563-6353 (Canada and USA);
fax: (709) 729-1965

Cross Country Skiing Organizations

Cross Country Canada - Newfoundland and Labrador division publishes an annual ski guide.
Newfoundland and Labrador Cross-Country Ski Association
PO Box 284, Gambo, NF A0G 1T0

Nfld/Lab

Newfoundland

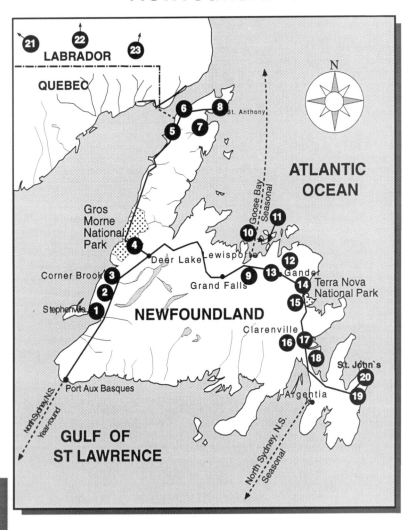

LABRADOR

QUEBEC

St. Anthony

ATLANTIC
OCEAN

Goose Bay
Seasonal

N

Gros
Morne
National
Park

Deer Lake

Lewisporte

Corner Brook

Grand Falls

Gander

Terra Nova
National Park

NEWFOUNDLAND

Stephenville

Clarenville

St. John's

Port Aux Basques

Argentia

North Sydney, N.S.
Year-round

North Sydney, N.S.
Seasonal

GULF OF
ST LAWRENCE

Nfld/Lab

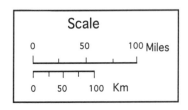

Scale

0   50   100 Miles

0   50   100   Km

Cross Country Ski Areas

Airport Nordic Ski Club	13	Menihek Nordic Ski Club	21
Aurora Nordic	8	Mt. St. Margaret Ski Club	5
Belvy Bay Cross Country	7	New World Island Ski Club	10
Birch Brook Nordic Ski Club	23	Northern Lights Ski Club	22
Butter Pot Provincial Park	19	Notre Dame Provincial Park	9
Clarenville Ski Club	17	Ski White Hills	16
Corner Brook Ski Park	3	Spruce Cove Ski Club	14
Deep Cove Ski Club	6	St. John's	20
Dildo Run Provincial Park	11	Stag Lake Provincial Park	2
Glenview Nordic Ski Club	18	Terra Nova National Park	15
Gros Morne National Park	4	Whaleback Nordic Ski Club	1
Jonathon's Pond Prov. Park	12		

Average Temperatures   Average Snowfall

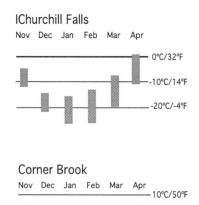

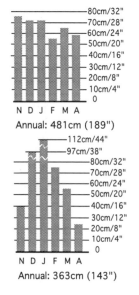

Annual: 481cm (189")

Annual: 363cm (143")

Average Temperatures   Average Snowfall

Gander

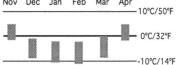

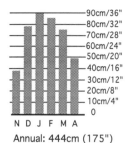

Annual: 444cm (175")

St. John's

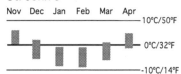

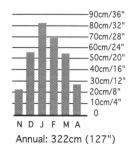

Annual: 322cm (127")

Loppets

Date	Event	Location
late Jan	Snowy Owl Classic	Stephenville
mid Feb	Notre Dame Ski Fest	Lewisporte
late Feb	Gambo Flop-It	Gambo
early Mar	Newfoundland Marathon	Stephenville
mid Mar	7-11 Ski Marathon	Corner Brook
mid Mar	Dildo Run Challenge	Summerford
early Apr	Don't Hang Up Your Skis Yet	St. Anthony
early Apr	*The Great Labrador Loppet	Labrador City

*Canadian Ski Odyssey

Nfld/Lab

Groomed Trails — Trail Fee · Total · ● ■ ◆ · Skating · Ungroomed · Lodge · Wax Room · Rentals · Food · Lessons · Shelters

1 Whaleback Nordic Ski Club, Stephenville, NF
In town of Stephenville.
Stacked loops of one-way trails.

Trail Fee	Total	●	■	◆	Skating	Ungroomed	Lodge	Wax Room	Rentals	Food	Lessons	Shelters
7^00	7	3	2	2	0		√	√	√		√	1
5^00	27.0	8.5	8.0	8.5	0.0							

2 Stag Lake Provincial Park, Corner Brook, NF
(709) 643-2541; c/o Dept. of Tourism and Culture, Parks Division, PO Box 8700, St. John's, A1B 4J
Approx 10 km S of Corner Brook on Trans-Canada Hwy
Trails vary in length and difficulty. Views of lake.

Trail Fee	Total	●	■	◆	Skating	Ungroomed	Lodge	Wax Room	Rentals	Food	Lessons	Shelters
NC	-											0
	9.3					0.0						

3 Corner Brook Ski Park, Corner Brook, NF
(709) 639-7279; PO Box 2100, RR 1, Corner Brook, A2H 2N2

Trail Fee	Total	●	■	◆	Skating	Ungroomed	Lodge	Wax Room	Rentals	Food	Lessons	Shelters
NA	-	-	-	-			√				√	0
	22.0					0.0						

4 Gros Morne National Park, Rocky Harbour, NF
(709) 458-2417, (709) 458-2066; PO Box 130, Rocky Harbour, NF A0K 4N0
30 km N of Deer Lake on R Rte 430. Three trailheads
Linear trails - one has loop at end.
Alpine touring and telemarking in the 600m-high tablelands for experts.

Trail Fee	Total	●	■	◆	Skating	Ungroomed	Lodge	Wax Room	Rentals	Food	Lessons	Shelters
Entry	3	1	2	0		-						4
Fee	27.0	7.0	20.0			Yes						

5 Mt. St. Margaret Ski Club, Plum Point, NF
1 km lighted trail. PO Box 93, Plum Point, A0K 2N0

Trail Fee	Total	●	■	◆	Skating	Ungroomed	Lodge	Wax Room	Rentals	Food	Lessons	Shelters
NA	-	-	-	-	0		√				√	0
	5.0					0.0						

6 Deep Cove Ski Club, Flowers Cove, NF
3 km S of Anchor Point. Deep Cove Ski Club, Flowers Cove, NF A0K 2N0

Trail Fee	Total	●	■	◆	Skating	Ungroomed	Lodge	Wax Room	Rentals	Food	Lessons	Shelters
NA	-	-	-	-			√	√	√		√	0
	7.0					3.0						

7 Belvy Bay Cross Country, Main Brook, NF
PO Box 8, Main Brook, A0K 3N0

Trail Fee	Total	●	■	◆	Skating	Ungroomed	Lodge	Wax Room	Rentals	Food	Lessons	Shelters
NA	-	-	-	-			√				√	0
	5.0					20.0						

Nfld/Lab

8 Aurora Nordic, St. Anthony, NF
Elevation and latitude extend season to May. Chance of viewing caribou

Trail Fee	Total	●	■	◆	Skating	Ungroomed	Lodge	Wax Room	Rentals	Food	Lessons	Shelters
NA	0	-	-	-		√						0
	0.0					Yes						

9 Notre Dame Provincial Park, Lewisporte, NF
(709) 535-2379; c/o Dept. of Tourism and Culture, Parks Division, PO Box 8700, St. John's, A1B 4J6
Wide trails thru rolling forest. forest.
11 km S of Lewisporte, 1 km W of Notre Dame on the Trans-Canada Hwy.

Trail Fee	Total	●	■	◆	Skating	Ungroomed	Lodge	Wax Room	Rentals	Food	Lessons	Shelters
NC	-	-	0	-	0	√	√			√		0
	5.0		5.0		0.0							

10 New World Island Ski Club, Summerford, NF
PO Box 10, Summerford, New World Island, A0G 4E0

Trail Fee	Total	●	■	◆	Skating	Ungroomed	Lodge	Wax Room	Rentals	Food	Lessons	Shelters
Yes	-	-	-	-	-	√				√		0
	4.0				8.0							

11 Dildo Run Provincial Park, Summerford,NF
(709) 629-3285; c/o Dept. of Tourism and Culture, Parks Division, PO Box 8700, St. John's, A1B 4J
New World Island 22 km N of Boyd's Cove.
Stacked loops along shore of Dildo Run bay. Varied terrain.

Trail Fee	Total	●	■	◆	Skating	Ungroomed	Lodge	Wax Room	Rentals	Food	Lessons	Shelters
NC	3	-	-	-	0							1
	7.0				0.0							

12 Jonathon's Pond Prov. Park, Gander NF
(709) 551-2224; c/o Dept. of Tourism and Culture, Parks Division, PO Box 8700, St. John's, A1B 4J6
16 km N of Gander on Rte 330.
Trail over campground thru mixed forest. Wildlife viewing.

Trail Fee	Total	●	■	◆	Skating	Ungroomed	Lodge	Wax Room	Rentals	Food	Lessons	Shelters
NC	-											0
	2.3					0.0						

13 Airport Nordic Ski Club, Gander, NF

Trail Fee	Total	●	■	◆	Skating	Ungroomed	Lodge	Wax Room	Rentals	Food	Lessons	Shelters
NA	-	-	-	-	0							0
	5.0				0.0							

14 Spruce Cove Ski Club, Gambo, NF
PO Box 495, Gambo, A0G 1T0
Host of the Gambo Flop-it.

Trail Fee	Total	●	■	◆	Skating	Ungroomed	Lodge	Wax Room	Rentals	Food	Lessons	Shelters
NA	-				0							0
	4.0				0.0							

Nfld/Lab

Trail Fee	Total	●	■	◆	Skating	Ungroomed	Lodge	Wax Room	Rentals	Food	Lessons	Shelters

Groomed Trails

15 Terra Nova National Park, Glovertown, NF
(709) 533-2801; Terra Nova National Park, Glovertown, NF A0G 2L0
80 km SE of Gander on Trans-Canada Hwy, 15 km from Glovertown.

Trail Fee	Total	●	■	◆	Skating	Ungroomed	Lodge	Wax Room	Rentals	Food	Lessons	Shelters
NC	3	0	3	0	-							0
	25.0		25.0			52.0						

16 Ski White Hills, Clarenville, NF
(709) 466-7773; PO Box 1118, Clarenville, A0E 1J0

Trail Fee	Total	●	■	◆	Skating	Ungroomed	Lodge	Wax Room	Rentals	Food	Lessons	Shelters
NA	5	-	-	-								0
	-					0.0						

17 Clarenville Ski Club, Clarenville, NF
Clarenville Ski Club, Clarenville, NF A0E 1J0

Trail Fee	Total	●	■	◆	Skating	Ungroomed	Lodge	Wax Room	Rentals	Food	Lessons	Shelters
Yes	-	-	-	-		-					√	0
	16.0					34.0						

18 Glenview Nordic Ski Club, Come By Chance, NF
Glenview Nordic Ski Club, Come By Chance, A0B 1N0

Trail Fee	Total	●	■	◆	Skating	Ungroomed	Lodge	Wax Room	Rentals	Food	Lessons	Shelters
NA	-	-	-	-		√					√	0
	10.0					0.0						

19 Butter Pot Provincial Park, St. John's, NF
(709) 551-2121; c/o Dept. of Tourism and Culture, Parks Division, PO Box 8700, St. John's, A1B 4J6
36 km SW of St. John's on Trans-Canada Hwy.
Trails on campground and around pond. "Butter pot" is a rounded hill.

Trail Fee	Total	●	■	◆	Skating	Ungroomed	Lodge	Wax Room	Rentals	Food	Lessons	Shelters
NC	2	0	2	0		0	√					0
	6.7		6.7			0.0						

20 Bowring Park & Rotary Park, St. John's, NF
(709) 576-8522; Rec. Dept., PO Box 908, St. John's, A1C 5M2
Bowring is 3 km W on Waterford Bridge Rd. Rotary Park is 7 km W on Thorburn Rd.
Bowring Park has 7 km trail. Rotary Park has 3 km trail & lessons.

Trail Fee	Total	●	■	◆	Skating	Ungroomed	Lodge	Wax Room	Rentals	Food	Lessons	Shelters
NC	7	-	-	-		0	√		√		√	0
	10.0					0.0						

21 Menihek Nordic Ski Club, Labrador City, LAB
(709) 944-5842; PO Box 38, Labrador City, LAB A2V 2L8
3 km W of Labrador City.
6 km lighted trail. 15 km trail designed by Bill Koch. Hosts the Great Labrador Loppet

Trail Fee	Total	Groomed Trails ●	■	◆	Skating	Ungroomed	Lodge	Wax Room	Rentals	Food	Lesons	Shelters
NA	-	-	-	-	0	√	√	√	√		√	2
	31.0				0.0							

22 Northern Lights Ski Club, Churchill Falls, LAB
PO Box 234, Churchill Falls, LAB A0R 1A0
1 km lighted trail.

Trail Fee	Total	Groomed Trails ●	■	◆	Skating	Ungroomed	Lodge	Wax Room	Rentals	Food	Lesons	Shelters
NA	1	-	-	-	0	√			√			0
	7.0				0.0							

23 Birch Brook Nordic Ski Club, Happy Valley-Goose Bay, LAB
PO Box 386, Station C, Happy Valley, Goose Bay, LAB A0P 1C0
13 km from Goose Bay on the Northwest River Road.
Black spruce, poplar and birch. Lookout over lake and bay.

Trail Fee	Total	Groomed Trails ●	■	◆	Skating	Ungroomed	Lodge	Wax Room	Rentals	Food	Lesons	Shelters
Yes	5	-	-	-	0	√						1
	30.0				0.0							

Nfld/Lab

Appendix A

Summary of Cross Country Ski Centres

Region	Number	Length of Groomed Trails
British Columbia	58	1560
Yukon	5	167
Northwest Territories	4	57
Alberta	70	1600
Saskatchewan	37	811
Manitoba	23	644
Ontario	127	3347
Quebec	129	6397
New Brunswick	28	601
Prince Edward Island	5	58
Nova Scotia	23	266
Newfoundland	23	266
Total	532	16,125

The above totals were compiled from the directory of this book. Actual numbers of centres would be greater if all the smaller centres were included. Total lengths of trails are those claimed by each centre so they may include some overlap, particularly those in the Quebec region.

Appendix B

Metric Conversion

1 centimeter = 0.39 inch   1 cm = 10 millimeters (mm)

1 inch = 2.54 cm   1 meter (m) = 1000 mm

1 m = 39 3/8 inches   1 kilometer (km) = 1000 m

1 km = 0.62 mile   1 mile = 1.61 km

1 kilogram (kg) = 1000 gm = 2.2 lb   1 lb = 454 grams

°C	°F
10	50
:	:
5	41
:	:
0	32
-1	30
-2	28
-3	26
-4	24
-5	23
-6	21
-7	19
-8	17
-9	15
-10	14
-11	12
-12	10
-13	8
-14	6
-15	5
:	:
-20	-4

cm	in
1000	394
800	315
600	236
400	158
300	118
200	98
150	79
100	40
80	32
60	24
50	20
40	16
30	12
20	8
10	4
5	2

Appendix C
Winter Olympics Nordic Results

1994 Olympics
Cross Country Skiing Results

Women

5 km Classic

L. Egorova	Rus	14:08.8
M. Di Centa	Ita	14:28.3
M. Kirvesniemi	Fin	14:36.0

Pursuit
5km Classic+10km Free

L. Egorova	Rus	41:38.1
M. Di Centa	Ita	41:46.4
S. Belmondo	Ita	42:21.1

15 km Free

M. Di Centa	Ita	39:44.5
L. Egorova	Rus	41:03.0
N. Gavriluk	Rus	41:10.4

30 km Classic

M. Di Centa	Ita	1:25:41.6
M. Wold	Nor	1:25:57.8
M. Kirvesniemi	Fin	1:26:13.6

4x5 km Relay

Rus	57:12.5
Nor	57:42.6
Ita	58:42.6

Men

10 km Classic

B. Daehlie	Nor	24:20.1
V. Smirnov	Kaz	24:38.3
M. Albarello	Ita	24:42.3
D. Bouchard	Can	49th

10km Classic+15km Free

B. Daehlie	Nor	1:00:08.8
V. Smirnov	Kaz	1:00:38.0
S. Fauner	Ita	1:01:48.6
D. Bouchard	Can	52nd

30 km Free

T. Alsgaard	Nor	1:12:26.4
B. Daehlie	Nor	1:13:13.6
M. Myllylae	Fin	1:14:14.0
D. Bouchard	Can	51st

50 km Classic

V. Smirnov	Kaz	2:07:20.3
M. Myllylae	Fin	2:08:41.9
S. Sivertsen	Nor	2:08:49.0
D. Bouchard	Can	51st

4x10 Relay

Ita	1:41:15.0
Nor	1:41:15.4
Fin	1:42:15.6

1924-1992 Olympics Cross Country Men

18 km Men
24	Haug	Nor 1:14:03
28	Groettums-	
	braaten	Nor 1:37:01
32	Utterstrom	Swe 1:23:07
36	Larsson	Swe 1:14:38
48	Lundstrom	Swe 1:13:30
52	Brenden	Nor 1:01:34

Pursuit
92	Daehlie	Nor 1:05:37.9

30 km Men
56	Hakulinen	Fin 1:44:06
60	Jernberg	Nor 1:51:03.9
64	Mantyranta	Fin 1:30:59.7
68	Nones	Ita 1:35:38.2
72	Vedenin	USSR 1:36:31.15
76	Saveliev	USSR 1:30:29.38
80	Zimiatov	USSR 1:27:02.80
84	Zimiatov	USSR 1:28:56.3
88	Prokourorov	USSR 1:24:26.3
92	Ulvang	Nor 1:22:27.8

4 x 10 km Relay Men
36	Fin	2:41:33
48	Swe	2:32:08
52	Fin	2:20:16
56	USSR	2:15:30
60	Fin	2:18:45.6
64	Swe	2:18:34.6
68	Nor	2:08:33.5
72	USSR	2:04:47.94
76	Fin	2:07:59.72
80	USSR	1:57:03.46
84	Swe	1:55:06.3
88	Swe	1:43:58.6
92	Nor	1:39:26.0

15 km Men
56	Brenden	Nor	49:39
60	Brusveen	Nor	51:55.5
64	Mantyranta	Fin	50:54.1
68	BroenningenNor		47:54.2
72	Lundback	Swe	45:28.24
76	Baukov	USSR	45:58.47
80	Wassberg	Swe	41:57.63
84	Svan	Swe	41:25.6
88	Deviatiarov	USSR	41:18.9

50 km Men
24	Haug	Nor	3:44:32
28	Hedlund	Swe	4:52:03
32	Saarinen	Fin	4:28:00
36	Vicklund	Swe	3:30:11
48	Karlsson	Swe	3:47:48
52	Hakuinen	Fin	3:33:33
56	Jernberg	Swe	2:50:27
60	Haemaelainen	Fin	2:59:06.3
64	Jernberg	Swe	2:43:52.6
68	Ellefsaeter	Nor	2:28:45.8
72	Tyldum	Nor	2:43:14.75
76	Formo	Nor	2:37:30.5
80	Zimiatov	USSR	2:27:24.6
84	Wassberg	Swe	2:15:55.8
88	Svan	Swe	2:04:39.9
92	Daehlie	Nor	2:03:41.5

1952-1992 Olympics Cross Country Women

5 km Women
64 Boyarskich USSR 17:50.5
68 Gustafsson Swe 16:45.2
72 Kulakova USSR 17:00.50
76 Takalo Fin 15:48.69
80 Smetanina USSR 15:06.92
84 Haemaelainen Fin 17:04.0
88 Matikainen Fin 15:04.4
92 Lukkarinen Fin 14:13.8

10 km Women
52 Widerman Fin 41:40

56 Kosyryeva USSR 38:11
60 Gusakova USSR 39:46.6
64 Boyarskikh USSR 40:24.3
68 Gustafsson Swe 36:46.5
72 Kulakova USSR 34:17.82
76 Smetanina USSR 30:31.41
80 Petzold Ger 30:31.54
84 Haemaelainen Fin 31:44.2
88 Ventsene USSR 30:08.3
92 Egorova Rus 42:20.8

15 km Women
92 Egorova Ita 42:20.8

20 km Women
84 Haemaelainen Fin 1:01:45.0
88 Tikhonova USSR 55:53.6

30 km Women
92 Belmondo Ita 1:22:30.1

3 x 5 km Women
56 Fin 1:09:01
60 Swe 1:04:21.4
64 USSR 59:20.2
68 Nor 57:30.0
72 USSR 48:46.15

4 x 5 km Women
76 USSR 1:07:49.75
80 Ger 1:02:11.10
84 Nor 1:06:49.7
88 USSR 59:51.1
92 Rus 59:34.8

7.5 km Women

1994 Olympics Biathlon

M. Bedard Can 26:08.8
S. Paramygina Bel 26:09.9
V. Tserbe Ukr 26:10.0

15 km Women
M. Bedard Can 52:06.6
Briand Fra 52:53.3
Disl Ger 53:15.3

3x7.5 Women
Rus 1:47:19.5
Ger 1:51:16.5
Fra 1:52:28.3

10 km Men
Tchepikov Rus 28:07.0
Gross Ger 28:13.0
Tarasov Rus 28:27.4

20 km Men
S. Tarasovs Rus 57:25.3
F. Luck Ger 57:28.7
S. Fischer Ger 57:41.9

4x7.5 km Men
Ger 1:30:22.1
Rus 1:31:23.6
Fra 1:32:31.3

1960-92 Olympics Biathlon

10 km Men			
80	Ullrich	Ger	32:10.69
84	Kvalfoss	Nor	30:53.8
88	Roetsch	Ger	25:08.1
92	Kirchner	Ger	26:02.3

20 km Men

60	Lestander	Swe	1:33:21.6
64	Melanjin	USSR	1:20:26.8
68	Solberg	Nor	1:13:45.9
72	Solberg	Nor	1:13:55.5
76	Kruglov	USSR	1:14:12.26
80	Aliabiev	USSR	1:08:16.31
84	Angerer	Ger	1:11:52.7
88	Roetsch	Ger	56:54.6
92	Redkine	Rus	57:34.4

4x7.5 km Men

68	USSR	2:13:02.4
72	USSR	1:51:44.9
76	USSR	1:57:55.64
80	USSR	1:34:03.27
84	USSR	1:38:51.7
88	USSR	1:22:30.0
92	Ger	1:24:43.5

7.5 km Women

92	Restzova	Rus	24:29.2

15 km Women

92	Misersky	Ger

3x7.5 km Women

92	Fra	1:15:55.6

1924-94 Olympics Nordic Combined

Individual

24	Haug	Nor
28	Groettumsbraaten	Nor
32	"	Nor
36	Hagen	Nor
48	Hasu	Fin
52	Slattvik	Nor
56	Sternesen	Nor
60	Thoma	Ger
64	Knutsen	Nor
68	Keller	Ger
72	Wehling	Ger
76	Wehling	Ger
80	Wehling	Ger
84	Sandberg	Nor
88	Kempf	Swe
92	Guy	Fra
94	Lundberg	Nor

Team

88	Ger
92	Jap
94	Jap

Appendix D

Ski Equipment and Clothing Sources

Ski Equipment Distributors

All ski equipment sold in Canada is imported. The following distributors sell wholesale only (except the distributors of Madshu and Ortovox):

Adidas boots, **Elpex** poles & roller skis, **Vauhti** waxes
Canada Winter Sports
31 Lakeview Ave.
Gormley, ON L0H 1G0
(905) 888–9102

Alpina boots, **Elan & Germina** skis, **Rottefella** bindings (NNN II)
Monark Sports, 81-H Brunswick Blvd., Dollard des Ormeau, QC H9B 2J5
(514) 421-7871

Atomic skis
Atomic Ski Canada
3345 Laird Rd., Unit 1
Mississauga, ON L5L 5R6
(905) 569-2300

Artex boots, **Exel** poles, **Peltonen** skis
Rottefella bindings (NNN II)
Exel Marketing Ltd.
56 Churchill Drive
Barrie, ON L4M 6E7
(705) 739-7690
1-800-461-6420

Fischer skis & boots, **SWIX** waxes & poles
Igloo Vikski, PO Box 180, Ste. Agathe, QC J8C 3A3
(819) 326-1664

Karhu skis, **Merrell** boots (NNN II & 3-pin)
Karhu Canada, 1200 - 55 Ave.
Lachine, QC H8T 3J8
(514) 636-5858

Madshu skis
Sport Dinaco Inc., 4330 Joseph Dubreuil, Lachine, QC H8T 3C4
(514) 636-8081

Ortovox avalanche beacons, probes and shovels
The Hostel Shop
1414 Kensington Rd. NW
Calgary, AB T2N 3P9
(403) 283-8311, 1-800-234-6711

Rossignol skis, boots, poles & bindings (NNN II)
955 André Line
Granby, QC J2J 1J6
(514) 378-9971

Salomon boots & bindings (SNS)
Salomon Canada Sports Ltd.
1904 St. Regis Blvd.
Dorval, QC H9P 1H6
(514) 684-2412
1-800-663-0629 (Manitoba & West)
1-800-361-3398 (Eastern Canada)

Toko waxes & **Uvex** Eyewear
Uvex Toko Canada Ltd.,
180 Industrial Parkway N.
Aurora, ON L4G 4C3
(905) 841-4001

Clothing Manufacturers (wholesale only)

Major Canadian manufacturers of active wear, including cross-country ski clothing, are :

Banff Designs
53A Fraser Ave.
Toronto, ON M6K 1K7
(416) 588-4839

Chlorophylle
250 Racine Est
Chicoutimi, QC G7H 5C2
(418) 549-7512
1-800-465-7512

Louis Garneau
30 rue de Grands Lacs, St.-Augustin-des-Desmaures, QC G3A 2E6
(418) 878-4135
66 Main St., Newport, VT 05855
(802) 334-5885

Mail Order

Companies that produce catalogues and handle mail orders of cross-country ski equipment and clothing in Canada are:

Mountain Equipment Co-op
130 W. Broadway
Vancouver, BC V5Y 1P3
(604) 876-6221 (Vancouver)
1-800-663-2667 (Canada)

Pecco's
78 Murray
Ottawa, ON K1N 5M6
(613) 562-9602

Silent Sports
113 Doncaster Ave.
Thornhill, ON L3T 1L6
(905) 889-3772, 1-800-661-7873

Velotique
1592 Queen St. East
Toronto, ON M4L 1G1
(416) 466-3171, 1-800-363-3171

Glossary

Alpine skiing - downhill skiing on equipment that locks the heel in place on the ski. Skiers are generally returned to the top of the hill by mechanical lifts (sometimes referred to as "yo-yo skiing" by cross-country skiers.)

Alpine touring - ski touring in mountainous regions, usually on alpine equipment with bindings that can be adapted to allow free vertical movement of the heel when ascending slopes. Climbing skins are generally used to provide traction when climbing.

Backcountry touring - cross-country skiing on ungroomed trails or in open wilderness areas.

Biathlon - a competition that involves both marksmanship and cross-country skiing. There are usually two individual and one relay event for both men and women. In the shorter individual events there are two shooting stations; the longer distances have four. At each station five targets must be knocked down with eight shots. For each missed target, a penalty loop must be skied.

Binder wax - the first layer of wax that is applied to grip zone to bind the following layers to the ski.

Breaking trail - creating the first tracks over fresh snow.

Classic technique - a term used to differentiate the original cross-country skiing techniques from the newer skating techniques. Also designates a cross-country ski competition that prohibits use of the skating technique.

Climbing skins - strips of material that are attached to the base of backcountry and telemark skis to prevent backsliding when climbing hills. Attachment is by means of hooks at the tip and tail of the ski plus a reusable adhesive backing that sticks to the ski base.

Cross-country skiing - skiing with nordic equipment on groomed trails or in the backcountry wilderness.

Diagonal stride - a classic cross-country skiing technique where traction is provided either by applying grip wax to the ski base or by the use of skis with waxless bases.

Fall-line - the steepest line down a slope, the path that a rolling object would follow.

Face plant - slang for taking a fall headfirst into the snow.

Fartlek - a training exercise for cross-country skiing that includes short intervals of intense running.

Free technique - designation for a cross-country ski competition that allows use of the skating technique.

Freestyle skiing - downhill skiing discipline that encompasses mogul skiing, ballet skiing and aerial acrobatics.

Glide wax - a wax that is applied, usually by heating, to the glide zones of classic skis and to the entire length of skating skis to increase the amount of glide.

Granular snow - snow that has thawed and refrozen, transforming it into kernels of ice. Gliding on granular snow is faster than on soft snow, but wax is quickly worn off the ski.

Grip wax - wax (either hard wax or klister) that is applied to the middle part of the ski base to provide grip when the skier kicks off during the diagonal stride.

Grooming - compaction of snow on trails for classic or skating technique by specialized machinery. Groomed trails have one or two track-set lanes for classic technique and sometimes a skating lane.

Hard wax - a solid wax that is applied to the wax pocket of classic skis to provide traction during the diagonal stride.

Klister - a paste wax that is smeared over the wax pocket of classic skis to provide traction during the diagonal stride when the snow is wet, granular or icy.

Loppet - a cross-country skiing race open to everyone, usually with a variety of distances for different abilities and ages.

Marathon - a cross-country skiing or running event that covers at least 40 km (25 miles).

NNN - (New Nordic Norm) a boot and binding system introduced by Rottefella in the early 1980s which has been superseded by the NNN II.

Nordic combined - competition that combines the results of a cross-country ski race held on one day and a ski jumping competition held on another day.

Nordic sports - ski sports that can be traced directly back to Scandinavia. Unlike alpine skiing, the heel is free to rise off the ski. Nordic sports include the disciplines of cross-country skiing, ski jumping, telemark skiing and biathlon.

Nordic World Ski Championship - a biennial competition with cross-country skiing, ski jumping and nordic combined events. The championships are held on years ending with an odd digit.

Pulk - sled for towing children or loads behind a skier.

Pursuit - a two-stage cross-country ski race with one classic and one free technique leg. The first stage is run in the same manner as other events with the skiers departing at 30-second intervals and racing against the clock. In the second stage, skiers leave the start at the time interval by which they trailed the leader in the first leg and race head-to-head to the finish line.

Riller - a tool for embedding a pattern in the base of a ski in order to make it glide faster. The structures or rills can be made fine (for fine snow) to coarse (for wet or granular snow).

SNS - (Salomon Nordic System) a boot and binding system manufactured by Salomon that was subsequently superseded by the SNS Profil system.

Sintered base - ski base material that has been sliced from a block of polyethylene, rather than extruded. Sintered bases are flatter, more durable and absorb wax better than extruded bases.

Sitzmark - an indentation in the snow caused by a falling skier. It should be filled in by the skier who created it to prevent it from causing other skiers to take a spill.

Skating - cross-country ski techniques where traction is provided by the edge of the ski rather than by grip wax. Since the skis are seldom parallel, trails intended for this technique have a flat-groomed surface at least two metres (six feet) wide.

Ski-joring - towing of a person on skis by horse, dogs or motorized vehicle.

Ski mountaineering - touring in alpine regions above the tree-line where there may be danger of avalanches, crevasses and rock faces.

Skinny skis - slang for the narrow skis used in cross-country skiing.

Structuring - creating a pattern in the base of ski to improve glide. Structuring can be done with a metal scraper, sandpaper, riller, wire brush or stone grinder.

Telemark position - a skiing stance with one foot forward and one behind and both knees bent almost 90 degrees. Its stability in the fore-aft direction makes it useful for the telemark turn and for the landing position in ski jumping.

Telemark skiing - downhill skiing on equipment with bindings that permit the heel to rise off the ski when performing the telemark turn. Sometimes referred to as "cross-country down-hill" or "nordpine", telemark skiing can be done either at lift-serviced centres or in the backcountry.

Three-pin binding - a binding system that clamps the extended front sole of the ski boot over three pins on base of the binding. Bindings with pins spaced at 75 mm (3 in.) were the original "Nordic Norm" and are still popular today for touring and telemarking equipment.

Track-set trail - a trail that has been groomed with one or more pairs of embedded grooves for classic technique.

Trailhead - the starting point of a trail.

Traverse - a line of travel up or down a slope that crosses the fall-line. Traversing a slope has the effect of reducing the steepness of ascent or descent. A lengthy linear trail between two points is sometimes also referred to as a traverse.

Wax pocket - the middle part of the base of classic skis where grip wax is applied to provide traction during the diagonal stride.

Waxless base - a ski base with an fishscale-type pattern embedded in the grip zone that acts as a substitute for grip wax to provide traction during the diagonal stride.

Yard sale - slang for a spectacular fall that leaves the skier's gear strewn about.

Index

Ordering Information

To order a copy of the *Canadian Cross Country Skiing Handbook* send $24.95 ($19.95 + $1.40 GST+ $2.50 S&H) cheque or money order and use the form on the back of this page. For each additional book, add $21.85 ($19.95+$1.40 GST+$0.50 S&H).

U.S. residents send $22.95 ($19.95 + $3.00 S&H) Canadian funds or $18.45 ($15.95 + $2.50 S&H) in U.S. funds. For each additional book, add $19.95 + $0.50 S&H Cdn or $15.95 + $0.40 U.S.

The second edition of the *Canadian Cross Country Skiing Handbook* is tentatively scheduled for October, 1998. *Cross Country Skiing USA* focuses on the American cross-country ski scene and is scheduled for publication in early 1997.

Save $4.00 ($3.00 U.S.) on the next edition of the *Canadian Cross Country Skiing Handbook*

Cannot be combined with any other discount. Limit of one per order.
Valid for mail orders only. Expiry: December 31, 1999
Send this coupon and $15.95 Cdn ($12.95 U.S.) plus appropriate
taxes and S&H with the order form on the next page after Nov. 1, 1998.

Name (Print): _____.

Signature _____.

Save $4.00 ($3.00 U.S.) on the first edition of *Cross Country Skiing USA*

Cannot be combined with any other discount. Limit of one per order.
Valid for mail orders only. Expiry: December 31, 1999
Send this coupon and $15.95 Cdn ($12.95 U.S.) plus appropriate
taxes and S&H with the order form on the next page.

Name (Print): _____.

Signature _____.

Order Form

To order fill out the following form and include cheque or money order payable to Polaris Guides. Send to:

Polaris Guides
P.O. Box 112, Station E
Montreal, Quebec H2T 3A5

Name (Print): _____.

Street Address: _____.

City: _____ Prov./State:_____ Pcode/Zip: _____.

QUANTITY	TITLE	PRICE	SUB-TOTAL
Total Before Taxes			
Canadian Residents Add 7% GST			
Sub-Total			
Shipping and Handling			
Total			